THE *Spoken* Blessing II

Influencing Generations

Ann Dews Gleaton & Family

True Potential
REACH THE WORLD

Copyright © 2025 Ann Dews Gleaton

All rights reserved.

No part of this publication may be reproduced, stored, or transmitted in any form or by any means, including written, copied, or electronically, without prior written permission from the author or her agents. The only exception is brief quotations in printed reviews. Short excerpts may be used with the publisher's or author's expressed written permission.

Unless otherwise indicated, all Scripture quotations are from the ESV® Bible (The Holy Bible, English Standard Version®), copyright© 2001 by Crossway Bibles, a publishing ministry of Good News Publishers. Used by permission. All rights reserved.

The Spoken Blessing 2: Influencing Generations

Cover design by Carolina Barber Gleaton

ISBN: (Paperback): 9781960024848

ISBN: (e-book): 9781960024855

LCCN:

True Potential, Inc.
PO Box 904, Travelers Rest, SC 29690
www.truepotentialmedia.com

"Ann Gleaton has thoroughly developed the Biblical concepts of spoken blessings. I recommend that everyone study her book on Biblical declarations and apply the Biblical blessings to their lives and the lives of their family members."

Pastor Bill Ligon, Brunswick, Georgia,
Author of Imparting the Blessing: Your Biblical Heritage

"Reading Ann Dews Gleaton's new book was a rare treat. I was deeply moved while reading it. She has tapped into a deep well of God's design for His world. Ann not only talks about it, but she shares personal stories from her family."

William L. Lyons, Ph.D.
Professor of Old Testament and Semitic Languages
College of Theology and Ministry
Oral Roberts University

"I have known Ann Gleaton since 2008, and she has consistently exemplified the importance of standing firm and speaking in faith based on God's Word, both in her own life and that of her family. Her new book, The Spoken Blessing: Influencing Generations, is not only grounded in biblical principles but also serves as a testament to a lifestyle that embraces the spiritual discipline of speaking life through the authority of God's Word. This practice has produced God-honoring results.

I strongly encourage readers to take the time to reflect on the biblical truths that have been tested and lived out by Ann and Cal Gleaton. Within the pages of this book, you will find biblical principles and testimonies that can awaken your faith, stir up hope, and motivate you to cultivate the discipline of speaking God's Word over your life, your family's life, and those whom God has placed in your path."

Bill Schwartz
Regional Director of Central & Eastern Europe
World Missions Ministries - IPHC

"Ann has done a marvelous job of letting Scripture interpret Scripture in this book. It is not a book of Ann's opinions, but a book of God's promises exegeted perfectly to fit today's culture.

Eleven and a half years ago, my wife and I met Ann and Cal Gleaton on our first trip to Tallahassee. At that time, Ann gave me a copy of her first book, The Spoken Blessing. It has been a source of encouragement during some very challenging times.

Also, in our first meeting, Ann gave me a blessing. I have kept it in the front of my Bible from that day to this. It reads as follows:

May the Lord increase the supernatural electrically charged current of power flowing from Him, depositing it into you.

May this powerful anointing strengthen you and fill you so completely that you become a lighthouse casting forth life-saving, hope-rescuing light.

May this brilliant light pierce the oppressive darkness, drawing the lost and confused out of darkness into His marvelous light.

Proverbs 24:5, 11; Acts 26:16-18; Romans 2:19; 1 Peter 2:9

Little did I know that December day in 2013, how I would need these words to fulfill God's assignment on my life. Truly His power has kept me going. He has strengthened me and filled me so completely with marvelous light that brings wisdom and direction. It has enabled me to make some of the toughest decisions of my life. His brilliant light has pierced oppressive darkness day after day.

So today, I am living proof of the power of a blessing.

Ann and Cal are now dear friends who I have learned to lean on, and trust for a word fitly spoken, when I need it most.

I highly recommend this book for every person and family as an essential that will nestle beside the Bible."

Steve Dow
Pastor All Nations Church Tallahassee, FL

Acknowledgments

To our Abba Father, our Lord and Savior Jesus Christ, and to Holy Spirit, our Teacher and Counselor: we give You all glory, honor, praise, and worship. There is none like You. You make known to us the path of life: in Your presence is fullness of joy; at Your right hand are pleasures forevermore!

To my wonderful husband, Cal: you have been and continue to be my best friend, my confidant, my helpmate, my prayer warrior, my behind-the-scenes supporter, and my true love. As our love for the Lord has grown and deepened, so has our love for each other! Thank you for walking with me into our future centered in the Lord.

To our amazing children, our supportive daughters-in-law and son-in-law, and our precious grandchildren: your families have enriched our lives and multiplied our joy. Thank you for joining us at our table, adding laughter and fun to our family gatherings! We are grateful that you embraced the power of speaking and releasing blessing declarations in and through your lives.

To our pastors, Steve and Yvonne Dow: your friendship has deeply touched our hearts and lives. Your leadership has kept us focused on following God and honoring Christ. Your teaching has enhanced our understanding of God's word and its application to our lives.

To our church family at All Nations Church in Tallahassee: your love and support have undergirded our journey with the Lord. You have linked arms with us in following the directive of Christ: *Go therefore and make disciples of all nations.*

To our publisher, Steve Spillman, and his team: thank you for embracing the vision of this book and running with its message. Your counsel and encouragement have been greatly valued. Your excitement and support have propelled our efforts and purpose.

To Dr. Bill Ligon: look what the Lord has done through your obedience! The Father's heart flowed into and through yours for the furtherance of His kingdom. You have eternally influenced many generations to the glory of God!

Ann Dews Gleaton

Contents

Acknowledgments	5
The Myrtle Tree	9
Foreword	11
Preface	17
Introduction	19
1. Generations Are Inside Blessing Declarations	25
2. What Happened within the Generations?	57
3. When Did Jesus Speak?	79
4. Where Did Jesus Speak?	109
5. Why Should We Speak Blessing Declarations?	135
6. How Do We Advance God's Kingdom through Blessing Declarations?	163
7. Engaging Blessing Declarations by the Next Generations	205
8. Creating Blessing Declarations	245
Examples of Blessings	249
Appendix	263
Author's Notes	265
About the Author	267
References	269

The Myrtle Tree

"Instead of the thorn shall come up the cypress; instead of the brier shall come up the myrtle; and it shall make a name for the LORD, an everlasting sign that shall not be cut off." (Isaiah 55:13)

The Myrtle tree is incorporated within the Blessings, etc. logo as a symbol of both God's blessings and His Saints. The Myrtle tree is highly valued and often planted in gardens. It yields choice and excellent fruit for oil and wine. This tree releases a sweet and fragrant scent, never shedding its leaves. The Myrtle tree can be compared to God's people as they are highly esteemed by Him. God plants His spiritual trees, His Saints, within His garden, the Church. They bear fruit to honor Him and to benefit others. Their leaves, which never wither, are for the healing of the nations. God's Saints produce a sweet and pleasing fragrance to Him and others.[1] (Psalm 1:3; Isaiah 60:21; 61:3; Ezekiel 47:12)

What does the myrtle tree mean in Hebrew?

In Hebrew, "myrtle tree" is hadas (הדס) and symbolizes prosperity, restoration, and the beauty that emerges from adversity. The related feminine name is Hadassah (הדסה), meaning "myrtle tree." Queen Esther was known as Hadassah. Her beauty was both natural and spiritual as she humbly served as God's deliverer, restoring His honor among the nations and the freedom of His people.[2]

1   Preaching from the Types and Metaphors of the Bible, Benjamin Keach, pp. 761-762
2   https://www.jewishvirtuallibrary.org/myrtle

It is from the heart of God that He restores, exchanging briers for the beauty, fragrance and fruit of the Myrtle Tree. His deep desire is that we prosper in all that we do as we serve Him and others. The longing of God's heart is to fellowship and walk in union with His Saints. He is the Master Gardener of our lives. May our love for Him grow, producing fruit to His glory.

Foreword

God has revealed himself to us clearly through a series of divine communications which are collectively called the Bible. This self-revelation came to various people in various circumstances and has been conveyed to us through various genres of written text called Scripture. These scriptures are the record of God's Word and the standard by which we measure all other information about God. God's word is not a burden to carry or a bondage to endure. Rather, it is a blessing to receive, understand, and proclaim. Through God's Word we are empowered rather than burdened; set free rather than bound up.

As mentioned above, receiving God's Word is just the beginning of our interaction with the Bible. We are also called to understand it and proclaim it. These should be lifelong and mutual pursuits. As long as we live, we should be students of God's Word. The Bible is not just a good book; it contains the words of life. God's self-revelation and communication should be examined thoroughly and often. No human can ever reach complete understanding in this life, but we can grow in our knowledge of the Word to ever-increasing levels of understanding with the help of the promised and ever-present Holy Spirit. Our efforts to learn are met with His promise to teach so that we can further grasp the content and meaning of the Bible. Understanding Scripture moves us beyond memorization and recitation. Even our enemy can recite scripture. Understanding includes discovering the heart of God behind every text. Like old love letters, we read and reread, accounting for every word to better understand not only what is written but what the writer meant. We want to know not only what God said but also God's intentions and their implications. This is understanding.

Those who have received and understood the Word are also called to proclaim that Word as witnesses in the world. Witnesses are simply called upon to testify to what they know to be true. Proclaiming God's Word is our primary form of verbal witnessing. We not only share God's words but we also explain God's heart and mission as revealed in the words. When we truly believe God's Word, sharing that Word becomes a natural response rather than a forced activity. We can't help but share what we have been given so graciously.

Nevertheless, we sometimes neglect one or more of our responsibilities regarding God's word. There are those who would seek to proclaim without giving adequate effort to understand. This can lead to shallow, incomplete, or even wrong information being conveyed about our beloved Lord. Others can dedicate themselves to learning but never share God's Word. Their minds are full of understanding, but they rarely open their mouths to proclaim what they know to be true. Thus, they are like those who hide their light under a basket.

Ann Gleaton, writing along with her family, has shown us why we must understand and declare God's Word. This book provides a great resource for those who believe and understand God's Word and want practical models for how we should proclaim God's Word for both personal and generational blessing. This book is about the enduring value of speaking the Word of God to yourself and sharing it with others with the intention of conveying the actual blessings found in scripture. When we speak from the context of genuine belief and right understanding, blessings overflow. It's a simple yet profound method of communicating truth.

Unfortunately, some have taken the practice of declaring God's Word in purely self-serving directions as a mere tool for getting what we want, even if those wants are out of harmony with God's heart. These misguided teachers suggest that we can harness the power of God's Word to serve or fulfill our self-centered desires. This is not that kind of teaching. This book is not about manipulating or misusing God and His Word for some selfish benefit. Rather, this is the demonstration of an obedient and faithful response to God's Word that arises from understanding God's loving heart and gracious mission toward all people.

Ann Gleaton's work, as you will see, is biblically based and practically experienced. She is describing to us the tangible benefits of blessing declaration. This is not using God's Word for self-promotion but finding in God's Word His own desires for us and accepting and conveying those divine desires. Once again, this is not mere memorization and recitation (although this is also valuable). This is proclaiming with understanding and faith God's own divine communication about himself and its implications for us.

Ann writes, "Within God's heart and design is found His desire to remain in constant, abiding communication with His creation. You and I are a part of His creation." In what follows, Ann gives us a method to facilitate God's desire to communicate His Word to His creation both now and into the future since "God's eternal nature and purpose continue throughout generations." God has anointed us to convey His message in our own voices. On the Day of Pentecost, we see the Spirit-filled believers using their newly empowered voices to powerfully declare God's Word. This is still God's plan for us today. God wants His Word spoken in our voices. We have the privilege of dedicating our voices to conveying God's eternal message. Why would we lend our voice to any other purpose or message?

Speaking up, however, can be difficult for some of us. There are many forces at work discouraging us from declaring God's Word. The enemy attempts to silence our voice through fear, condemnation, and bitterness. Sometimes, we even allow our voices to communicate the enemy's evil intentions. This ought not to be. The reality is that every believer is called by God to convey his Good News. Certainly we are not all called to be preachers, but everyone is equipped to declare blessings arising from God's Word. Most of God's people will not be placed in a pulpit to deliver a sermon, but every believer is positioned in a place of influence where our voices can be heard with authority and credibility. Most of us should begin declaring God's Word in our homes—both around the table and in the mirror. Many will find further opportunities to speak blessings from the context of understanding of and faith in God's Word. God has entrusted us with His Word to help us carry out His mission and convey His heart with our voices. Isn't it amazing that God wants His messages to be heard by others in your voice? Indeed, I believe some people are prepared by God to receive His Word in our voice. They can hear it from others on TV, radio, and street corners, but there is something about your voice that will make the difference. That should excite us rather than frighten us.

How can we do this amazing and important work? This book gives us a viable and practical model for declaring the wonders and blessings of God. Ann has given us both the why and the how. She explains why blessing declaration is important and how we can do it rightly.

I can affirm from personal experience that Ann is teaching what she and her family practice. My wife and I have known Ann and Cal for 17 years. From the early days of our friendship until now, the Gleaton family has been a source of encouragement and blessing for us. We were challenged by their example and sought to participate in their practice of speaking and sharing blessings with others. With Ann and Cal's help, we have been able to share blessings (many of which she prepared and gave to us) with hundreds of people from at least 14 different countries while we served as missionaries in East Africa. We gave rolled blessing cards to church family, young students, college graduates, new converts, neighbors, and visitors. We made these written blessings available in our home and placed them in gifts for others. Back in the USA, we have shared the rolled blessing cards with elderly members of our church who are unable to attend our in-person gatherings so they could have a tangible expression of our love and God's desires for them. We still give these to those who are celebrating important milestones as gifts. In this book, Ann acknowledges that God's Word is not limited by time or space. We see that in both the generational and geographical impact of these blessings, and I pray that through this book, the ministry of declaring blessings will be carried even further.

I want to commend Ann and the Gleaton family for their transparency. Throughout the book, you will find powerful testimonies from Ann, Cal, their children, and even their grandchildren. These testimonies reveal the challenges and tragedies that this family has faced. Yet we also see the hope and victory that arose when the Word of God was declared as blessings and reality for and over one another. There are details in this book that we would never have known about this family, but we are invited to see these things in order that we may appreciate the redemptive and life-giving results of God's Word when it is embraced, understood, and proclaimed by individuals and families. I am grateful to the Gleaton family for yielding themselves for God's purpose and our benefit.

We believe that God sees us not only for who we are today but for who we shall be in eternity when His redemptive work is made complete in us. When we speak or share blessings, we are affirming by faith what God has promised to do and is doing for those who trust in Him. As you begin this study of blessing declarations, may you find God's truth and vision for you, your family, and your community, and may you begin to see everything else through the lens of God's truth. Our study of the Word of God reveals the heart of God. Through our declaration of God's heart for humanity, individuals will be drawn toward Christ and start to become the person God has called them to be. We can actually participate in and facilitate this great work of God by using our voices to proclaim God's message, and the impact can indeed touch generations.

Kevin Sneed, President, Holmes Bible College

Preface

"Our Faithful God" is how I know Him. When I replay the memory movies of my life, I watch Him working behind the scenes, introducing people into my life, reconciling difficult consequences that my choices created, holding my heart that was shattered. There are scenes in my life that cannot be edited or cut. They exist—sudden tragic death, deep loss, and even anger with God. He always showed Himself faithful, no matter how bewildered, angry, or ugly I was. He was, He is, and He will always be faithful.

Dear Reader, you are holding our family's story. It's very tender and personal, as is yours. You have a story. Would you walk with us for a while? As you listen to us, may we hear from you? Would you jot down your thoughts and responses to our stories? Feel free to share your lives with us at: www.spokenblessing.com. As you consider the past events of our lives, may you take nuggets of truth and God's wisdom to help you move forward with renewed focus and purpose. May God's heart touch yours.

Conversation: that's truly at the core of God's original relationship with His creation. He walked and talked with Adam and Eve. The three talked, listened, and responded. That's at the core of our faithful God—relationship, personal, one-on-one time.

May I invite you to "practice the presence" of God. Make room for Him, every day, throughout the day. Create a time, place, and space to remain and sustain His presence. For you see, *"You make known to me the path of life; in your presence there is fullness of joy; at your right hand are pleasures forevermore."* (Psalm 16:11) Do you want more joy in your life? Our culture provides countless suggestions for obtaining the "good life" that is brimming full of "pleasures."

Yet, God offers you and me so much more.

Just hours before Jesus submitted Himself to the Cross, He encouraged His disciples: *"Peace I leave with you; my peace I give to you. Not as the world gives do I give to you. Let not your hearts be troubled, neither let them be afraid."* (John 14:27)

May the peace of God rule and reign within and through your life! May the promised peace of Christ be your secure foundation. May Holy Spirit's presence direct your next step and the path of your future. In Jesus' Name. Amen.

Introduction

"Let this be recorded for a generation to come, so that a people yet to be created may praise the LORD:... The children of your servants shall dwell secure; their offspring shall be established before you." (Psalm 102:18, 28)

The psalmist looked toward the future. He focused on "a people yet to be created," that is, subsequent generations. His vision was cast beyond simply one more age group, but toward "their offspring." He not only prophesied about the existence of the next generations, but he also pronounced a prosperous and secure future. As you advance through our family's anecdotal experiences of using blessing declarations, you will gain greater recognition and understanding of how these declarations influence generations.

Speaking and releasing blessing declarations into lives and situations can become a generational strength. Engaging and trusting the power of the word of God and the authority and dominion of Jesus' Name re-establishes the original directive of God to "be fruitful and multiply"—His image.

"For those whom he foreknew he also predestined to be conformed to the image of his Son, in order that he might be the firstborn among many brothers."
(Romans 8:29)

"Foreknew" means the same as "foreloved" or "loved beforehand." It is used in the sense that God *chose to show his love toward us before we came into being and before we knew God (cf. 5:8; Ex.* 2:25; Ps. 1:6; Hos. 13:5; Matt. 7:23; 1 Cor. 8:3; Gal. 4:9; 1 John 3:1).[1]

1 FireBible™, p. 1905, note on Romans 8:29

Foreknowledge means that God purposed and decided from eternity (i.e., the infinite past, without beginning) to love the human race, to rescue them from their own way and to restore them to a relationship with himself through Christ (5:8; John 3:16).[1]

"...and have put on the new self, which is being renewed in knowledge after the image of its creator." (Colossians 3:10)

And have clothed yourselves with the new [spiritual self], which is [ever in the process of being] renewed and remolded into [fuller and more perfect knowledge upon] knowledge after the image (the likeness) of Him Who created it. (Colossians 3:10 AMPC)

Image—this continues to be the desire of God's heart and purpose. His image is to be "wrought" within our lives. "Wrought" is a powerful word picture when considering a metalworker—heating, hammering, and reheating, rehammering the metal as he or she shapes the image desired.

The shaping and reshaping of our lives within the crucible of God has recognizable "generations" of our personal faith and walk with Him. Today we have multiple "generations" of computers, cell phones, automobiles, etc. Each new generation of these items includes improvements, discoveries, greater effectiveness, and efficiencies. We can reflect on our journeys with God and easily identify progressions of our faith. Just as some of those products in our society have had flaws, we may recognize errors in our perception of God and our interpretation of His activity within our lives. If we are willing and submit our thoughts and ways to Him, God will reveal Himself to us. He will refine and purify our understanding of Him, our relationship with Him, and our future in Him.

"Submit yourselves therefore to God…" "Draw near to God, and he will draw near to you…" (James 4:7,8)

Isaiah calls "thirsty" people to the LORD: *"Come, everyone who thirsts, come to the waters;…listen diligently to me…incline your ear, and come to me: hear, that your soul may live…seek the LORD while he may be found; call upon him while he is near…"* (Isaiah 55:1,2,3,6)

As God's word is eternal and continues to accomplish its purpose, Jesus, the Divine and Living Word, spoke the same eternal truth: *"On the last*

---

1   ibid

day of the feast, the great day, Jesus stood up and cried out, 'If anyone thirsts, let him come to me and drink.'" (John 7:37)

Isaiah explains the grandeur and supremacy of our God:

> *For my thoughts are not your thoughts, neither are your ways my ways, declares the LORD. For as the heavens are higher than the earth, so are my ways higher than your ways and my thoughts than your thoughts. For as the rain and the snow come down from heaven and do not return there but water the earth, making it bring forth and sprout, giving seed to the sower and bread to the eater, so shall my word be that goes out from my mouth; it shall not return to me empty, but it shall accomplish that which I purpose, and shall succeed in the thing for which I sent it.* (Isaiah 55:8-11)

Consider with me the effect of God's thoughts, ways, and word being released from His mouth: His purpose is accomplished. You may ask: "How is it accomplished?" God's word requires activity and movement toward the fulfillment of His word.

Please read verses 20 and 21 in the writings of David as recorded in Psalm 103: *"Bless the LORD, you His angels, who excel in strength, who do His word, heeding the voice of His word. Bless the LORD, all you His hosts, you ministers of His, who do His pleasure."* (Psalm 103:20,21 NKJV)

Prayers & Decrees that Activate Angel Armies, by Tim Sheets, offers insight into verse 20:

> The Hebrew word for heeding is shama, which means 'to come to attention like a soldier, to perceive intelligently and obey, and to give undivided attention for the purpose of obeying or fulfilling' (Strong, H8085). Angels stand to attention when the Word of the Lord is declared. They heed it. Sons and daughters speak the voice of God's Word on this earth. When we speak the Scriptures, we are speaking God's Word. When we make decrees, angels snap to attention to bring that Word to pass. They don't hearken to our word; they hearken to and obey the Word of God that we declare. An angel network is laboring to bring about the decrees of the saints, the bold declarations of Scripture.[1]

---

1   p. 57, underline added

Walking in and experiencing the New Covenant that Jesus' blood purchased, the writer of Hebrews challenged us to consider: *"Are they not all ministering spirits sent forth to minister for those who will inherit salvation?"* (Hebrews 1:14 NKJV)

The New Spirit Filled Life Bible explains: *They are ministering spirits, or heavenly assistants, who are continually active today in building the body of Christ—advancing the ministry of Jesus and the building of His church."*[1] God's angels cause, make happen, the will and intent of God to occur.

God's purpose succeeds for the good, for the benefit of His creation. Look what occurs within others and their surroundings when God's purpose is fulfilled:

> *For you shall go out in joy and be led forth in peace; the mountains and the hills before you shall break forth into singing, and all the trees of the field shall clap their hands. Instead of the thorn shall come up the cypress; instead of the brier shall come up the myrtle; and it shall make a name for the LORD, an everlasting sign that shall not be cut off.* (Isaiah 55:12,13)

The curse is reversed. Sorrow is replaced by joy. The spoken, released word of God breaks forth life, joy, excitement, refreshment, renewal, peace. His angels do His word, accomplishing His purpose and honoring His Name. You and I will bring honor to His Name as we speak and release His word. God's presence, His majesty, His beauty will be magnified within our lives as we focus our attention on and place our trust in Him.

Hear the words of God's only Son, Jesus:

> *Ask, and it will be given to you; seek, and you will find; knock, and it will be opened to you. For everyone who asks receives, and the one who seeks finds, and to the one who knocks it will be opened.*
> (Matthew 7:7,8)

> *Keep on asking and it will be given you; keep on seeking and you will find; keep on knocking [reverently] and [the door] will be opened to you. For everyone who keeps on asking receives; and he who keeps on seeking finds; and to him who keeps on knocking, [the door] will be opened.* (Matthew 7:7,8 AMPC)

---

1   *The New Spirit Filled Life Bible*, p. 1731

Introduction

You and I ask in faith, we seek with faith, we find because He is faithful to open the door allowing us to enter. Jesus is the Door through which we enter God's presence. Jesus provides the privilege of meeting with God.

"I am the door. If anyone enters by me, he will be saved and will go in and out and find pasture." (John 10:9)

"And without faith it is impossible to please him, for whoever would draw near to God must believe that he exists and that he rewards those who seek him." (Hebrews 11:6)

> *And without faith living within us it would be impossible to please God. For we come to God in faith knowing that he is real and that he rewards the faith of those who give all their passion and strength into seeking him.* (Hebrews 11:6 TPT)

In the Gospel According to Luke, he shared one man's reward for seeking Jesus. The rather short man used his strength to climb a sycamore tree to obtain a better viewpoint of Jesus. Zacchaeus was seeking to discover more about Him.

Read what happened next:

> *And when Jesus came to the place, he looked up and said to him, "Zacchaeus, hurry and come down, for I must stay at your house today." So he hurried and came down and received him joyfully. And when they saw it, they all grumbled, "He has gone in to be the guest of a man who is a sinner." And Zacchaeus stood and said to the Lord, 'Behold, Lord, the half of my goods I give to the poor. And if I have defrauded anyone of anything, I restore it fourfold." And Jesus said to him, 'Today salvation has come to this house, since he also is a son of Abraham.* (Luke 19:5-9)

"For the Son of man is come to seek and to save that which was lost."
(Luke 19:10 KJV)

Are you willing to seek God, the Father, God, the Son, and God, the Holy Spirit? You will be rewarded as you do. Zacchaeus experienced awe-filled reverence and humility before Jesus. His heart was changed. His life was redirected to follow Jesus. As you read, seek Him.

During an interview with Steve Shultz on Elijah Streams, Robin D. Bullock identified: *"God is constantly dealing in the future. God preaches to us from our future. He is there..."*[1]

Walk with God into your future. Enjoy His fellowship. He enjoys yours.

---

[1] https://elijahstreams.com/, October 5, 2023

Chapter 1

Generations Are Inside Blessing Declarations

As God spoke over the formless void, He purposed eternity within His creation. Within eternity are generations of the various kingdoms within our world. God spoke and released the Word of Life into His creation.

> *In the beginning was the Word, and the Word was with God, and the Word was God. He was in the beginning with God. All things were made through him, and without him was not any thing made that was made.* (John 1:1-3)

> *For by Him all things were created that are in heaven and that are on earth, visible and invisible, whether thrones or dominions or principalities or powers. All things were created through Him and for Him.* (Colossians 1:16 NKJV)

"But in these last days he has spoken to us by his Son, whom he appointed the heir of all things, through whom also he created the world." (Hebrews 1:2)

God released His breath of life, which contained certain DNA that would replicate that unique creation. God's purpose and will were deposited within His creation so that they would be fruitful and multiply.

The Spoken Blessing II: Influencing Generations

And God said, "Let the earth sprout vegetation, plants yielding seed, and fruit trees bearing fruit in which is their seed, each according to its kind, on the earth." And it was so." "...And God saw that it was good. (Genesis 1:11,12)

God enabled mankind to discover the accuracy and inerrancy of His word when He revealed the molecule later known as DNA to a Swiss chemist named Johann Friedrich Miescher in the 1860s. Miescher was researching the key components of the white blood cell.[1] His investigation led to the recognition of self-replicating material, confirming God's word and work.

DNA: noun BIOCHEMISTRY

1. a self-replicating material that is present in nearly all living organisms as the main constituent of chromosomes. It is the carrier of genetic information.

2. the fundamental and distinctive characteristics or qualities of someone or something, especially when regarded as unchangeable.

DNA: The molecule inside cells that contains the genetic information responsible for the development and function of an organism. DNA molecules allow this information to be passed from one generation to the next.

What is DNA and its function? DNA (Deoxyribonucleic acid—dee-AAK-see-RIGH-boh-noo-KLAY-uhk A-suhd) is a molecule that contains the biological instructions that make each species unique. DNA, along with the instructions it contains, is passed from adult organisms to their offspring during reproduction.[2]

When we consider the declaration of the Godhead when He spoke to His creation: *"Be fruitful and multiply,"* we recognize this is true. God intentionally infused our DNA with His purpose. Multiplication indicates more and more and more, moving from one generation to the next.

Dear Reader, as you continue through this book, may I encourage you to remain in a prayerful posture before God. May you invite Him to reveal

---

1 https://www.nature.com/
2 https://my.clevelandclinic.org/health/body/dna

His word of truth as you read this message of speaking blessing declarations. May the eyes of your heart be enlightened to know and understand the God of Creation and His steadfast purpose and love for you.

Make a note of this: Creation was accomplished with God's speaking, i.e., a voice-activated work. During Creation the Life-depositing Word was released with a demonstration of the power of God's Spirit.

> *In the beginning, God created the heavens and the earth...And the Spirit of God was hovering over the face of the waters. And God said, "Let there be light," and there was light. And God saw that the light was good. And God separated the light from the darkness.*
> (Genesis 1:1-4)

God declared, He spoke His decree. "What does decree mean in the Bible?"

> *Decrees cause truths from the Word and the heavenly realm to be manifested in our earthly realm. In Hebrew, decree, means 'to divide, separate and destroy.' When we decree for example 'I am blessed' (based on Psalm 112:1) we establish blessing while separating from anything purposed against it by the enemy.*[1]

"Declare" is the translation of a variety of Hebrew and Greek words in the Old Testament and New Testament, appearing to bear uniformly the meaning "to make known," "set forth," rather than (the older meaning) "to explain." (Deuteronomy 1:5)

Consider the writings of Paul, the apostle, as he declared to the believers in Corinth:

> *And my speech and my preaching was not with enticing words of man's wisdom, but in demonstration of the Spirit and of power: That your faith should not stand in the wisdom of men, but in the power of God.* (1 Corinthians 2:4,5 KJV)

> *And my speech and my preaching were not with persuasive words of human wisdom, but in demonstration of the Spirit and of power, that your faith should not be in the wisdom of men but in the power of God.* (1 Corinthians 2:4,5 NKJV)

---

[1] www.heavolutionintl.org

"But we impart a secret and hidden wisdom of God, which God decreed before the ages for our glory." (1 Corinthians 2:7)

> *But rather what we are setting forth is a wisdom of God once hidden [from the human understanding] and now revealed to us by God---[that wisdom] which God devised and decreed before the ages for our glorification [to lift us into the glory of His presence].* (1 Corinthians 2:7 AMPC)

Let's revisit John's description of Jesus at the beginning of his gospel. John 1:1-5:

> *In the beginning was the Word, and the Word was with God, and the Word was God."* (2) *"He was in the beginning with God."* (3) *"All things were made through him, and without him was not any thing made that was made."* (4) *"In him was life, and the life was the light of men."* (5) *"The light shines in the darkness, and the darkness has not overcome it.*

As Scripture explains Scripture, consider what Jesus *declared, made known* about Himself:

"Again Jesus spoke to them, saying, 'I am the light of the world. Whoever follows me will not walk in darkness, but will have the light of life.'"

(John 8:12)

"Jesus said to her, 'I am the resurrection and the life. Whoever believes in me, though he die, yet shall he live,'" (John 11:25)

"Jesus said to him, 'I am the way, and the truth, and the life. No one comes to the Father except through me.'" (John 14:6)

Speaking to His disciples, Jesus made known His relationship with the Father: *"I and the Father are one."* (John 10:30)

In John 14:9: *"Jesus said to him, 'Have I been with you so long, and you still do not know me, Philip? Whoever has seen me has seen the Father. How can you say, "Show us the Father"?'"*

Jesus continued to set forth the unity of the Godhead as He presented His promise to send the Holy Spirit to those who loved and obeyed Him.

Generations Are Inside Blessing Declarations

"True love for God cannot be separated from obedience."[1]

> *If you love me, you will keep my commandments." "And I will ask the Father, and he will give you another Helper, to be with you forever," "even the Spirit of truth, whom the world cannot receive, because it neither sees him nor knows him. You know him, for he dwells with you and will be in you.* (John 14:15-17)

Within God's heart and design is found His desire to remain in constant, abiding communion with His creation. You and I are a part of His creation. In describing the One whom the Father would send, i.e., the Helper, Holy Spirit, Jesus explained: *"…to be with you forever."* (John 14:16) FOREVER is from generation to generation. You and I are one of those generations.

May I return your attention to John 14:15: *"If you love me, you will keep my commandments."*

May I ask you a question: Do you love Jesus? Do you believe that He is the only begotten Son of God? Do you believe that Jesus lived a perfect life and chose to die on the cross to pay the penalty for your sins? Do you believe that after three days He arose from the dead and is now seated at the right hand of the Father in heaven?

If you are not able to answer those questions with "Yes," may I encourage you to pause for a moment to ask the Father to help you discover His love and His Son throughout all the Scriptures that you will read and review. The Holy Trinity has a purpose-filled, abundant life for you to live, here on earth and for eternity. To enjoy and experience your abundant life, a decision is required: believe on the Lord Jesus Christ.

Consider the fact that God spoke to Adam and Eve, releasing over them His blessing, His will, and His purpose for their lives (Genesis 1:28-30). Genesis 3:8 describes God walking in the Garden in the cool of the day. God had placed Adam in the Garden of Eden to work it and keep it (Genesis 2:15). We could conclude that God, Adam, and Eve enjoyed the fellowship of one another. Jesus walked and talked with His disciples during His time on earth. Jesus promised to send His Holy Spirit to abide and dwell within everyone who believed in Him.

---

1   *FireBible*™, p. 1762, note on John 14:15

The desire of the Holy Trinity to fellowship with mankind has not diminished throughout the generations.

You can become someone who walks and talks with God, the One True God who is overflowing with wisdom and counsel. You can become someone who is seen and heard by a loving Father, a forgiving Savior, and a Truth-filled Companion. Why wouldn't you want to become that someone who experiences the Holy Trinity's abiding love, continual forgiveness, and steadfast fellowship?

Are you experiencing this relationship with God?

Please read Paul's words of truth, which he wrote to the believers in Ephesus:

> *But God, being rich in mercy, because of the great love with which he loved us," "even when we were dead in our trespasses, made us alive together with Christ—by grace you have been saved—" "and raised us up with him and seated us with him in the heavenly places in Christ Jesus," "so that in the coming ages he might show the immeasurable riches of his grace in kindness toward us in Christ Jesus." "For by grace you have been saved through faith. And this is not your own doing; it is the gift of God," "not a result of works, so that no one may boast.* (Ephesians 2:4-9)

As Paul described the forgiveness that Jesus offers and provides as the "gift of God," he continued by identifying a wonder-filled, power-filled future for you in Christ Jesus:

"For we are his workmanship, created in Christ Jesus for good works, which God prepared beforehand, that we should walk in them." (Ephesians 2:10)

Look again at verse 10! Generations ago (before time, as we know it, began), God prepared all these wonderful, good works for us to experience and accomplish. We are His creation! He takes great delight in us. As we are walking within His "prepared beforehand" good works, we are fulfilling God's destiny specifically created for us!

This passage screams loudly about PURPOSE. No one is a "mistake." God does not create "mistakes." Our Sovereign God does not say, "Oops… back to the drawing board."

"Now the word of the LORD came to me, saying, 'Before I formed you in the womb I knew you, and before you were born I consecrated you; I appointed you a prophet to the nations.'" (Jeremiah 1:4-5)

Jeremiah was born, lived, and fulfilled God's purpose generations before Paul wrote his letter to the Ephesian believers. The unchanging character of God is that He has an awe-filled, power-packed purpose and "good works" for every person.

Your mind may begin to think of numerous reasons why you "can't" or are "not qualified" to accomplish wonderful and powerful works throughout your life. So did Jeremiah! He didn't just think those thoughts; he spoke them to the Omniscient, All-knowing God!

"Then I said, 'Ah, Lord GOD! Behold, I do not know how to speak, for I am only a youth.'" (Jeremiah 1:6)

Do you hear Jeremiah's excuse for not doing the *good works* of God? Follow the conversation between our Sovereign LORD and one of His creations:

"But the LORD said to me, 'Do not say, "I am only a youth"; for to all to whom I send you, you shall go, and whatever I command you, you shall speak.'" (Jeremiah 1:7)

The LORD did not want Jeremiah to shrink back and remain in the mindset of "I can't." The LORD corrected Jeremiah's declarations about himself. Our declarations, our words, reflect our mindset concerning ourselves, others, and situations around us and the greatness and power of God. Those mindsets can bind and restrict us. Those mindsets can create a stronghold within our thinking and thus control our actions and future. They can be a stumbling block to fulfilling our destinies in Christ Jesus. Our damaging declarations hinder us from becoming ALL that He created us to be! Self-defeating, negative words stifle angels who are poised and ready to assist us in fulfilling all that God has purposed!

The LORD reassured Jeremiah that He had a plan and purpose for Jeremiah and He would direct Jeremiah's life. There were places to which the LORD would send Jeremiah. There were people with whom Jeremiah would speak to advance His kingdom purposes.

Then the LORD addressed another emotion of Jeremiah: fear and trepidation.

"Do not be afraid of them, for I am with you to deliver you, declares the LORD." (Jeremiah 1:8)

"Be not afraid of their faces: for I am with thee to deliver thee, saith the LORD." (Jeremiah 1:8 KJV)

The LORD promised His presence and protection to Jeremiah. He counseled Jeremiah not to allow the people's countenance to create fear within him. During interactions with people, have you ever thought: "Whoa, he just shot me one of those looks" or "Ooo, she did not like what I just said"? Such thoughts often circulate in your mind after a verbal exchange with someone. You notice some type of reaction on the other person's face or hear the tone of their voice or words. Remember that the LORD told Jeremiah: *"Do not be afraid of their faces..."* as He reassured him.

Consider the meaning of LORD: "(the) self-Existent or eternal; Jehovah, Jewish national name of God: - Jehovah, the Lord."[1]

Jehovah, the LORD, is eternal. He has always existed and will exist forever. He governs all. He is not leaving you. He will continue to direct your ways if you allow Him. Jeremiah had to allow the LORD to be the Leader and Director of his life. Watch what happened next:

"Then the LORD put out his hand and touched my mouth. And the LORD said to me, 'Behold, I have put my words in your mouth.'" (Jeremiah 1:9)

Make note of this: the LORD empowers us with the presence of His Spirit and His word as it richly dwells within us. As Holy Spirit resides within everyone who has called on the Name of Jesus for salvation, He will give you the word of God to release through your mouth as you speak blessing declarations over people and situations. That specific work of His Spirit was explained by Jesus as He taught His disciples about the coming Helper:

"But the Helper, the Holy Spirit, whom the Father will send in my name, he will teach you all things and bring to your remembrance all that I have said to you." (John 14:26)

---

1 Strong's Concordance, H3068: LORD

Generations Are Inside Blessing Declarations

Let's return to the conversation between the LORD and young Jeremiah:

"See, I have set you this day over nations and over kingdoms, to pluck up and to break down, to destroy and to overthrow, to build and to plant."
(Jeremiah 1:10)

The LORD was making young Jeremiah an overseer of nations and to exercise dominion over kingdoms for a specific work. Doesn't that sound like the same directive and appointment given to Adam and Eve in the Garden of Eden? The LORD, the Sovereign Ruler, exercised all authority and governance over His creation. He appointed people to govern, to oversee the control and direction of His world.

God's eternal nature and purpose continue throughout generations. He desires to enjoy fellowship and communion with mankind. As His conversation and fellowship with Jeremiah progressed, the LORD placed before Jeremiah an almond tree that was blossoming and asked His young spokesman a question. As Jeremiah responded, the LORD confirmed His eternal purpose:

"Then the LORD said to me, 'You have seen well, for I am watching over my word to perform it.'" (Jeremiah 1:12) His word is eternal and *will be accomplished*, no matter what happens. For further confirmation of God's fulfilling His word, read Isaiah 55:11: *"So shall my word be that goes out from my mouth; it shall not return to me empty, but it shall accomplish that which I purpose, and shall succeed in the thing for which I sent it."*

As God is eternal, Jeremiah's life had always been known by Him—the same is true of your life. He has the continuation of life and purpose for you as well. He releases His word of sustaining life into and over you! You are His next generation through which blessings will flow. His good pleasure is to pour into your life the blessings of salvation through His Son, Jesus Christ.

Keep in mind, His salvation is a gift to you (Ephesians 2:8). As with any gift, you must accept this gift. Then, as you receive His gift and blessings, you use His gift and pour into others blessings of His Life, His Light, His Hope, His Peace. You receive from God so that you can give to others. You can become an active participant in speaking blessing declarations based on the life-depositing word of truth.

Everyone is searching and seeking truth. Jesus declared to Thomas: *"I am the way, and the truth, and the life. No one comes to the Father except through me."* (John 14:6)

If you have not accepted Jesus as your Savior, now would be a great time for you to repent of your sins, to place your faith in Him (and not in yourself), to trust in His provision for your life, and to receive all the benefits of His salvation.

"For everyone who calls on the name of the Lord will be saved."
(Romans 10:13)

As you pray a prayer of repentance and acceptance of Jesus' forgiveness, there is transformation that occurs within your spirit. Old things have passed away; new things have been birthed within you. Holy Spirit does His work of regeneration within you.

"Therefore, if anyone is in Christ, he is a new creation. The old has passed away; behold, the new has come." (2 Corinthians 5:17) Now read this declaration from the Amplified™ Bible:

> Therefore if any person is [ingrafted] in Christ [the Messiah] he is a new creation (a new creature altogether); the old [previous moral and spiritual condition] has passed away. Behold, the fresh and new has come.

Your DNA has been made new with His life producing good fruit in and through you!

Jesus forgives you of your sin. He sends His Holy Spirit to indwell you. His Spirit will never leave nor forsake you. Jesus will continually pray for you as He is seated in Heaven at the right hand of the Father. His Spirit, living within you, also continually prays for you. (Romans 8:26)

Now that's Prayer Power. He invites you to walk and talk with Him all the time. He wants you to ask Him questions. He has answers. Do you recall Jeremiah? Consider God's instruction, challenge, and reassurance for Jeremiah:

"Call to me and I will answer you, and will tell you great and hidden things that you have not known." (Jeremiah 33:3)

"Call unto me, and I will answer thee, and shew thee great and mighty things, which thou knowest not." (Jeremiah 33:3 KJV)

It is within and through our oneness with God, the Father, God, the Son, and God, the Holy Spirit that we will experience and have knowledge of the Way we are to follow, the Truth of who we are and who God is, and the Life to live within this union.

During the last few hours before His crucifixion, Jesus explained and confirmed this union: *"Jesus answered him [Judas, not Iscariot], 'If anyone loves me, he will keep my word, and my Father will love him, and we will come to him and make our home with him.'"* (John 14:23, brackets added)

Now read it from The Amplified™ Bible Classic Edition:

> *Jesus answered, If a person [really] loves Me, he will keep My word [obey My teaching]; and My Father will love him, and We will come to him and make Our home (abode, special dwelling place) with him.*

Just moments before making this statement, He identified the continuing fellowship of God, the Holy Spirit:

> *If you love me, you will keep my commandments. And I will ask the Father, and he will give you another Helper, to be with you forever, even the Spirit of truth, whom the world cannot receive, because it neither sees him nor knows him. You know him, for he dwells with you and will be in you.* (John 14:15-17)

Recall in Ephesians 2:10 that God prepared beforehand the good works we are to accomplish. This is the same principle that was operating within Jeremiah's life and his future. God operates and communicates with the future in His mind and focus. He is omniscient; that is, He is all-knowing. He knows the details of every time—past, present, and future. As LORD, He governs them all. He has appointed and released ambassadors into every *generation* to achieve His original directive to Adam and Eve: *"Be fruitful and multiply and fill the earth and subdue it, and have dominion over..."* (Genesis 1:28)

Let's reference Ephesians 2:10 one more time:

> *For we are* (we have our being in) *his workmanship* (His tapestry of life and creation), *created* (skillfully designed) *in* (inside a position of rest, having given oneself wholly to the authority of) *Christ Jesus for good works* (for the purpose of accomplishing the power-filled, wonder-filled acts, occupation, labor, deeds), *which God prepared beforehand* (prepared and provided for in advance), *that we should walk in them* (tread about with the ability to do so, living in those good labors).

I added parenthetical notes derived from Strong's Concordance for various words in the Greek language.

On a side note: you and I have purpose and good works to accomplish in this world. *One* of those wonder-filled good works is to help others recognize their purpose and value in the Father's heart. We can assist them in discovering why they are on this earth at this time and place. In helping their discovery, we turn their focus to Jesus, the Author and Finisher of their faith, their loving Abba Father and Holy Spirit, their faithful companion in life.

Paul, author of the book of Ephesians, instructed his child in the faith, Titus, to accomplish works that would benefit others, for their good. Paul's instruction was this: *"Show yourself in all respects to be a model of good works, and in your teaching show integrity, dignity, and sound speech that cannot be condemned."* (Titus 2:7,8)

Then, Paul directed his attention to the Cretans who would be under the leadership of Titus. Paul exhorted Titus to remind these believers *"…to be ready for every good work, to speak evil of no one, to avoid quarreling, to be gentle, and to show perfect courtesy toward all people."* (Titus 3:1,2)

Please read Titus 3:2: *"to speak evil of no one, to be peaceable, gentle, showing all humility to all men."* (NKJV)

Our words can release life or death, encouragement or condemnation, hope for the future or despair. Our verbal communication can direct others toward God's goodness, mercy, and love OR our words can demean others as we attempt to elevate ourselves. It is our choice how we use our words and works.

Generations Are Inside Blessing Declarations

"Death and life are in the power of the tongue,..." (Proverbs 18:21)

"Your words are so powerful that they will kill or give life..."
(Proverbs 18:21 TPT)

Tim Sheets identified: "We must understand that we are destined to live the life we speak."[1] Please read Tim's quote a few more times. Think about it.

Our words can edify or tear down ourselves and others.

David, our son, has applied this biblical principle in his life:

> As a kid into my current stage of life, I have always been hyperaware of calling people negative names because I know the impact that it has. Growing up with the Blessings, I wouldn't use them in the "Blessing declaration" format; I would just speak positively to others because that's what I gathered was the purpose of the Blessings. God has shown me that speaking Blessings over people is probably more important for them than they realize. It is similar to speaking positive affirmations; it plants a seed in them. It may get them curious about God, or it could make their day. But it is something positive, and they know that.

Carolina, David's wife, shared insight from a recent work environment:

> God showed me during my time as a therapist the importance of language. What is said and how it is said. In the mental health realm, the idea of diagnoses is very accepted. You bring in your issue, and the provider is meant to give you a label for what you are experiencing. I found this to be problematic because it mirrors, at times, speaking a curse over someone. While some people may find it healing, as they gain language to describe what they are feeling, for others it becomes an identity that represents brokenness. "I am my symptoms. There is nothing I can do to change this, because it is who I am." This takes away hope. You are finding identity in something that isn't God.

Currently Carolina serves as an Academic Advisor for a college in their area. She engages the Blessings in this way:

---

1   *Prayers & Decrees that Activate Angel Armies*, p. 43

I have a container of Blessing scrolls sitting on my desk. So when students ask what they are, I am able to engage them in a quick dialogue about speaking positively and speaking life in accordance with our faith and beliefs.

If we submit to God's authority to weave His purpose and good pleasure within the tapestry of our lives, then we will walk about sharing His goodness from generation to generation. We will propel and deposit His blessings and benefits into their lives and futures with the words of Christ:

"Thy kingdom come. Thy will be done in earth, as it is in heaven."
(Matthew 6:10 KJV)

"Manifest your kingdom realm, and cause your every purpose to be fulfilled on earth, just as it is fulfilled in heaven." (Matthew 6:10 TPT)

If you are not experiencing God's goodness, then invite Him and allow Him to remove old habits and mindsets, permitting His best to operate within your life.

Pray this: God, help me. Show me what needs to go so that Your good works can be accomplished and manifested in my life. I am willing to trust You for my life and what You want me to do. I reject old habits and mindsets that oppose Your truth and Your goodness. I need Your Holy Spirit to do a good work in me so I can advance Your Kingdom directives! Work Your best in me. In Jesus' Name, I pray. Amen.

Remember: God does not change, even with the passing of generations. Through His Holy Spirit, He speaks to you as you read His word of truth, the Holy Bible. May you enjoy the fellowship of His presence every day! God's desire and good pleasure is to be in close communion with you, moment by moment. Enjoy His friendship. He wants to be so close that He kisses your face.

Consider the LORD's instruction to Moses:

> *The LORD spoke to Moses, saying, "Speak to Aaron and his sons, saying, Thus you shall bless the people of Israel: you shall say to them, The LORD bless you and keep you; the LORD make his face to shine upon you and be gracious to*

> *you; the LORD lift up his countenance upon you and give you peace. So shall they put my name upon the people of Israel, and I will bless them."* (Numbers 6:22-27)

Take note that the LORD, in the governance of His people, engaged successive *generations* to impart His blessings upon others, i.e., *"Speak to Aaron and his sons.....So shall they put my name upon the people of Israel, and I will bless them."* (verse 27)

Consider the meaning of "put my name." The LORD directed Aaron and his sons, the next generation, to convey, to transfer, to transmit God's name, which includes the entirety of His nature, into the lives of His people. The LORD desired that the totality of His nature be imparted to one person, and to another, and to another. His name is His nature; His nature is His image. Revisit the passage about God's creation of mankind in Genesis 1:26-28. God's plan, purpose, and desire continue throughout generations.

If we fast forward several generations to the final days of King David, we discover that the household or family of Aaron was advancing this directive of the LORD. King David identified the continuance of the duties of Aaron and his sons: *"Forever should make offerings before the LORD and minister to him and pronounce blessings in his name forever."*
(1 Chronicles 23:13)

Read verse 24 of Numbers 6 again: *"The LORD bless you and keep you;"* and consider the *FireBible's*™ note:

> To 'bless' (Heb. *barak*) carries the idea of God's presence, activity and love are brought into a person's life and environment. (1) This blessing was set before God's faithful servants under the conditions he had established (Deut. 11:27).

If you were to say: "I am not a king nor priest, so I can't…" May I draw your attention to the Apostle Peter's declaration over every believer in Christ Jesus:

> *But you are a chosen race, a royal priesthood, a holy nation, a people for his own possession, that you may proclaim the excellencies of him who called you out of darkness into his marvelous light.* (1 Peter 2:9)

Take a moment to read that verse from the Amplified™ Bible:

> *But you are a chosen race, a royal priesthood, a dedicated nation, [God's] own purchased, special people, that you may set forth the wonderful deeds and display the virtues and perfections of Him Who called you out of darkness into His marvelous light.*

Let's add to the understanding of our position in Christ by reading Romans 5:17:

> *For if, because of one man's trespass, death reigned through that one man, much more will those who receive the abundance of grace and the free gift of righteousness reign in life through the one man Jesus Christ.*

> *For if because of one man's trespass (lapse, offense) death reigned through that one, much more surely will those who receive [God's] overflowing grace (unmerited favor) and the free gift of righteousness [putting them into right standing with Himself] reign as kings in life through the one Man Jesus Christ (the Messiah, the Anointed One). (AMP)*

I gain comfort in knowing that I receive "[God's] overflowing grace."

I gain confidence that through His gift of righteousness, He puts me in "right standing with Himself."

I gain renewed excitement for reigning as a king in life through Jesus Christ, the Messiah.

Those are just three benefits we receive "through the free gift of righteousness."

As you and I live within God's grace provided through His Son, Jesus, we shall enjoy our freedom within His kingdom to decree, declare, and establish His kingdom on earth as it is in heaven. One way to accomplish this advancement is to speak and release blessing declarations over people, places, and circumstances. We are to establish the authority of the word of God and His Christ.

Listen to the apostle Peter's declaration as found in his first writings:

Generations Are Inside Blessing Declarations

"But the word of the Lord remains forever. And this word is the good news that was preached to you." (1 Peter 1:25)

Peter was echoing the prophet Isaiah: *"The grass withers, the flower fades, but the word of our God will stand forever."* (Isaiah 40:8) "Forever" indicates the unending advancement of God's word, generation to generation.

From the very beginning, God declared a blessing over and flowing *into* His creation, which includes mankind. His nature, His word carries and deposits His power and authority to accomplish His purpose. You and I can walk inside His blessing declaration.

So, what's your decision? Now is the time to lay down everything you've been holding sacred, not allowing God to touch or "deal with it." Now is the time to surrender every area of your being: body, soul, and spirit. Now is the time to release your clenched fist on your self-prescribed future and allow God to accomplish His will and good pleasure within you.

You and I will walk in and will be covered with His blessings if we abide in Him. Within the framework of His commandments includes the privilege of walking and talking with God, the Creator of the Universe. Our Sovereign God is much more awesome than any Hollywood star, celebrated athlete, powerful politician, or religious leader. Let's remind ourselves that from the very beginning of Creation, God, our Creator, set before Adam and Eve the principles of following His directives, i.e., the principles of life or death—a blessing or a curse. Such principles of living in communion with Him and His creation (including other humans) are enumerated in Deuteronomy 11.

Let's pause for a quick moment and discuss this idea: living in communion with Him and His creation, which includes other humans. Most of us live within some type of community, whether it be in a Peruvian jungle village along the Amazon River, in the hills of Tennessee, in New York City, in a suburb of a metropolitan city or in a quiet country town. Within these various groups of people, there is a framework of rules, regulations, and directives that are followed. These guidelines may be written or simply understood. In fact, our communities suffer greatly when rules or laws are not in force. Chaos, bloodshed, abuse, and death occur.

What am I saying? Don't allow the word "commandments" to become a stumbling block to you. If you want to drive a car within a community, you must adhere to certain laws or "commandments." These laws are intended to help drivers and pedestrians reach their destination safely and in a timely fashion.

God's commandments are intended to establish guidelines in our relationship with others and with Him. God deeply desires to live in communion, in relationship with us. He created us for the pleasure of knowing and communing with us. He loves us. God loves you. He set us within a community of people so that we could bless them, and, in turn, we could be blessed by them. He placed within us certain gifts which can encourage the lives of people (1 Corinthians 12:4-11; Hebrews 2:4). As we follow His leading, we will discover the optimum use and benefits of the Spirit's gifts. Allowing His gifts to operate in and through us honors Christ as we express God's grace and declare the good news of Salvation. Following God's directives is not burdensome.

From my personal experience, I recognize that if I adhere to and assimilate His commandments in my daily living, I save myself from self-defeating attitudes, mindsets, and behaviors. I acknowledge that His ways are better than mine (Isaiah 55:8-9).

Let's return to God's commander, Moses, who served as His governing official and ambassador to the descendants of Abraham, Isaac, and Jacob. Advancing the will of the LORD, he issued this instruction found in Deuteronomy 11:

> (1) *You shall therefore love the LORD your God and keep his charge, his statutes, his rules, and his commandments always. (2) …consider the discipline of the LORD your God, his greatness, his mighty hand and his outstretched arm, (7) For your eyes have seen all the great work of the LORD that he did.*

Verses 3 through 6 enumerate the provision and protection the LORD supplied the generations of Abraham, Isaac, and Jacob to advance His original plan and desire for mankind. Even in the harsh environment of Egyptian slavery, God faithfully furnished His people with fruitfulness and multiplication. As a family of seventy, Jacob and his descendants entered Egypt accepting the Pharaoh's invitation. More than four-hundred years later, the subsequent generations of Jacob exited Egypt numbering over one million!

"Behold, the LORD's hand is not shortened, that it cannot save, or his ear dull, that it cannot hear;" (Isaiah 59:1). God's open hand, full of His power, His provision, and His direction is able to save His people.[1]

He loves His creation. He longs for mankind to respond to His love with love. Moses repeated this idea several times throughout the eleventh chapter of Deuteronomy. This ambassador of the Sovereign LORD also reiterated the principle of obeying God's original directive to go forth, subdue the land, occupy, and possess it.

Read Moses' instruction found in subsequent verses of Deuteronomy 11:

(8) "You shall therefore keep the whole commandment that I command you today, that you may be strong, and go in and take possession of the land that you are going over to possess," (9) "and that you may live long in the land that the LORD swore to your fathers to give to them and to their offspring, a land flowing with milk and honey." (11) "…the land that you are going over to possess is a land of hills and valleys, which drinks water by the rain from heaven," (12) "a land that the LORD your God cares for. The eyes of the LORD your God are always upon it, from the beginning of the year to the end of the year."

Do you hear the attention the LORD, who is also our God, gives to His people and the land He directs them to occupy and possess? Do you recognize the partnership involved in this God-to-mankind, mankind-to-God relationship? If you have ever suffered a drought, you know the power and significance of the rain that comes from heaven. Droughts severely affect crop production. No crops, no food. No food, no life. These people had just left over four-hundred years of the grueling, torturous daily "grind" of the treadwheel which was used by the Egyptians to irrigate the land drawing water from the Nile River.* The Egyptians had forced God's people to be the manpower of those treadwheels. To be delivered from this grueling task and to be supplied heavenly rain was a powerful promise![2]

---

1 Strong's Concordance H3027: hand
2 https://www.e-sword.net/mac/

For God's people to be provided a land to possess was another power-packed promise. They had suffered for hundreds of years the harshness of being possessed by the Egyptians. The LORD, in His governance, was giving them the opportunity to be those who "possess," to occupy, to subdue a land "flowing with milk and honey." What an invitation! What a provision! What was the LORD requiring from His people? Relationship, relationship, relationship with Him. He delivered them from a polytheistic culture. The Egyptians worshipped a plethora of little gods, manmade idols. The God of Abraham, Isaac, and Jacob wanted His people to trust Him, and Him alone, for their provision, their future, and their influence within the land into which He sent them. The original desire for His image to be multiplied across the face of the earth was still active, still in force. The promise He made to Abraham and reconfirmed to Isaac, Abraham's son, was being fulfilled.

Generations are always involved as God's faithful plan and lovingkindness are revealed. God's eternal plan of reconciling, reuniting mankind with his Creator has been in existence before the foundations of the world were established, that is, before Creation.

God's love, His desires, His plans for mankind are eternal. Eternal means without a beginning nor an end. Our minds may have a hard time grasping eternity, but we can consider God's faithful involvement and provision for generations of mankind.

As you choose to lay down the control of your life and submit to the leading and guiding of His Holy Spirit, you choose to participate in God's continuing story! You become one of His KEY players! You become a beacon of light to the world! You begin sharing the knowledge of God's love through His Son, Jesus Christ. God makes His appeal to others through you!

These passages written through the hand and heart of Paul, guided by God's Holy Spirit, declare to us what God's purpose and will are for our lives.

"For those who live according to the flesh set their minds on the things of the flesh, but those who live according to the Spirit set their minds on the things of the Spirit." (Romans 8:5)

Paul had chosen to surrender his life to the saving grace of Jesus Christ and to the Lordship of His Spirit. Paul lived "according to the Spirit." He walked in the natural and supernatural. You and I can do the same. Our Father God calls us to do the same.

Our son, David, and his wife, Carolina, choose to serve as "beacons of light." Recently Carolina shared how they engage Paul's truth in their daily lives:

> For me, blessing declarations are about speaking LIFE. This to me means highlighting hope, encouragement, and strength. I will often write blessing-like statements on a whiteboard in our kitchen, such as "Since we live by the Spirit, let us keep in step with the Spirit." The purpose of this being to invite the presence of God into our home, and I do similarly in my office. David and I have a habit of sharing blessing scrolls in public when an opportunity arises in conversation. We are able to explain to others the power of words.

We no longer live to follow the desires of our self-centered flesh, but we choose to submit to the leading and all-wise counsel of Holy Spirit. That's one way to experience His peace and confidence for each day.

"I will instruct you and teach you in the way you should go; I will counsel you with my eye upon you." (Psalm 32:8)

"Let me give you some good advice; I'm looking you in the eye and giving it to you straight: 'Don't be ornery like a horse or mule that needs a bit and bridle to stay on track.'" (Psalm 32:8-9 The Message)

Jesus gave His disciples a new identity which contained a new purpose for living:

"You are the light of the world. A city set on a hill cannot be hidden."
(Matthew 5:14)

Then Jesus explained the disciples' participation and continuation of God's blessing of life:

"In the same way, let your light shine before others, so that they may see your good works and give glory to your Father who is in heaven." (Matthew 5:16)

The Amplified™ Bible Classic Edition provides:

> *Let your light so shine before men that they may see your moral excellence and your praiseworthy, noble, and good deeds and recognize and honor and praise and glorify your Father Who is in heaven.* (Matthew 5:16)

The Apostle Paul explained the "before" and "after" reality of not believing in Jesus Christ as your Savior and then placing your life and future in His saving hands of forgiveness and abundant life: *"For at one time you were darkness, but now you are light in the Lord. Walk as children of light."* (Ephesians 5:8) Walking with the Lord transforms our lives!

Psalm 37 contrasts the life of a person walking in darkness and doing evil works with the person who commits his or her way to the LORD and trusts in Him.

Psalm 37:5 *"Commit your way to the LORD; trust in him, and he will act."*

Psalm 37:23 *"The steps of a man are established by the LORD, when he delights in his way;"* (TPT) *"The steps of the God-pursuing ones follow firmly in the footsteps of the Lord, and God delights in every step they take to follow him."*

Psalm 37:30 *"The mouth of the righteous utters wisdom, and his tongue speaks justice."* (TPT) *"God-lovers make the best counselors. Their words possess wisdom and are right and trustworthy."*

Wow! Look at The Passion Translation's description of those of us who love God and follow His ways: we are "the best counselors." Our words that others hear us speak "possess wisdom and are right and trustworthy." I want to share God's counsel, don't you?

Read Philippians 2:

> (13) *For it is God who works in you, both to will and to work for his good pleasure."* (15) *...that you may be blameless and innocent, children of God without blemish in the midst of a crooked and twisted generation, among whom you shine as lights in the world...* (16) *...holding fast to the word of life.*

Generations Are Inside Blessing Declarations

May I encourage you to ask God "to will and to work for his good pleasure" through your life? I assure you that as you invite and submit to His good pleasure, you will experience a deep joy and awe of Him. Release the adoration expressed through Mark Altrogge's song: "I Stand In Awe Of You."

May I share with you an awe-filled time I spent with the Lord? This is related to the generational aspect of God's work. I will "set the stage" for when this occurred.

This experience unfolded when our children's ages ranged from preschool to college. (Our four children fall into three generational groups: Generation X, Millennials, and Generation Z.) Our habit was to share a Sunday meal together. Seated around our large, oval table, everyone was talking, laughing, and enjoying the food and fellowship. Suddenly, and I stress suddenly, Holy Spirit began to speak to me. Other voices were somewhat muted as His voice became the dominant one that I heard. He directed my attention to each child, one by one. As He highlighted each one, He focused on their strengths. He described their impact upon our family. He identified their personalities, their God-created abilities, and enhancements to our family. As I listened to Holy Spirit's words, I was filled with awe and reverence for God. The Spirit was enlarging my heart toward God and our children.

May I turn our attention to the living, active word of God found in Psalm 127?

"Behold, children are a heritage from the LORD, the fruit of the womb a reward." (v. 3)

"Children are God's love-gift; they are heaven's generous reward." (v. 3, TPT)

"Like arrows in the hand of a warrior are the children of one's youth." (v. 4)

"Children born to a young couple will one day rise to protect and provide for their parents." (v. 4, TPT)

"Blessed is the man who fills his quiver with them! He shall not be put to shame when he speaks with his enemies in the gate." (v. 5)

The Spoken Blessing II: Influencing Generations

Happy will be the couple who has many of them! A household full of children will not bring shame on your name but victory when you face your enemies, for your offspring will have influence and honor to prevail on your behalf! (v. 5, TPT)

The psalmist continued his declarations as recorded in Psalm 128:

"Blessed is everyone who fears the LORD, who walks in his ways!" (v. 1)

"You shall eat the fruit of the labor of your hands; you shall be blessed, and it shall be well with you." (v. 2)

"Your wife will be like a fruitful vine within your house; your children will be like olive shoots around your table." (v. 3)

"Your wife will bless your heart and home. Your children will bring you joy as they gather around your table." (v. 3, TPT)

Remember, I was simply sitting around our dining table enjoying time with my husband and children when God, the Holy Spirit, began to speak to me. It was as though He had pulled up a chair next to me, leaned over to whisper His wisdom, and to deposit a deeper depth of God's love for our family. He loves your family as well!

Again, I sing: "I stand in awe of You."[1]

Join me in releasing this blessing declaration as written in Psalm 144:12: *"May our sons in their youth be like plants full grown, our daughters like corner pillars cut for the structure of a palace;"*

Let's follow the wisdom and direction of David as provided in Psalm 145:4: *"One generation shall commend your works to another, and shall declare your mighty acts."*

Twenty-plus years after this tender, life-changing time with Holy Spirit, I testify to God's faithfulness in His working within and through the lives of our children. As adults, our four children are incredible blessings to Cal and me. Their four wonderful spouses bring additional gifts, talents, and personalities to enhance our family's wealth. Remember, wealth far exceeds monetary assets. All eight of these young adults pour into our lives great joy, laughter, love, acceptance, forgiveness, generosity, fellow-

---

1   Mark Altrogge, 1987

ship, "free labor," medical advice, investment counsel, encouragement, patience, comforting hugs, grandchildren, and on and on I could go.

"God's love-gifts" arise "to protect and provide for" Cal and me. Our children's lives bring honor to ours and to God. Our offspring influence their spheres of employment, education, recreation, faith, and family. Our eight young men and women enlarge our family's "tent pegs" and "push back boundaries" for the advancement of God's kingdom on earth. As I write about our children pushing back or enlarging boundaries, I recall a prayer that Cal and I have prayed for many years.

Read the prayer of Jabez found in 1 Chronicles 4: *"Jabez was more honorable than his brothers; and his mother called his name Jabez, saying, 'Because I bore him in pain. Because I bare him with sorrow.'"* (vs. 9 KJV)

> *Jabez called upon the God of Israel, saying, 'Oh that you would bless me and enlarge my border, and that your hand might be with me, and that you would keep me from harm so that it might not bring me pain!' And God granted what he asked.* (vs. 10)

Notice that God lovingly responded to the prayers of a desperate man. Jabez understood that his name meant sorrow or pain. Think about it: when Jabez was greeted, he would hear that malediction spoken over his life: "Hello, Sorrow," "How is your day going, Pain?" Yet "Sorrow and Pain" desperately wanted to experience a better, more fulfilling life than what his given name declared over him and his future. In brokenness this descendant of Judah (which means praise) looked UP, for he knew that his help would come from the LORD, the God of Israel. The author of Chronicles emphasized Jabez's dependence upon the LORD to bless him and to create a better future for him. The author succinctly stated:

"And God granted what he asked." (vs. 10)

God's blessing changed the atmosphere and future of Jabez.

Let's consider what God's response indicates:

1. As we believe God and trust that HE is the source of our help, He hears and responds to our cries for His help. Jabez's prayer pleased God because it was based on faith in Him.

The Spoken Blessing II: Influencing Generations

"And without faith it is impossible to please him, for whoever would draw near to God must believe that he exists and that he rewards those who seek him." (Hebrews 11:6)

But without faith it is impossible to please and be satisfactory to Him. For whoever would come near to God must [necessarily] believe that God exists and that He is the rewarder of those who earnestly and diligently seek Him [out]. (Hebrews 11:6 AMPC)

"…the righteous shall live by his faith." (Habakkuk 2:4)

Jabez's heart aligned with God's desire to bless. This desire is described in the beginning of Creation as God blessed mankind to be fruitful and multiply, fill the earth and subdue it, and have dominion over the fish, the birds, and every living thing on the earth. (Genesis 1:28)

Thus, our hearts must align with His heart. We discover and understand "what's on His heart" as we read His word and listen to His Spirit. He willingly reveals Himself, His heart, His nature to us. God's word is abundantly rich with His self-revelation throughout the generations of His people.

2. As Genesis 1:28 reminds us, God's plan for us is to "fill the earth," which indicates that He wants us to occupy it with His image since we were created in His image. Our purpose is to increase and enlarge His image, His nature across the earth.

3. Jabez recognized the power and authority of God in his life and in the world. God's provision was strong and complete, originating from "His hand."

4. This humble man ascribed to God the power to deliver him from harm and danger. God, the Son, taught His disciples to pray to our heavenly Father.

Jesus instructed: *"Pray then like this: 'Our Father in heaven, hallowed be your name……And lead us not into temptation, but deliver us from evil.'"* (Matthew 6:9,13)

5. Jabez petitioned God to deliver him from harm that would cause him pain. Recall that his name means: sorrow, pain. When spoken,

that reality is released over his life. Proverbs 18:21 reminds us of the power of our words: *"Death and life are in the power of the tongue, and those who love it will eat its fruits."*

Now, read this sobering principle in The Message: *"Words kill, words give life; they're either poison or fruit---you choose."* Jabez did not want to walk inside of that curse-filled name. He wanted deliverance from that burdensome, heavy-laden life. He desperately implored God to reverse that curse and to bless him. The life application discovered within Proverbs 18:21 should call us to place a guard over our mouths and to think before we speak!

Jesus implored people to come to Him: *"Come to me, all who labor and are heavy laden, and I will give you rest."* (Matthew 11:28)

"Come to Me, all you who labor and are heavy-laden and overburdened, and I will cause you to rest. [I will ease and relieve and refresh your souls.]" (Matthew 11:28 AMPC)

The "come to me" part of Jesus' call indicates that a person must make the decision and choice to change. In taking those steps to "come alongside" Jesus, an individual will receive the benefits of His peace, rest, and refreshment.

6. Let's consider this: faith as small as a mustard seed will grow. Jesus is the Author and Finisher of our faith. He inscribes faith upon our hearts. Such dedication to engraving His precepts upon the hearts of mankind is not a new work for God.

    In fact, He promised to fulfill and strengthen His covenant relationship with Israel by accomplishing that work:

    For this is the covenant that I will make with the house of Israel after those days, declares the LORD: I will put my law within them, and I will write it on their hearts. And I will be their God, and they shall be my people. (Jeremiah 31:33)

7. This idea of enlarging our place and space of influence and effectiveness for God is echoed in Isaiah 54:2 : *"Enlarge the place of your tent, and let the curtains of your habitations be stretched out; do not hold back; lengthen your cords and strengthen your stakes."*

The Spoken Blessing II: Influencing Generations

I recognize that Isaiah 54:2 follows the preceding verse that addresses barren, childless women, encouraging them to enlarge the size of the tent in expectation of bearing children.

God's heart is for His people to be fruitful and multiply not just in the producing of children in the natural sense, but in the spiritual realm of influencing the realm in which we live and in which we "do life." From the beginning, His desire is for us to bring His kingdom to earth in the same way that it rules and reigns in heaven.

(Matthew 6:9-13)

Recall that Jesus pronounced God's kingdom principle over His followers: *"You are the light of the world. A city set on a hill cannot be hidden."* (Matthew 5:14)

"Here's another way to put it: You're here to be light, bringing out the God-colors in the world. God is not a secret to be kept. We're going public with this, as public as a city on a hill." (Matthew 5:14 The Message)

Jesus declared, prophesied, proclaimed the influence His followers were to have across the world. He released a blessing declaration over and into their lives and future. You and I fulfill Jesus' prophecy when we act upon His words and broadcast His light, His truth, His hope, His peace, and the knowledge of His heavenly Father.

Jesus continued: *"Nor do people light a lamp and put it under a basket, but on a stand, and it gives light to all in the house."* (v. 15)

Consider The Message's wording: *"If I make you light-bearers, you don't think I'm going to hide you under a bucket, do you? I'm putting you on a light stand. Now that I've put you there on a hilltop, on a light stand---shine!"*

Jesus places us on a light stand to "shine!" Everyone benefits from our light. Now consider who receives the honor and glory for the light we share. *"In the same way, let your light shine before others, so that they may see your good works and give glory to your Father who is in heaven."*

(Matthew 5:16)

Now read it from The Message: *"Keep open house; be generous with your lives. By opening up to others, you'll prompt people to open up with God, this generous Father in heaven."*

"Before others" includes the generations of our families. Here's a thought: many times, when we think of generations, we think "down the family line." Yet, many of us have siblings, and we all have parents! What's stopping us from shining brightly before them? They would benefit from hearing and receiving our blessing declarations over them!

You may think: "My sister (brother) lives clear across the States," or "I'm not on speaking terms with my dad." Remember that distance or proximity in the natural realm does not control effectiveness and influence in the spiritual realm. Whose faith caught the attention and stirred a response from Jesus?

Read this narrative provided in Luke 7:2-10:

> *Now a centurion had a servant who was sick and at the point of death, who was highly valued by him. When the centurion heard about Jesus, he sent to him elders of the Jews, asking him to come and heal his servant. And when they came to Jesus, they pleaded with him earnestly, saying, "He is worthy to have you do this for him, for he loves our nation, and he is the one who built us our synagogue." And Jesus went with them. When he was not far from the house, the centurion sent friends, saying to him, "Lord, do not trouble yourself, for I am not worthy to have you come under my roof. Therefore I did not presume to come to you. But say the word, and let my servant be healed. For I too am a man set under authority, with soldiers under me: and I say to one, 'Go,' and he goes; and to another, 'Come,' and he comes; and to my servant, 'Do this,' and he does it." When Jesus heard these things, he marveled at him, and turning to the crowd that followed him, said, 'I tell you, not even in Israel have I found such faith.' And when those who had been sent returned to the house, they found the servant well.*

Distance was no barrier for Jesus, and it should not be for us. Read Jesus' revelation regarding our activity (works) while living on earth:

"Truly, truly, I say to you, whoever believes in me will also do the works that I do; and greater works than these will he do, because I am going to the Father." (John 14:12)

The Spoken Blessing II: Influencing Generations

If you are not "on speaking terms" with someone, then begin praying for God to work in your heart first, then in theirs. Declare this blessing over yourself:

> May my heart, _____ (insert your name), be flooded with the forgiveness of Christ. May the cleansing Blood of Jesus Christ wash away all pain, offense, bitterness, and unforgiveness. May my sin of unforgiveness be remembered no more.
>
> May my heart be changed. May my thoughts be cleansed and renewed toward _____ (insert name of those who offended you).
>
> May my relationship with _____ be recreated and restored. In Jesus' Name. Amen.

You will experience a change internally and externally; in the natural and in the spiritual.

Our son-in-law, Kyle Del Vecchio, testified that blessings "always change the atmosphere."

Don't stop there! Consider your spiritual descendants! Your light can greatly influence those around you: *"All your children shall be taught by the LORD, and great shall be the peace of your children."* (Isaiah 54:13)

In the widest sense of the word, *children* references "grandson, subject, nation, quality or condition, etc...." That term can also refer to those with whom you work and serve.[1]

What happens when you throw a rock into a pond? Yes, ripples are created. Those ripples spread outward, affecting the water's surface beyond the point of entry. The first ripple creates another; then, the second ripple creates a third, and so it goes. This progression of ripples began with one rock that you chose to cast.

Your life affects many others in all "walks" of life: family, work, church, recreational activities, community, military service. You have a wonderful destiny to fulfill within the kingdom of God that touches innumerable lives. How will you move forward? Will you "cast a rock" of blessing declarations into their waters? Others need to hear and receive the bedrock

---

1   Strong's Concordance, H1121: children

truth of the Gospel of Jesus Christ. People need to be touched by the truth that Jesus loves them.

Our family met Kyle when he and Elizabeth began dating as teenagers. Elizabeth invited him to one of our Sunday lunch gatherings. Soon after that, he was introduced to hearing and receiving blessings. Kyle shared this: "Along with God's grace, the blessings have saved my life and kept me strong in my faith."

May I encourage you to join the apostle Paul in declaring: *"I press on toward the goal for the prize of the upward call of God in Christ Jesus."* (Philippians 3:14)

Reflecting on Chapter 1

1. What did you discover about the nature of God?
   _____
   _____
   _____

2. What did you learn about His love for you?
   _____
   _____
   _____

3. How will your new understanding of Him affect your future?
   _____
   _____
   _____

4. How will you touch the generations within your life for their good?
   _____
   _____
   _____

Chapter 2

What Happened within the Generations?

As God's Creation progressed from day to day, He saw that it was "good." As He beheld the entirety of His created world, He saw it was "very good." His Creation brought Him very good pleasure.

We may ask: "So what happened?"

Recall what the apostle Paul wrote to the believers in the church at Philippi:

> *For it is God who works in you, both to will and to work for his good pleasure....that you may be blameless and innocent, children of God without blemish in the midst of a crooked and twisted generation, among whom you shine as lights in the world, holding fast to the word of life,* (Philippians 2:13,15,16).

In the beginning, Adam and Eve experienced being filled with and surrounded by God's words of life. God actively, effectively worked His mighty purpose and design within and around them. He showed Himself mighty as an expression of His good pleasure and purpose for them. As their Creator, the Sovereign One, provided a beautiful, amply supplied Garden of Eden to be a place of work (vocation) and a source of sustenance.

From the beginning, Adam and Eve were called to be partners with the Divine Creator, the Master of the Universe, in governing His world. They were to participate with Him as they established His authority and dominion across the face of the earth. As the Senior Partner, God created for His coworkers a bountiful provision which included His protection:

"And God said, 'Behold, I have given you every plant yielding seed that is on the face of all the earth, and every tree with seed in its fruit. You shall have them for food.'" (Genesis 1:29) That sounds like an incredible and delicious provision.

> *The LORD God took the man and put him in the garden of Eden to work it and keep it. And the LORD God commanded the man, saying, "You may surely eat of every tree of the garden, but of the tree of the knowledge of good and evil you shall not eat, for in the day that you eat of it you shall surely die."* (Genesis 2:15-17)

God's protection was included within His provision. Yet, Adam and Eve were tempted and deceived with the idea that God was "holding out on them." The first couple was enticed with the idea that once they ate and consumed the restricted and protected fruit, they would be as wise and powerful as their Creator. That sounds like mutiny within the bounty of God's blessing. They were fed the lie of Satan that God's word could not be trusted. Satan sowed seeds of doubt, unbelief, and rebellion. He convinced Adam and Eve that God was not truly GOOD. He cast the seed of not believing that there would be a penalty for disobedience. Satan invited them to join in his rebellious narrative, forsaking the purity of God's nature.

Eve and Adam were persuaded by Satan to NOT hold fast to the word of life.

By not holding fast to the word of life, in placing Satan's lie in authority above God's word, Adam and Eve forfeited God's provision and protection. They relinquished their dominion and authority, their title deed, over God's created world to the enemy, Satan. They were no longer innocent and blameless. They chose to enter the enemy's darkness, departing the majestic beauty of God's light and glory: His Presence. They chose to leave the pleasure of walking and talking with the Creator of the Universe to become ensnared in the enemy's "crooked and twisted generation."

Satan lured them into focusing on themselves versus looking to their Creator *"both to will and to work for his good pleasure."* (Philippians 2:13) Instead of viewing their future in the realm of being fruitful and multiplying God's holy image, Adam and Eve's perspective turned inward, centered on themselves. That's when they saw how naked they were. Their focus, their devotion and desire changed from looking BEYOND themselves, to looking only AT themselves. Their destinies were doomed; their DNA became corrupted.

God originally deposited within and around Adam and Eve a complete, "lacking nothing" future of being fruitful and multiplying His image, His character across the face of the earth. Adam and Eve carried within them the potential of producing generations of God's nature. God is good, loving, faithful, kind, compassionate, trustworthy, holy, creative, full of joy.

God also gave this couple a free will, the choice of obedience. The choice to love or not to love Him.

When Adam and Eve devalued their destiny and partnership within God's design and plan, shunning their privilege of abiding in the presence of their Creator, their future drastically changed. Since that destiny-altering decision, the generations born from the first couple have carried their sin-filled, self-centered life.

> *"Therefore, as sin came into the world through one man, and death as the result of sin, so death spread to all men, [no one being able to stop it or to escape its power] because all men sinned."* (Romans 5:12 AMPC) Adam's sin affected the entire human race.

Is all hope for a better future lost? Must our destinies remain doomed, our DNA flawed?

The Apostle Paul answered that troubling question in Romans 5:8:

> *But God shows his love for us in that while we were still sinners, Christ died for us."* (ESV) *"But God shows and clearly proves His [own] love for us by the fact that while we were still sinners, Christ (the Messiah, the Anointed One) died for us.* (AMP)

The Apostle Peter confirmed Paul's message of hope and redemption:

> *For you know that your lives were ransomed once and for all from the empty and futile way of life handed down from generation to generation. It was not a ransom payment of silver and gold, which eventually perishes, but the precious blood of Christ—who like a spotless, unblemished lamb was sacrificed for us. This was part of God's plan, for he was chosen and destined for this before the foundation of the earth was laid, but he has been made manifest in these last days for you.* (1 Peter 1:18-20 TPT)

Our God, our Creator, is Eternal. He views our lives with Eternal Eyes. He is Omniscient—that means He is All-knowing. In God's Omniscience, Jesus, the Living Word, agreed to die in our place, to pay the penalty of our sin, before the foundation of the earth was created. God's Eternal Eyes are on you and me! Doesn't knowing that bring you comfort? As I learn more about the depths of God's love and Jesus' sacrifice for us, I am humbled. My perspective changes. The focus of my daily living shifts from me to God, the Father, God, the Son, and God, the Holy Spirit.

Jesus shared this truth with a large crowd who had gathered on the countryside to hear Him teach as is noted in Matthew 5:1:

"One day Jesus saw a vast crowd of people gathering to hear him, so he went up the slope of a hill and sat down. With his followers and disciples spread over the hillside." (TPT)

"Seeing the crowds, he went up on the mountain, and when he sat down, his disciples came to him."

On that hillside, Jesus presented a heavenly perspective for living life on the Earth. He described the way of thinking, living, and interacting with others that would provide heavenly benefits. This instruction reminds me of God, the Creator and Benefactor, walking and talking with Adam and Eve. God instructed the first couple in the way they should think (obedient to His directive of being fruitful and multiplying His image and character), in the way they should live (be a worker and watchman for His garden which incorporated their provision), and in the way they should interact with each other *"and they shall become one flesh."* (Genesis 2:24)

Jesus' instruction presented His listeners with an alternative to their current way of life:

"Blessed are the poor in spirit, for theirs is the kingdom of heaven."
(Matthew 5:3)

To experience God's kingdom within their lives, their hearts must become humble, recognizing their need for God, not arrogant and self-reliant, not spiritually self-sufficient.[1]

Jesus continued to describe the nature of God's kingdom as found in Matthew 5:7, *"Blessed are the merciful, for they shall receive mercy."*

Being merciful means being compassionate, willing to express and show sympathy. As we demonstrate mercy toward others, our focus and actions will reflect a desire to reduce or eliminate their hardship. Expressing mercy will require time, focus, resources, and love.

That is the change of focus Jesus was describing in Matthew 5:7. Yes, you may be experiencing some very HARD places in your life, yet, if you are willing to redirect your focus outward toward others, your situation becomes less glaring in your eyes. Jesus assures you that as you extend mercy, you will receive mercy. Will you elevate His word, His truth as the standard for your daily living?

Are you willing to trust Him?

Consider the words of Jesus as noted in Matthew 6:26, *"Look at the birds of the air: they neither sow nor reap nor gather into barns, and yet your heavenly Father feeds them. Are you not of more value than they?"*

The answer is: "Yes, yes and yes!"

After Jesus had carefully and prayerfully selected twelve men to serve Him as disciples, He instructed and assured them of the omniscience of the Father: *"Are not two sparrows sold for a penny? And not one of them will fall to the ground apart from your Father."* (Matthew 10:29)

Jesus added more comfort by stating: *"But even the hairs of your head are all numbered. Fear not, therefore; you are of more value than many sparrows."* (Matthew 10:30,31)

---

1   *FireBible*™, p. 1521, note on Matthew 5:3

He builds their confidence in His love and care for them: *"So everyone who acknowledges me before men, I also will acknowledge before my Father who is in heaven,"* (Matthew 10:32)

You are important to the Father. He showed you just how important by sending His only begotten Son into the world, so that the world, that's you and me, might be saved from the "crooked and twisted generation." (John 3:16)

The Father treasures you and desires to share a precious relationship with you because you are priceless to Him. Have words to the contrary of that truth been spoken against or over you? Are you questioning your value and worth? Have you accepted an alternative identity?

Right now, this very moment, kneel before Jesus, the One who shed His blood for your life so that your sins and the sins of others could be forgiven. Give Him all those hurtful and condemning words and offenses. Ask Jesus to heal your heart and to forgive those who caused such pain and rejection. How can you forgive those who have hurt you?

Follow Jesus' heart and example:

After being brutally tortured, having His body torn to shreds, Jesus was nailed to the Cross. As He hung, suspended over the earth, He cried out to His Father, saying: *"Father, forgive them, for they know not what they do."* (Luke 23:34 KJV)

Yes, you may need to cry out: "Jesus, help me forgive as You did." In that moment of your willingness to forgive, in your cry for help, He will help you. Jesus has come to set the captives free; to heal the brokenhearted.

My Blessing Declaration for you:

> *May you accept the Risen Savior's touch of restoration.*
>
> *May you allow Him to reach into the depths of your pain to extract the trauma and suture the wound.*
>
> *May the Master Surgeon use His red thread of mercy to carefully knit together the mangled pieces of your soul.*
>
> *May Holy Spirit comfort you as you rest in His care and companionship.*

May He bring to your remembrance the word of life and truth: by the stripes, the scourging of Jesus, you are healed.

May you arise and walk in wholeness and newness of life.

In Jesus' Name. Amen.

Isaiah 53:5

Isaiah prophesied about the coming Messiah:

> *The Spirit of the Lord GOD is upon me, because the LORD has anointed me to bring good news to the poor; he has sent me to bind up the brokenhearted, to proclaim liberty to the captives, and the opening of the prison to those who are bound;* (Isaiah 61:1).

Jesus, the Messiah, fulfilled Isaiah's prophecy. Allow Jesus' good news to penetrate your heart, soul, and body. Receive the healing of your brokenness, setting you free from the captivity of offenses, unforgiveness, and bitterness. Walk through the open door of a new liberated life in Him.

Jesus taught a new way of living life to those who surrounded Him: a life within the kingdom of God. He declared; He announced that the kingdom of God was among them. When He came to earth, He brought the kingdom of God with Him.

In Mark's gospel he wrote: *"Now after that John was put in prison, Jesus came into Galilee, preaching the gospel of the kingdom of God, And saying, The time is fulfilled, and the kingdom of God is at hand: repent ye, and believe the gospel."* (Mark 1:14,15 KJV)

Catch this: Jesus declared the fulfillment of prophecy by His bringing the "right here, right now" reality of the kingdom of God.

Those listening to Jesus had a decision to make: to repent and believe, to accept or reject God's kingdom. There is no room for confusion over His words.

Consider this definition for <u>declaration</u>: "the <u>formal announcement of the beginning of a state or condition</u>."[1] This accurately describes what was occurring. Jesus was formally announcing the beginning of the state and condition of God's kingdom coming to earth.

---

1   https://languages.oup.com/dictionaries/

Each of us has a decision to make. Do we repent and believe in the Gospel, the Good News that Jesus brought into our earth? Jesus brought it; it remains.

Listen to Jesus' instruction to His disciples about praying: *"After this manner therefore pray ye: Our Father which art in heaven, Hallowed be thy name. Thy kingdom come. Thy will be done in earth, as it is in heaven...."* (Matthew 6:9,10 KJV)

Not only did Jesus bring the kingdom of God to earth, He taught and instructed His disciples to *"...pray to God, that is, supplicate, worship: - pray (...earnestly, for), make prayer."*[1]

You and I have an important role in advancing God's kingdom across the face of the earth, i.e., into the lives of those around us. Each of us has a sphere of influence as we live our lives in the "marketplace." Every day we interact with others wherever we go. Every day you and I have divine appointments to impart God's truth into others.

You and I can shine, as Paul proclaimed, "as lights in the world." Our lives will become a beacon of light to those who are suffering. Our words of truth and life will redirect others as they look to the future. Cultural "norms," works of darkness and lies of defeat will no longer bind nor restrict them. Our blessing declarations of the word of God will prepare the way for their freedom. As we speak Jesus' living word over others, they will hear Him through us. Light overpowers darkness. Truth evicts lies and destroys "false narratives."

Tim Sheets shared this:

> Our great God has promised, "I will be an enemy to your enemy and an adversary to your adversary. I'll be on your side. My angels will go before you and lead you into My promises. Live in such a way that you construct an atmosphere for My Kingdom advancement. Do not provoke My angels. Do not ground them. Launch them! Release them with words of faith!"[2]

May I encourage you to move forward into speaking and releasing blessing declarations over your life, the lives of others, and into prevailing

---

1   Strong's Concordance, G4336: pray
2   *Prayers & Decrees that Activate Angel Armies*, p.44

circumstances. Advance the kingdom of God; broadcast His image into your world. Jesus declared the way for powerful change to be experienced within people, families, communities, nations. He infused hope for a better tomorrow, and the path through which it could become a reality.

From the beginning God directed mankind to function as His co-laborers and representatives on the earth. The specific assignments given in the Garden of Eden are still in force and are to be accomplished. Consider Paul's letter to the believers in Corinth. 1 Corinthians 3:9 references our assignment:

"For we are labourers together with (G4904) *God:..."* (KJV, Strong's number added)

"For we are God's fellow workers...."

"For we are fellow workmen (joint promoters, laborers together) with and for God..." (AMPC)

Strong's Concordance provides this for G4904: "a co-laborer, that is, coadjutor: - companion in labour, (fellow-) helper (labourer, -worker), labourer together with, workfellow."

Before Paul wrote his first letter to the believers in Corinth, he sent a message to the young believers within the church of Thessalonica. Within Paul's writing he referenced a similar partnership between God and man. Read Paul's description of Timothy:

"And we sent Timothy, our brother and God's coworker in the gospel of Christ, to establish and exhort you in your faith." (1 Thessalonians 3:2)

"...and sent Timothy, our brother and minister of God, and our fellow laborer in the gospel of Christ, to establish you and encourage you concerning your faith." (1 Thessalonians 3:2 NKJV)

Did you notice the expected result of Timothy's coworking with God? Paul was confident in Timothy's ability to preach the gospel of Christ which was based upon the word of God. Earlier in Paul's letter, he noted the power of God's word: *"...the word of God, which effectually worketh also in you that believe."* (1 Thessalonians 2:13 KJV)

"Effectually worketh" means *"...to be active, efficient: - do, (be) effectual (fervent), be mighty in, shew forth self, work (effectually in)."*[1]

Thus, Paul was quite confident in the effectiveness of Timothy's sharing God's word and fully anticipated the good work that would be accomplished within the lives of the believers. Paul had the assurance that the believers' faith would be strengthened and encouraged within their hearts. Paul recognized that these believers were experiencing fierce persecution. He trusted the power of God's word to establish His truth and to keep their focus fixed on the Lord Jesus. Paul knew from experience the comfort of Holy Spirit's presence within his life. Holy Spirit would take the word of God that Timothy shared and would cause it to become fruitful and multiplied in and through those Thessalonian believers. Timothy would teach and train them how to advance the kingdom of God in the face of extreme challenges.

Fast forward into our lives—as you and I speak and release blessing declarations based upon God's word, the effectiveness of His word will be accomplished. God's word is living and active, full of power to accomplish His mighty and loving purpose!

Let's read one more message that Paul penned to the believers in Philippi.

> *Yes, I ask you also, true companion, help these women, who have labored side by side with me in the gospel together with Clement and the rest of my fellow workers, whose names are in the book of life.* (Philippians 4:3)

Again, Paul described others as his fellow workers or co-laborers in sharing the gospel of Jesus Christ. *"...whose names are in the book of life"* references a record of individuals who have placed their faith in the salvation of Jesus Christ and trusted Him as Lord of their life.

As a co-laborer of the Gospel, we reverence the God of the Gospel. We speak often about Him and His Good News. We exalt and magnify Him over ourselves and others. As we speak and release blessing declarations, we honor Him before others, pointing them to entrust their lives, their future to Him. We regard Him as the Sovereign One possessing the highest, most supreme value. His character is unsurpassed. As we declare our

---

1   Strong's Concordance, G1754: effectually worketh

trust in God and esteem His Holy Name, we receive a great reward: our names are written in the book of life.

Jesus remembers and discusses us with His Father: *"So everyone who acknowledges me before men, I also will acknowledge before my Father who is in heaven, but whoever denies me before men, I also will deny before my Father who is in heaven."* (Matthew 10:32,33)

My Blessing Declaration for you:

May you be filled with the empowering Holy Spirit to confidently speak the truth that sets men, women, and children free.

May you not be ashamed of the Gospel of Jesus Christ.

May you be confident in this very thing: that He who has begun a good work in you shall complete and perfect it until the day of Jesus Christ.

In Jesus' Name. Amen.

Engaging Blessing Declarations within My Life:

Declare this:

> I choose to evict lies and defeating mindsets that oppose God's word of truth. I choose to turn my back on the old way of thinking that blocks my walking in the freedom that Jesus has purchased for me. I choose to place my trust in His love and future for me.

Make note of lies that have been spoken or written about you. Destroy those lies with God's truth.

Lie:

_____

_____

_____

Truth:

_____

_____

_____

Lie:

_____

_____

_____

Truth:

_____

_____

_____

Lie:

_____

_____

_____

Truth:

_____

_____

_____

Reference these scriptures for God's word of truth.

- **I am saved by grace through faith.** Ephesians 2:8 *"For by grace you have been saved through faith. And this is not your own doing; it is the gift of God,"*

- **I am forgiven.** Acts 10:43 *"…everyone who believes in him receives forgiveness of sins through his name."* 1 John 1:9 *"If we confess our sins, he is faithful and just to forgive us our sins and to cleanse us from all unrighteousness."*

- **I am delivered from the power of darkness.** Psalm 18:17 *"He rescued me from my strong enemy and from those who hated me, for they were too mighty for me."*

- **I am casting down vain imaginations that come against the knowledge of God.** 2 Corinthians 10:5 *"We destroy arguments and every lofty opinion raised against the knowledge of God, and take every thought captive to obey Christ,"*

- **I am being transformed by the renewing of my mind.** Romans 12:2 *"Do not be conformed to this world, but be transformed by the renewal of your mind, that by testing you may discern what is the will of God, what is good and acceptable and perfect."*

The Spoken Blessing II: Influencing Generations

Using God's word of truth, create blessing declarations to speak and release into your life to <u>establish</u>: to set fast, to turn resolutely in a certain direction, to fix, to confirm and strengthen your faith in God.[1]

Remember the power of hearing the word of God. *"So then faith cometh by hearing, and hearing by the word of God."* (Romans 10:17 KJV)

Let's use John 1:12 to create a blessing declaration to speak over yourself: *"But to all who did receive him, who believed in his name, he gave the right to become children of God,"*

"As I have received and believed in the Name of Jesus, may I always remember that I have been given the right to become a child of God. In Jesus' Name. Amen."

Put that blessing declaration into action and speak it in faith over yourself.

Now use Romans 8:15, *"For you did not receive the spirit of slavery to fall back into fear, but you have received the Spirit of adoption as sons, by whom we cry, 'Abba! Father!'"*

"May I no longer accept the bondage of fear but recognize and receive my adoption into the family of God. May I run into the loving arms of my Abba Father. In Jesus' Name. Amen."

Now speak it over yourself.

> The reason we use the word, "may," is that the Hebrew language has two verb tenses: past and present/future. The English language has three verb tenses: past, present, future. The English word, "may" is used to convey the Hebrew verb tense—present/future.[2]

Use 2 Corinthians 5:17, *"Therefore, if anyone is in Christ, he is a new creation. The old has passed away; behold, the new has come."* Add John 14:26, *"But the Helper, the Holy Spirit, whom the Father will send in my name, he will teach you all things and bring to your remembrance all that I have said to you."*

---

1   1 Thessalonians 3:2, Strong's Concordance, G4741: establish
2   *The Spoken Blessing—A Spiritual Posture*, Ann Dews Gleaton

What Happened within the Generations

Speak and release it over yourself:

> May I continually walk in the newness of a life centered and grounded in Jesus. May I allow the Helper, Holy Spirit, to teach me all things and to bring to my remembrance the words of Christ. In Jesus' Name. Amen.

Have you noticed that these examples of blessing declarations conclude with "In Jesus' Name. Amen"? There's a reason! As co-laborers with Jesus Christ, He sent us to people to reconcile them to the Father through Him. He gave us authority to continue His ministry here on earth. We go in His Name and speak in His Name with His power and love working through us. We are His ambassadors. Let us speak His word in His Name.

Would you pause your reading for a moment and immerse yourself in worshipping Jesus? Please search YouTube for Tommy Walker's worship-filled song: "Speak the Word." Listen carefully to its message. Replay it. Listen and worship Jesus.

Consider what you want to occur within your life. You may think: "What does she mean by that?" Let me tell you about a blind beggar named Bartimaeus who was sitting along the roadside between Jericho and Jerusalem. Bartimaeus means honorable or son of Timaeus. Timaeus means highly prized.[1]

From all outward appearances, Bartimaeus was not living a highly prized life. Yet, when people called his name, they declared him to be a highly prized person! Bartimaeus' future was being prophesied!

Jesus, His disciples, and a very large crowd were walking toward Jerusalem. Bartimaeus heard that Jesus of Nazareth was approaching. He became excited. Had Bartimaeus <u>seen</u> the miraculous events that surrounded Jesus? No, he had <u>only heard</u> about the Son of David. Yet, Bartimaeus began calling out to Jesus, asking Him to have mercy on him. The crowd tried to silence Bartimaeus, but Jesus instructed those rebukers to call him. This blind beggar, with a plethora of needs, jumped up, cast his cloak aside, and made his way to Jesus. <u>His hearing helped him locate Jesus</u>. He moved in the direction of the voice of Jesus. (Precious reader,

---

1   Herbert Lockyer, D.D.: *All the Men of the Bible*, pp. 69, 328

there is a power-filled lesson in calling out, listening to, and moving in the direction of the voice of Jesus.)

> *And Jesus said to him, "What do you want me to do for you?" And the blind man said to him, "Rabbi, let me recover my sight." And Jesus said to him, "Go your way; your faith has made you well." And immediately he recovered his sight and followed him on the way.* (Mark 10:51, 52)

This is a brief encounter between a person in need and the Need-Meeter. It may be brief, yet it speaks volumes and sets a wonderful example of the power of hearing and believing.

Notice how Bartimaeus addressed Jesus: "Jesus, Son of David." Using this title, Bartimaeus declared his belief that Jesus was the One who would fulfill every promise and prophecy given to God's people over many generations.[1]

Honorable Bartimaeus honored Jesus with faith in who He was. Jesus heard faith and responded to it by asking what Bartimaeus wanted, i.e., what he would take delight in. Then, Jesus heard allegiance in Bartimaeus' response: "Rabbi…" That title indicated that Bartimaeus ascribed to Jesus the revered position of being his Master or Lord. This blind man placed himself in submission to Jesus' authority. Again, Jesus heard the heartfelt faith of this one who was just sitting along the dirty road that led to the Cross.

What more can we learn from this divine appointment? Listen to Jesus' instruction to Bartimaeus: *"Go your way; your faith has made you well"* (G4982). (Mark 10:52, Strong's number added)

Jesus released him to depart, to go his way. Jesus identified the power of Bartimaeus' faith that had been wrought within his heart simply by hearing about Jesus. (There's a lesson to learn about hearing!)

Jesus used the word "sozo" as He spoke of Bartimaeus' healing. Strong's Concordance provides this definition: G4982 - "to save, that is, deliver or protect (literally or figuratively): - heal, preserve, save (self), do well, be (make) whole."

---

1   Herbert Lockyer, D.D.: *All the Divine Names and Titles in the Bible*, p. 254

Consider the fact that Jesus responded to Bartimaeus' faith and a healing occurred; salvation came to this "once blind and now I see" man. Then, He released the healed man to go forth! Yet, look at the decision of Bartimaeus: *"And immediately he recovered his sight and followed him on the way."* Strong's Concordance provides this definition for "followed," G190: "…to be in the same way with, that is, to accompany (specifically as a disciple): - follow, reach." Look at that: Bartimaeus became a follower or disciple of Jesus, his Master.

Bartimaeus' life was renewed, made whole. From one moment to the next, his future changed.

From Bartimaeus' perspective, his most pressing need was the healing of his eyes, i.e., his sight restored. Yet, Jesus looked deeper into this beggar's life and saw the seed of faith which had begun to germinate. The water from the Living Word, Jesus, poured onto this seed of faith and caused it to break through the soil. Bartimaeus' faith was released. He honored Jesus, Son of David, with faith-filled action.

What do you want Jesus to do for you? Are you willing to walk by faith and not by sight? What do you need from Jesus? Do you need peace in your life?

Jesus spoke these words of comfort to His disciples during their last supper together before going to the Cross. *"Peace I leave with you; my peace I give to you. Not as the world gives do I give to you. Let not your hearts be troubled, neither let them be afraid."* (John 14:27)

Listen carefully to the words provided by the Amplified™ Bible:

> *Peace I leave with you: My [own] peace I now give and bequeath to you. Not as the world gives do I give to you. Do not let your hearts be troubled, neither let them be afraid. [Stop allowing yourselves to be agitated and disturbed; and do not permit yourselves to be fearful and intimidated and cowardly and unsettled.]* (John 14:27 AMPC)

Jesus continued to offer words of encouragement as He spoke:

"I have said these things to you, that in me you may have peace. In the world you will have tribulation. But take heart; I have overcome the world."
(John 16:33)

> *I have told you these things, so that in Me you may have [perfect] peace and confidence. In the world you have tribulation and trials and distress and frustration; but be of good cheer [take courage; be confident, certain, undaunted]! For I have overcome the world. [I have deprived it of power to harm you and have conquered it for you.]* (John 16:33 AMPC)

Let's create a blessing declaration to speak and release over your life:

May I hear and believe the words of Christ that He sends forth to me that I will prosper in Him. May I trust His gift of quietness and rest. May my heart not be agitated nor timid. May I not shrink back in uncertainty of His love and peace for me but walk in His oneness. May I trust in His victory and authority. In Jesus' Name. Amen.

As a side note: I use Strong's Concordance to discover the meaning of various words within each scripture verse. Then I incorporate that deeper understanding into the blessing declarations.

Are you anxious about circumstances in your life?

Matthew 6:25 allows us to hear the words of Christ:

> *Therefore I tell you, do not be anxious about your life, what you will eat or what you will drink, nor about your body, what you will put on. Is not life more than food, and the body more than clothing?*

The Passion Translation provides this wording:

> *This is why I tell you to never be worried about your life, for all that you need will be provided, such as food, water, clothing—everything your body needs. Isn't there more to your life than a meal? Isn't your body more than clothing?*

Add Paul's words of instruction to the believers at Philippi:

> *Do not be anxious about anything, but in everything by prayer and supplication with thanksgiving let your requests be made known to God. And the peace of God, which surpasses all understanding, will guard your hearts and your minds in Christ Jesus.*
>
> (Philippians 4:6,7)

Let's consider the wording of The Passion Translation:

Don't be pulled in different directions or worried about a thing. Be saturated in prayer throughout each day, offering your faith-filled requests before God with overflowing gratitude. Tell him every detail of your life, then God's wonderful peace that transcends human understanding, will make the answers known to you through Jesus Christ. (Philippians 4:6,7 TPT)

Paul's words are instructive, cautionary, and encouraging. We can create a blessing declaration using these scriptures. Speak and release it over yourself and others!

May I not allow worry or anxiety to enter nor control my thoughts. May I recognize the greatness of my God, the Creator of the universe, the One who has given me life. May I cast aside all fears and trepidation of the "what ifs" of my future. May I allow Holy Spirit to reveal the plans God has for me. May I offer Him a heart of gratitude and words of praise. In Jesus' Name. Amen.

Do you need wise counsel and guidance?

Holy Spirit is your guide. He is the One who hears the wise counsel from Jesus and the Father, then shares it with you. Read Jesus' explanation He gave to His disciples just hours before He submitted Himself to the Cross.

When the Spirit of truth comes, he will guide you into all the truth, for he will not speak on his own authority, but whatever he hears he will speak, and he will declare to you the things that are to come. He will glorify me, for he will take what is mine and declare it to you. All that the Father has is mine; therefore I said that he will take what is mine and declare it to you. (John 16:13-15)

Understanding and allowing Holy Spirit to operate as Jesus described is essential to our growth and maturity as we "do life." Strong's Concordance provides this definition for "guide," G3594: "...to show the way (literally or figuratively [teach]): - guide, lead."

Holy Spirit shows us the way to move forward in life because He hears, He listens. Then, He speaks. In speaking to us, He declares or tells us about the future. Strong's Concordance defines His declaring or showing us the way, G312: "…to announce (in detail): - declare, rehearse, report, show, speak, tell."

I love that about Holy Spirit—"to announce in detail." In His hearing, listening, speaking, and announcing, Holy Spirit glorifies and magnifies King Jesus which, in turn, glorifies the Father. Isn't that our desire?

Don't we want to enlarge Jesus and the Father within our lives and within the lives of others?

My answer is: "YES!" So, what are we waiting for? Let's follow the leading of Holy Spirit and hear what He wants to declare to us. Then, as we hear Him, we choose to walk it out immediately!

When blind Bartimaeus heard that Jesus wanted him to come, did he remain seated in his lowly, defeated position? Did he think, "Well, let me think about it…"? NO! He cast aside that old, filthy cloak of defeat and despair, jumped to his feet, and moved in the direction of the Son of David, the One who would fulfill ALL the promises and prophecies of the Messiah.

So, when we hear Holy Spirit guiding us in all truth and announcing to us things concerning the future, then we had better jump to our feet and move in that direction! *"So faith comes from hearing, and hearing through the word of Christ."* (Romans 10:17)

As we listen, i.e., hear, the word of Christ through the leading and guiding of His Spirit, faith is being germinated, developed, and matured within us. By faith we can speak and release blessing declarations over ourselves and others to advance the kingdom of God!

In advancing the kingdom of God, we move forward into our future in Christ Jesus! In releasing the truth of God's word, we magnify Jesus within lives, ours and others. Our relationship with the Spirit of Christ, Holy Spirit, is vital. Listen for His voice of wisdom.

Holy Spirit began to "replay" a hymn I sang as a child: "Open My Eyes, that I May See."

Clara H. Scott penned this hymn of petition in 1895. I memorized three stanzas in the mid-1960s. Some 60 years later, Holy Spirit gave it new life within my heart and released it through my mouth!

Clara H. Scott's hymn perfectly describes what our position and posture should be before God. I can "place" the story of blind Bartimaeus within this hymn of petition. He lived centuries before Clara H. Scott was prompted by Holy Spirit to create this hymn. You and I are living over a century beyond Clara, yet we can still sing this song, asking Holy Spirit, Spirit Divine, to open our eyes, ears, mouths, and hearts. Will you join Clara H. Scott in asking to see "glimpses of truth," to hear "voices of truth," to speak the "warm truth," and to "prepare love" in our hearts to share with God's children, everywhere?[1]

If you just responded with a resounding "YES," then position and posture yourself as Bartimaeus did, sing the song of Clara H. Scott, and join me in asking God to touch our eyes, ears, mouths, and hearts to advance His kingdom here on earth as it reigns supreme in Heaven.

Receive this blessing declaration over and into your life:

> May God, the Father of our Lord Jesus Christ, the Father of glory, give you the Spirit of wisdom and knowledge of Him. May the eyes of your heart be enlightened, that you may know what is the hope to which He has called you, what are the riches of His glorious inheritance in the saints. May you see and experience the immeasurable greatness of His power He showers on us who believe. May you witness the operation of His dominion and power that was at work in Christ when He raised Him from the dead and seated Him at His right hand in the heavenly places. May God show you the immeasurable riches of His grace in kindness toward you as you believe in Christ Jesus. In Jesus' Name. Amen. (Ephesians 1:17-20; 2:7)

Mark your place in the book. Then spend time with God. He is worthy of your time and love. He calls you worthy of His.

---

[1] The Hymnbook, p. 330

Make a note of what you hear the Spirit of God say:

_____

_____

_____

Carefully consider this: the Spirit of God, Holy Spirit, is "an active member of the Godhead." He is "the direct Agent between heaven and earth in this present age in salvation and sanctification." Holy Spirit is "the Administrator of the affairs of the Church Jesus purchased by His precious blood."[1]

Lockyer added: "Our conception of the Spirit determines our attitude toward Him." (p. 297)

May we allow Holy Spirit to prevail and preside in us. May our hearts and lives remain willing vessels through which Holy Spirit may operate. May our lives of clay continually submit to the shaping and correcting of the Potter's Hands. May we become vessels of honor for Him. In Jesus' Name. Amen.

---

1   Lockyer: *All the Divine Names and Titles in the Bible*, p. 284

Chapter 3

When Did Jesus Speak?

Jesus' disciples had the privilege of listening to His words and wisdom. As these followers walked with Jesus, they watched His ways. Their "school of grace," their "classroom of mercy" moved across the countryside of Judea, along fields of grain, inside a fishing vessel on the Sea of Tiberias, within the walls of a synagogue, at Jacob's well in Samaria, under the towering trees on the Mount of Olives, along a path within the Kidron Valley. Jesus took advantage of their present location and surroundings to teach and train the disciples for their future assignments. His careful instruction has been set before us as the perfect pattern to follow.

In fact, Jesus had been speaking for centuries, before He walked on the earth in human flesh. Consider with me these notable events: when Adam and Eve sinned, they lost their intimate relationship with God and His purity, needing their shame or nakedness covered. God sacrificed an animal to create garments of skin. Blood was shed to cover their sin. (Genesis 3:1-24) The principle of shedding blood as payment for sin was demonstrated in the presence of mankind. Adam and Eve witnessed the sacrifice of a life to cover their rebellion, their dishonoring of the authoritative word of God. Before mankind was created, the Godhead designed a plan for their salvation and restoration to an intimate relationship with God. Creating and building, restoring, and advancing a relationship with mankind is at the core of God's heart.

1 Peter 1:20 explains God's plan: *"He was foreknown before the foundation of the world but was made manifest in the last times for the sake of you,"*

The Amplified™ Bible Classic Edition offers:

> *It is true that He was chosen and foreordained (destined and foreknown for it) before the foundation of the world, but He was brought out to public view (made manifest) in these last days (at the end of the times) for the sake of you.*

God's plan, which began before the world was created, includes YOU.

Earlier in the life of Peter, on the Day of Pentecost, he declared before a large gathering of people: *"this Jesus, delivered up according to the definite plan and foreknowledge of God, you crucified and killed by the hands of lawless men."* (Acts 2:23)

Let's read from The Amplified™ Bible:

> *This Jesus, when delivered up according to the definite and fixed purpose and settled plan and foreknowledge of God, you crucified and put out of the way [killing Him] by the hands of lawless and wicked men.* (Acts 2:23 AMPC)

An earlier "school of grace" and "classroom of mercy" occurred during the time of Noah.

Evil and wicked acts were running amuck across the earth. In Genesis 6:5-10 we read:

> *The LORD saw that the wickedness of man was great in the earth, and that every intention of the thoughts of his heart was only evil continually. (6) And the LORD regretted that he had made man on the earth, and it grieved him to his heart. (7) So the LORD said, "I will blot out man whom I have created from the face of the land, man and animals and creeping things and birds of the heavens, for I am sorry that I have made them." (8) But Noah found favor in the eyes of the LORD. (9) These are the generations of Noah. Noah was a righteous man, blameless in his generation. Noah walked with God. (10) And Noah had three sons, Shem, Ham, and Japheth.*

The ark that God instructed Noah to build was his training place of grace and his atmosphere of mercy. God described with detail the design, size, and contents of the ark: God's tangible, touchable expression of grace and mercy. Noah carefully followed God's pattern and instructed his family accordingly. His obedience and honor of God allowed the second generation to witness and experience God's blessings of grace and mercy.

"Grace" is often defined as "God's unmerited, unearned favor." "Mercy" is God's lovingkindness at work within people's lives to deal with the consequences of their sin. Noah was highly favored in God's eyes and was provided a refuge of deliverance from God's impending judgment. Noah obediently and carefully followed God's directive, and he included his family as he worked for decades on the ark. Noah recognized the power and importance of propelling God's plan into the next generation and those yet to be born.

Consider how many days are involved in decades. Now, consider the persistent, dedicated trust in God's word of instruction which Noah displayed as he created this floating vessel, this place of refuge. The construction of the ark was no easy task. There were no chainsaws, no power drills, no massive cranes for lifting logs. This family of eight planted, harvested, and stored whatever food would be needed for themselves and the animals. Within Noah's family, I expect that hearts were being carefully crafted, molded, and shaped to follow God and trust His plan. Their dedication and obedience stood in stark contrast to those around them.

As Noah continued to rely on God and His faithful presence in his life, he earnestly urged his neighbors to turn their hearts to God. Many generations later Peter described Noah as a "preacher of righteousness" warning others about the approaching judgment. (2 Peter 2:5) Being a "preacher of righteousness" describes Noah's communication with others as being a herald of divine truth. This does NOT describe a person just "minding their own business," "waiting for his ticket out of the mess," allowing the world to perish. Quite the contrary, Noah spoke boldly to those around him, amidst the jeers and taunting words. His words would have conveyed to others their need to change the intents of their hearts from wickedness to righteousness, from darkness to light. Noah continually warned those around him about the impending judgment and the right way of living and relating to God.

When did Noah speak and declare the words of divine truth? He spoke publicly and privately about the righteous ways of God; in his going out and in his coming in. He spoke words of truth to neighbors and to family members. When should we declare the words of divine truth? **Daily**. God calls us to bear the fruit of His Spirit's presence within our lives and to multiply His kingdom principles across the face of the earth; in our going out and our coming in, publicly and privately. We are called to leave a legacy of light and truth, of holiness and righteousness.

Let's hit the "pause" button on the story of Noah's obedience and God's faithfulness for a moment. May I stress the importance of trust and obedience I mentioned earlier: "…consider the persistent, dedicated trust in God's word of instruction which Noah displayed as he created this floating vessel, this place of refuge." There will be occasions when our blessing declarations include a word of instruction which, if followed, will provide a place of refuge. Consider these examples:

> *May you hoe out of your garden the rocky worries of the world, the thorny deceitfulness of riches and the pestilence of desires for other things. May only God's fruit be produced within your garden: love, joy, peace, patience, kindness, goodness, faithfulness, gentleness and self-control.*©

Mark 4:19; Galatians 5:20

"The Seed of God's Word" Blessing Set

> *May you be steeped in the Word of God, infused with His love, and sweetened by His Spirit. May the bitter brews of your life be given to Him, so that in return, He may be able to give to you. May you, then, offer cups of kindness to others and help satisfy their thirst for the true Living Water, Jesus.*©

John 4:14-15

"Intimacy with Jesus" Blessing Set

Let's return to the saga of Noah fulfilling God's word of instruction and receiving His provision of salvation:

God publicly displayed and confirmed the divine truth of which Noah had declared for decades as the waters broke forth and covered the earth. *"In the six hundredth year of Noah's life, in the second month, on the seven-*

teenth day of the month, on that day all the fountains of the great deep burst forth, and the windows of the heavens were opened." (Genesis 7:11)

Verses 17 and 22 describe the extent of the waters and the destruction of life: *"The flood continued forty days on the earth. The waters increased and bore up the ark, and it rose high above the earth." "Everything on the dry land in whose nostrils was the breath of life died."* Catch that: *"everything....died."*

Now, consider for a moment, during such chaos, did Noah abandon his trust and faith in God's word and plan? Was God still on the "throne of Noah's heart"? Reflect on the duration of confinement within this floating vessel: *"And the waters prevailed on the earth 150 days."* (Genesis 7:24)

I love the next statement and declaration of God's faithfulness: *"But God remembered Noah and all the beasts and all the livestock that were with him in the ark. And God made a wind blow over the earth, and the waters subsided."* (Genesis 8:1) More time was required for the waters to recede from the face of the earth. Noah, his family, and the creatures on board the ark remained there for approximately 371 days!

Then God released mankind and beasts from His place of refuge, saying: *"...be fruitful and multiply on the earth."* (Genesis 8:17) God's instructions and His desire for creation that were declared and released in the Garden of Eden were propelled into the generations of Noah and his family.

Noah's three sons and their wives would bear children who would become the third generation to be taught and trained within the Noahic Covenant that God established and sustained as noted in Genesis 9:12-15.

In the scope of God's eternal plan, there is a timing for events to occur. Did you notice that the writer of Genesis provided detailed information: *"...on that day all the fountains of the great deep burst forth..."* (Genesis 7:11). God is Sovereign; He is Supreme; He knows when the time is right. Consider the timing of His Son, Jesus, entering our humanity.

"But when the fullness of time had come, God sent forth his Son, born of woman, born under the law, to redeem those who were under the law, so that we might receive adoption as sons." (Galatians 4:4-5)

Consider the timing of Jesus beginning His public ministry:

> *Now after John was arrested, Jesus came into Galilee, proclaiming the gospel of God, and saying, "The time is fulfilled, and the kingdom of God is at hand; repent and believe in the gospel."* (Mark 1:14-15)

Noah was a foreshadow of Jesus as he was a "preacher of righteousness." Jesus' ministry on earth:

> Brought both the message and the evidence of God's kingdom near to people. His coming fulfilled and completed many purposes of God's kingdom on earth. God's kingdom was the theme of Jesus' earthly message (Matt. 4:17). It appears and develops through several stages throughout history as part of God's overall plan to bring people into a relationship with himself.[1]

Watch the timing of people's response when Jesus spoke to them:

> *Passing alongside the Sea of Galilee, he saw Simon and Andrew the brother of Simon casting a net into the sea, for they were fishermen. And Jesus said to them, 'Follow me, and I will make you become fishers of men.' And immediately they left their nets and followed him. And going on a little farther, he saw James the son of Zebedee and John his brother, who were in their boat mending the nets. And immediately he called them, and they left their father Zebedee in the boat with the hired servants and followed him.* (Mark 1:16-20)

Jesus was intentional in his "going out and in his coming in." He prayed continually, submitting Himself to the Father's will. The Son sought guidance from His Father. Jesus spent one-on-one time with His Father, communing with Him.

The prophet Isaiah spoke about the coming Messiah as One who would advance the kingdom of God on earth:

> *Yet it was the will of the LORD to crush him; he has put him to grief; when his soul makes an offering for guilt, he shall see his offspring; he shall prolong his days; the will of the LORD shall prosper in his hand.* (Isaiah 53:10)

---

1   FireBible™, p. 1601, note on Mark 1:15

When Did Jesus Speak?

As Jesus walked, He followed the leading of God's Spirit. You will recall that as Jesus arose from being baptized by John the Baptist in the Jordan River, the Spirit of God descended from the heavens and rested on Him.

> *In those days Jesus came from Nazareth of Galilee and was baptized by John in the Jordan. And when he came up out of the water, immediately he saw the heavens being torn open and the Spirit descending on him like a dove. And a voice came from heaven, 'You are my beloved Son; with you I am well pleased.' The Spirit immediately drove him out into the wilderness.* (Mark 1:9-12)

Another gospel writer, Matthew, provided additional insight into the conversation between John the Baptist and Jesus:

> *Then Jesus came from Galilee to the Jordan to John, to be baptized by him. John would have prevented him, saying, "I need to be baptized by you, and do you come to me?" But Jesus answered him, "Let it be so now, for thus it is fitting for us to fulfill all righteousness." Then he consented.* (Matthew 3:13-15)

Let's read verse 14 in the King James Version: *"But John forbad him, saying, 'I have need to be baptized of thee, and comest thou to me?'"* The word "forbad" means to hinder altogether, that is, utterly prohibit: - forbid.[1]

In today's vernacular we would describe John's response as "pushing back" against Jesus' plan and desire. John resisted Jesus. Yet, Jesus called him to join Him in His desire and fulfillment of all righteousness. Jesus redirected John's focus and sharpened his vision to accomplish God's plan within both their lives. Eternal destinies were involved.

If you reread John's description of the baptism of Jesus (Mark 1:9-12), you will recognize the powerful consequence of their united obedience. God, the Father, spoke an affirmation and recognition of Jesus' being His beloved Son. God, the Holy Spirit, empowered God, the Son. The Holy Trinity was audible and visible at one time. God, the Father, God, the Son, and God, the Holy Spirit were manifest for mankind to witness and to experience! The Godhead desires to share our lives and to be very real to us. He is not a distant God. He is right here with us! Immanuel, God with us!

---

1   Strong's Concordance, G1254: forbad

We can help others see, hear, and experience our Holy God every day!

The writer of Hebrews encourages us in this way:

> *Watch over each other to make sure that no one misses the revelation of God's grace. And make sure no one lives with a root of bitterness sprouting within them which will only cause trouble and poison the hearts of many.* (Hebrews 12:15 TPT)

The word used for God's grace refers to *"...the divine influence upon the heart, and its reflection in the life; including gratitude): - acceptable, benefit, favour, gift...."*[1] We are the ones to be diligent, serving and helping others to not miss seeing, hearing, and experiencing communion with our Holy Trinity.

As we speak and release blessing declarations over and into people's lives, we can redirect their focus and offer clarity to their vision concerning their circumstances, their love relationship with God, their lives, future, and their eternal destinies being fulfilled.

Tim Sheets adds this insight:

> We miss awesome Kingdom benefits when we don't speak the Word of God. We certainly miss out on angels assisting God's Word to come to pass. While we have not been given authority to command angels to do whatever we want them to do (we have to have Scripture and biblical principle behind it), they are listening. Words we speak in agreement with God's Word, which we do not negate, activate angels to begin to amass the goodwill and concrete benefits of God in our lives. Promises can materialize when we stand in faith.[2]

How can you do this? During our daily prayers, Cal and I speak and release a blessing declaration for whomever is celebrating a birthday on that day. We also include Birthday Blessings within our greeting cards to our children and spouses, and our grandchildren.

We enhance the theme of the birthday card's sentiments and its illustrations by including scripture-based blessing declarations.

---

1   Strong's Concordance, G5485: grace
2   *Prayers & Decrees that Activate Angel Armies*, p. 35

Our grandchildren have mentioned that the Blessings written within their birthday cards are "different for each person, they're special…" (Zachary); "they're personalized…Nana and Papa know what you're going through…" (Andrew); "it makes me feel great and happy…" (Victoria); "it helps me have peace…" (Isaac); "and joy" (Daniel Del Vecchio); "feel joyful" (Joseph).

"They're special because I don't get them from anyone else…I've never heard them before…" (Daniel Gleaton).

During his teenage years, our eldest son, Anthony, was intrigued by lighthouses. Throughout his life, Anthony has continued to shine God's light of truth and to provide guidance for others. We have sent him birthday cards that include drawings of lighthouses; then, we have written blessing declarations based upon scriptures relating to being a light to the world, shining forth God's light of truth in the midst of darkness.

Our Birthday Blessing Declaration:

> Anthony, may the Lord continue to use you as a beacon shining forth His light of truth and righteousness. May your words of truth reveal the rocky, hard places within people's lives, helping them choose the direction that leads to safety and salvation. May others see your life, your commitment to integrity, honesty, and service as a shining example of being a follower of the Light of the World, Jesus. In Jesus' Name. Amen.

Let's return to the shoreline of the Sea of Galilee and consider that the calling of the four fishermen to "follow me," was not a casual call. Jesus had sought the Father's will and His directive and received Holy Spirit's empowerment to fulfill kingdom advancement purposes. You and I are called by Him to advance kingdom purposes in this day and in this hour. Both gospel writers, Mark and John, described the timing of speaking and responding by using the word: <u>immediately</u>. Let's not miss this lesson. Submit daily to Holy Spirit's guidance and voice; then, follow Him. Put "feet" to His directive. Speak when He directs you. Send that text, make that phone call. Pray that prayer. Release blessing declarations.

Recently I sent an email to a friend who leads an intercessory group within our church. This email included a YouTube video of a worship team's song based on Psalm 139. My husband had asked for my help to send it to this friend. With a "copy," "paste," and "send," the link to the video flashed through the airways to this intercessor. Within minutes Amy Johnson responded, indicating that she had just prayed for Abba Father to provide an answer. Then, my email popped up on her screen. She rejoiced in God's perfect timing and thanked me for my obedience. (Remember, I was simply helping my husband by using whatever computer skill I had.)

I gave thanks to our Abba, Father. He hears when we call. He responds to our requests and recognizes our needs. Jeremiah, the prophet, received this message from the LORD:

"Call unto me, and I will answer thee, and shew thee great and mighty things, which thou knowest not." (Jeremiah 33:3 KJV) The English Standard Version provides this wording:

"Call to me and I will answer you, and will tell you great and hidden things that you have not known."

If you read verse 1 of Jeremiah 33, you will note where Jeremiah was when he received the message of hope and reassurance:

"Moreover the word of the LORD came unto Jeremiah the second time, while he was yet shut up in the court of the prison, saying...."

Jeremiah's movement may have been restricted by an angry king, guards, and prison courtyards, but his ability to receive a timely message was not. God's message of truth, His words of guidance are never restricted by earthen walls, manmade confinements, nor physical barriers.

I am reminded of the restrictions imposed by the COVID shutdowns during 2020. Schools were closed, students were sent home, teachers learned quickly how to hold Zoom classes. Employees created workspaces within their homes and apartments to conduct business "offsite." The daily personal contact with others was abruptly altered. God created mankind to be relational beings. We need to communicate and associate with others, face-to-face. That's in our human nature, our DNA.

Anthony's wife, Cassidy, being a band director for a local high school, was sent home to "conduct" (pun intended) her classes online. Cassidy not only was forced to create online assignments; she and Anthony, who also had been sent home to work, created "learning stations" for their three sons. Many of you remember those days of <u>immediate</u> changes.

During these worldwide efforts to separate mankind, Cassidy's perseverance to strengthen friendships prevailed. Her desire to have fellowship with other women and her love for reading scaled the walls of confinement. Several of her friends and their relatives created a Bible-Book Study group in which they used the Zoom platform for their meetings. A camaraderie among these ladies developed to the depth that they chose to continue their regular Zoom meetings after teachers, students, and employees returned to their in-person settings. As Cassidy incorporated my first book within their study, I had the delight and privilege of participating in one of their Zoom calls. I met her friends in a quasi-"face-to-face" conversation. I was deeply moved to discover that one participant was bedridden due to an illness, but she actively engaged in the group's discussion. Her physical restrictions did not confine her mind, nor her heart in desiring to learn and to grow closer to God. Additionally, I was touched with the women's receptivity for the word of God to be active and real within their lives. The deeper they dove into the word of God, the Word, Jesus, became "closer than a brother." Their hunger and thirst were satisfied by Him. These women began to activate blessing declarations within the lives of their families and friends. In doing so, these women began to create another generation of imparting blessing declarations.

Now consider the generations of speaking blessing declarations which preceded this Bible-Book Study group. Anthony received God's word declared over him by his parents. He spoke and released blessing declarations over his wife; she shared the same with her friends. Being fruitful and multiplying the word of God, advancing His kingdom and purposes are profitable outcomes of blessing declarations. Familial and relational generations advance God's kingdom purposes and blessings. Blessing declarations help people get to know Jesus. As they get to know Jesus, they meet God, the Father.

The Apostle Paul reminded the Corinthian believers that their reconciliation to God was accomplished through Christ who, in turn, had given them the ministry of reconciliation. The next generation of believers was to come through their witness and testimony of Jesus Christ, the Anointed One, who sets the captives free. Paul continued to explain: *"Therefore, we are ambassadors for Christ, God making his appeal through us. We implore you on behalf of Christ, be reconciled to God."* (2 Corinthians 5:20)

Paul continued to broaden the understanding of their responsibility: *"Working together with him, then, we appeal to you not to receive the grace of God in vain."*(ESV) The Passion Translation provides this version: *"Now, since we are God's coworkers, we beg you not to take God's marvelous grace for granted, allowing it to have no effect on your lives."*
(2 Corinthians 6:1 TPT)

The Passion Translation continues to explain the perfect timing of God's work within lives:

"For he says, I listened to you at the time of my favor. And the day when you needed salvation, I came to your aid. So can't you see? Now is the time to respond to his favor! Now is the day of salvation!" (2 Corinthians 6:2 TPT)

Our God listens. He gives audience to and attends to our prayers and cries for help. As He listens and responds to us, He does the same for others. You and I can serve as God's ambassadors, His representatives on earth. As we allow His Spirit to lead us throughout our days, we can follow His prompting to speak, write, text, and release blessing declarations based on God's word. Enlarging who God is within people's perspective is life changing.

He created the universe; nothing is too difficult, nor too big for Him!

Our God is a "right on time" God. His timing is impeccable. His salvation comes at that moment of need and crisis. What's interesting is that we may not recognize our need, our lostness; while, at other times, we may cry out for His deliverance and safety!

The word "salvation" in verse two of 2 Corinthians 6 refers to the salvation that Jesus Christ provides; additionally, it means: *"...rescue or safety (physically or morally): - deliver, health, salvation, save, saving."*[1]

As we have received Jesus' gift of salvation, we are called to tell others about Him, serving as God's ministers of reconciliation. Paul cautions us

---

1   Strong's Concordance, G4991: salvation

as we go forth. The Passion Translation offers Paul's cautionary words in this way:

> *We will not place obstacles in anyone's way that hinder them from coming to salvation so that our ministry will not be discredited. Yet, as God's servants, we prove ourselves authentic in every way. For example: We have great endurance in hardships and in persecutions. We don't lose courage in a time of stress and calamity.*
> (2 Corinthians 6:3,4 TPT)

You and I must be courageous.

Consider verse ten which identifies a treasure for us: we can enrich others through our lives as we point them to Jesus and His saving grace. "*We may suffer, yet in every season we are always found rejoicing. We may be poor, yet we bestow great riches on many. We seem to have nothing, yet in reality we possess all things.*" (2 Corinthians 6:10 TPT) Our witnessing will cost us time, effort, money, self-pleasures, yet consider the generations of believers coming to faith in the resurrected Lord because of our partnering with God.

Please hear the heart of our grandson, Reed, as he commented on the Birthday Blessings: "I like the Birthday Blessings because it shows that she really loves us a lot and she also takes time with them." Generations of hearts are being sown with Jesus' love.

Paul wrote to the Thessalonian believers:

> *For you know, brothers and sisters, that our coming to you has not been ineffective (fruitless, in vain), but after we had already suffered and been outrageously treated in Philippi, as you know, yet in [the strength of] our God we summoned the courage to proclaim boldly to you the good news of God [regarding salvation] amid great opposition.* (1 Thessalonians 2:1,2 AMPC)

Catch that: "in the strength of our God," we receive courage and confidence "to proclaim boldly" the good news of God's salvation even in the face of "great opposition."

Paul and his companions had suffered along their path of ministry, yet they remained faithful and resolved to share their faith which produced great spiritual fruit. Not only had the Gospel been presented, but these ambassadors for God had also shared their lives. Listen to verse eight of that passage: *"Having such a deep affection for you, we were delighted to share with you not only God's good news but also our own lives, because you had become so very dear to us."* (1 Thessalonians 2:8 AMP)

Let's follow Paul's letter a bit further:

> *For you know how we were exhorting and encouraging and imploring each one of you just as a father does [in dealing with] his own children, [guiding you] to live lives [of honor, moral courage, and personal integrity] worthy of the God who [saves you and] calls you into His own kingdom and glory.* (1 Thessalonians 2:11,12 AMP)

Paul conveyed Jesus' invitation: *"Come to me, all who labor and are heavy laden, and I will give you rest."* (Matthew 11:28) Jesus' invitation of "Come to me" was authoritative and carried the idea that it was vital for the people to draw near in relationship to Him.

His words carried an urgency of "Come to Me now!"

Who was He inviting "to come now"? He called all who were wearied and fatigued by hard work. Jesus authoritatively directed those who were overloaded in their bodies and spirits. Then, He announced a benefit of responding to His invitation and drawing close to Him: repose and refreshment.[1]

Parents and grandparents, our children and grandchildren can feel overloaded and need refreshment and encouragement. Our eldest grandchild, Andrew, reflected on his parents' speaking blessing declarations over him:

> It makes me feel good that other people are supporting me through my problems. Sometimes when you're going through something you feel like it's all on you to fight through it. [With the Blessings] you feel like there's people behind you that also want you to win. It makes you feel supported.

Zachary, Andrew's brother, commented about his parents' blessings: "It reminds me that God has my back and I think to pray for it. And I ask God and He will help me."

---

1   Strong's Concordance, G373: rest

Matthew's gospel also provided a time frame for Jesus' instructing and releasing His carefully chosen Twelve. The Gospel writer described the chronology of Jesus' sending forth His twelve disciples to prepare the way for His message. In Matthew 10 we read when and how Jesus prepared His delegated ambassadors: *"And when he had called unto him his twelve disciples, he gave them power against unclean spirits, to cast them out, and to heal all manner of sickness and all manner of disease."* (Matthew 10:1 KJV)

When Jesus called his twelve disciples to "come unto" Him, He was summoning them. When they came to Him, then He empowered them. Jesus emboldened them with His authority and power to accomplish God's will and purpose: to:

> *...bring good news to the poor; ...to bind up the brokenhearted, to proclaim liberty to the captives; and the opening of the prison to those who are bound; to proclaim the year of the LORD's favor..."*
> (Isaiah 61:1-2)

Jesus' disciples, His ambassadors, would prepare the way within the hearts of people for the King to enter! His ministers of reconciliation would cast out unclean spirits, evict the lies of old mindsets, destroy the constraints of traditions, and remove spiritual stumbling blocks, and accomplish the works of deliverance and healing. People's hearts would be prepared for the King of Glory to transform their lives from darkness to everlasting light. Jesus' seeds of kingdom truth would be sown into the soil of their hearts.

Consider the honor and authority those Twelve carried as they served the King! You and I have that same honor, delegated authority, and empowerment to go forth with His word of truth, hope, and salvation as we speak and release blessing declarations into the soil of people's hearts. The word of truth can remove weeds of despair, cast aside rocks of depression, eliminate hardened clumps of disappointment, and pour over hearts the water of God's word. (Ephesians 5:26, John 15:3)

Use this blessing declaration as you minister to someone:

> May you always remember that nothing can separate you from the love of Christ; not even depression, disappointment, lack of funds, sadness (add what you heard the person mention as you listened to them).

> May you be confident that Jesus makes continual intercession for you as He is seated at the right hand of the Father.
>
> May you be assured that Jesus' intercession will reach the Father's ears and touch His heart. Jesus' prayers are effective and secure His goal for you.
>
> May you focus on the goodness of God and receive His mercies that are new and fresh every morning. Great is His faithfulness. In Jesus' Name. Amen.
>
> (Romans 8:34,35; Lamentations 3:22,23; Psalm 145:9 KJV)

Listening to people is vital as you minister. Listen to the Spirit of Christ as you hear others' needs and situations. Holy Spirit knows how to meet their needs. He knows the words of Christ which will satisfy the longing of their hearts. He knows the truth they need to hear that will counteract and remove the restrictions and falsehoods controlling their hearts, thoughts, and actions. During your daily life, you have the privilege of operating in the natural and supernatural realms, simultaneously. During an ordinary conversation, you may hear someone's fear of going to sleep at night. They may express a fear of storms or being alone or being attacked at night. Holy Spirit knows the depth of that person's needs. Listen to the person and to the Spirit. Then speak and release a blessing declaration:

> May you diligently ask the LORD for His wisdom and gain His perspective about your situation.
>
> May you focus on knowing Him, gaining His understanding, and experiencing His love and the depth of His goodness.
>
> May you trust Him with your care and protection, and He will give you rest, and sleep that is sweet and peaceful.
>
> May the LORD be your shelter, your strong tower into which you run and find safety.
>
> In Jesus' Name. Amen.
>
> (Proverbs 3:13,19,21,24,26; 18:10; 1 Peter 5:7; Psalm 61:3)

Out of a heart filled with gratitude and worship, the psalmist declares: *"I will sing of the steadfast love of the LORD, forever; <u>with my mouth I will make known your faithfulness to all generations.</u>"* (Psalm 89:1, underline added)

Shall we not dedicate our lives to do the same? From the depths of our gratitude and love, our mouths shall make known God's faithfulness to all generations. Our blessing declarations share the richness of God's mercies and grace which transform the lives of people. As they are transformed, they, in turn, touch the lives of others. There is a ripple effect; one touches another, who touches another, etc. Generations of transformations occur.

Asaph, the psalmist, reminded God's people to continually teach their children the commands and standards of God. He encouraged parents

> *Tell to the coming generation the glorious deeds of the LORD, and his might, and the wonders he has done"* so *"that the next generation might know them, the children yet unborn, and arise and tell them to their children.*

Consider the purpose of Asaph's exhortation to God's followers: *"so that they should set their hope in God and not forget the works of God, but keep his commandments."* (Psalm 78:4,6,7)

Shall we not pass on to the lives of our families, friends, and associates the joy of knowing Jesus? How satisfying it is to witness others as they experience the love and care of our heavenly Father! Shall our legacy include helping others believe on our Lord Jesus as their Savior? Shall we desire to daily reflect and relay our dependence upon and union with Holy Spirit? You and I have the privilege and calling to nurture, yes, cultivate a love for the Godhead, the Holy Trinity: Father, Son, and Holy Spirit. Let us cultivate a **generational strength of faith in God**.

Amy, our son Peyton's wife, shared her remembrances and impact of our Blessings:

> Over the past 11 years, the blessings you've spoken over our family have consistently uplifted us. Your words have a way of highlighting the goodness in our lives, helping us focus on gratitude and positivity. Each blessing has been a reminder of the strength

we share, the love we have for one another, and the many gifts we often overlook. Your thoughtful words have inspired us to embrace joy and appreciate life's blessings more deeply.

Blessing declarations can express the heart of Jesus and direct others' focus on Him.

Paul's letter to the believers in Corinth captures the profoundness of Jesus' love as it describes the depth of sacrifice He made for us: 2 Corinthians 8:9 : *"For you know the grace of our Lord Jesus Christ, that though he was rich, yet for your sake he became poor, so that you by his poverty might become rich."*

Read this passage from The Amplified Bible Classic Edition:

> *For you are becoming progressively acquainted with and recognizing more strongly and clearly the grace of our Lord Jesus Christ (His kindness, His gracious generosity, His undeserved favor and spiritual blessing), [in] that though He was [so very] rich, yet for your sakes He became [so very] poor, in order that by His poverty you might become enriched (abundantly supplied).* (2 Corinthians 8:9)

"Enriched (abundantly supplied)." May I ask you a question? Are you living inside of "His kindness, His gracious generosity, His undeserved favor and spiritual blessing"? Let's just pause right here for a moment. The rest of this chapter can wait. Jesus' **when** is **right now** for you.

We began this chapter considering Jesus' "school of grace" which He invited ordinary people to attend. Yes, it required them to leave their ordinary, daily routines to immerse themselves in His presence and training. During their journey with Jesus, they arose early in the mornings, accompanied Him along the dusty roads, gathered around their campfire at night and heard His wonderful wisdom. Every day they witnessed and experienced His extravagant grace. Their lives became enriched and abundantly supplied. These individuals were transformed as they pressed closer to hear every word He spoke. At times His words were corrective and firm, other times, gentle and forgiving. Jesus knew how and when to admonish, affirm, inspire, and convict because He immersed Himself in the Father's presence and allowed Holy Spirit to lead Him.

When Did Jesus Speak?

When did Jesus speak? He spoke **when** transformation from the kingdom of darkness into the kingdom of His marvelous light was needed. Holy Spirit allowed Him to hear what was being said and often whispered. He confronted the kingdom of darkness with the light of revelation—revealing the presence and power of the kingdom of God.

Matthew described a confrontation between the two kingdoms as Jesus first healed (set free) a demon-possessed man, a man being controlled by the kingdom of darkness. *"Then a demon-oppressed man who was blind and mute was brought to him, and he healed him, so that the man spoke and saw."* (12:22)

The demon-controlled man was transformed from darkness to light.

Let's follow Matthew's narrative a bit further:

> (23) *And all the people were amazed, and said, "Can this be the Son of David?" (24) But when the Pharisees heard it, they said, "It is only by Beelzebul, the prince of demons, that this man casts out demons." And Jesus knew their thoughts, and said unto them, "Every kingdom divided against itself is brought to desolation; and every city or house divided against itself shall not stand:"* (12:25 KJV)

Empowered by Holy Spirit, Jesus knew what the Pharisees were thinking, and He confronted the kingdom of darkness with the light of truth and life. He continued the revealing of truth: *"But if it is by the Spirit of God that I cast out demons, then the kingdom of God has come upon you."* (Matthew 12:28)

May I share with you the treasure within Jesus' words? Jesus clearly identified the source of His power to cast out demons: "by the Spirit of God." The kingdom of God confronts darkness. Listen to Jesus' confronting the darkness of the Pharisees' religious spirit: *"You brood of vipers! How can you speak good, when you are evil? For out of the abundance of the heart the mouth speaks."* (Matthew 12:34)

The Amplified™ Bible Classic Edition offers this rendering:

> *You offspring of vipers! How can you speak good things when you are evil (wicked)? For out of the fullness (the overflow, the superabundance) of the heart the mouth speaks.* (Matthew 12:34)

Jesus teaches us as He confronts the rottenness of the religious leaders' hearts. His confrontation challenges us to examine the contents of our hearts. What do we hear ourselves speaking? What attitudes do we express when we speak? What is our overflow?

Listen to our Master Teacher: *"The good person out of his good treasure brings forth good, and the evil person out of his evil treasure brings forth evil."* (Matthew 12:35)

We may question if our negative, faithless words have any consequence. Jesus speaks very plainly regarding their effect on our future and on the future of others:

"I tell you, on the day of judgment people will give account for every careless word they speak, for by your words you will be justified, and by your words you will be condemned." (Matthew 12:36,37)

The Passion Translation provides this explanation:

> *You can be sure of this: when the day of judgment coes, everyone will be held accountable for every careless word he has spoken. Your very words will be used as evidence against you, and your words will declare you either innocent or guilty.* (Matthew 12:36,37)

When is a good time for repentance? **Right now**. Right this minute, pray with me.

> Heavenly Father, I repent of the sin in my heart. It's ugly to You and to me. Jesus, I ask You to apply Your Blood to cover my sin so that my sin can be forgiven. Holy Spirit, I invite You to create in me a clean heart, renewing a right spirit, a good treasure within me. I pray this in Jesus' Name. Amen.

Take a moment to listen to the voice of the Good Shepherd. Allow Him to lead you beside quiet waters to restore your soul. Lean into Him. Be quiet. Listen. What is He saying to you?

_____

_____

_____

When Did Jesus Speak?

Let's remain in the atmosphere of quiet waters refreshing and restoring us, making us new.

Would you stand with me around Jacob's well which was located outside the Samaritan city of Sychar? The scene was this: Jesus, in His humanity, was weary from walking miles and miles with His disciples. He remained at the well while His disciples sought food in that city. When Jesus rested was around noontime, in the heat of the day, when the sun was at its brightest glory. A Samaritan woman approached the well to draw water. (1. women usually drew water in the evening.) Jesus, being led by the Spirit, initiated a conversation with the woman. (2. typically men did not converse with women who were not their wives.) Consider when this conversation occurred. Jesus desired a one-on-one, heart-to-heart conversation with this individual. There would be no outside interference. (3. Jesus placed value on those marginalized by society.) He flooded her day with the light of truth for eternal life. Jesus' words created a thirst within this woman who spoke honestly with Him. When the Son's words illuminated her sin, she confessed. (John 4:1-43)

1 John 1:9 declares this powerful truth: *"If we confess our sins, he is faithful and just to forgive us our sins and to cleanse us from all unrighteousness."*

Please read it from The Amplified™ Bible:

> *If we [freely] admit that we have sinned and confess our sins, He is faithful and just [true to His own nature and promises], and will forgive our sins and cleanse us continually from all unrighteousness [our wrongdoing, everything not in conformity with His will and purpose].*

This woman's life was parched and dry. She wanted Jesus' living water. Her need for forgiveness was great, and so was her thirst for His newness of life.

Consider another **when** of this powerful, life-changing story: when in the course of daily events, when doing the menial tasks required, a woman met the Lover of her soul, the Savior of her life. Jesus chose to spend time with an emotionally bound, sin-entangled soul. He came to set the captive free. He spoke the truth of God's kingdom. He set before her LIFE, deliverance from evil, freedom from shame and rejection.

The Spoken Blessing II: Influencing Generations

How do I know and recognize the power and effectiveness of Jesus' conversation?

Read verses 28-30:

> *So the woman left her water jar and went away into town and said to the people, "Come, see a man who told me all that I ever did. Can this be the Christ?" They went out of the town and were coming to him.* (John 4:28-30)

Could their inner thirst have driven them to the well to see if her words were truthful? Were her words reaching the depths of their needs, their longings?

Psalm 42:1 *"...as the deer pants for the water, so my soul longs after Thee."*

The townspeople hurried out to see the man who had a profound, recognizable impact on this outcast person of the community. They listened and responded to her words, her testimony. We can testify of our discovery of the Anointed One as we speak about Jesus' truth, His love, His goodness. John, a disciple of Jesus, began his testimony about Jesus:

> *In the beginning was the Word, and the Word was with God, and the Word was God. He was in the beginning with God. In him was life, and the life was the light of men. The light shines in the darkness, and the darkness has not overcome it. The true light, which gives light to everyone, was coming into the world. He was in the world, and the world was made through him, yet the world did not know him.* (John 1:1-5, 9, 10)

How can we help the world know Jesus?

The "woman at the well" literally dropped what she was doing and ran toward people who needed to hear about the One who might be the Christ. Most of us live in a community with others. Consider those individuals whose paths you regularly cross: family members, business associates, sales associates at stores you frequent, bank tellers, delivery people, Uber drivers, neighbors, friends, church members. When in the course of human events, your life, your testimony, your words will have an impact on others. What is your mindset toward these people? Are you willing to lay aside your daily tasks to reach into their lives with the truth, the compassion, and the goodness of Jesus?

When Did Jesus Speak?

Jesus laid down His heavenly glory when He entered our human realm on this earth.

In Paul's letter to the believers at Philippi, he described the incomprehensible sacrifice made by Jesus when He left His heavenly glory.

> *Have this mind among yourselves, which is yours in Christ Jesus, who, though he was in the form of God, did not count equality with God a thing to be grasped, but emptied himself, by taking the form of a servant, being born in the likeness of men. And being found in human form, he humbled himself by becoming obedient to the point of death, even death on a cross.* (Philippians 2:5-8)

The Amplified Bible provides this wording for verse 5: *"Have this same attitude in yourselves which was in Christ Jesus [look to Him as your example in selfless humility]."* (Philippians 2:5 AMP)

You and I are called to follow Jesus' example of self-surrender. "He emptied Himself, that is, refused to avail Himself of the use of His divine attributes, that He might teach the meaning of absolute dependence on the Father. He obeyed as a servant the laws which had their source in Himself. He became man—a humble man, a dying man, a crucified man."[1]

When do we speak, releasing blessing declarations into and over people? **When** we are led by the Holy Spirit; when we surrender our self-centered motivations and depend upon the wisdom and counsel of God's Spirit. Jesus explained this quite plainly and bluntly to the religious leaders. Jesus depended upon the empowerment and leading by the Spirit of God. So should we.

Were the Pharisees the only ones to receive Jesus' rebuke and correction?

Let's return to the "school of grace" in which Jesus was teaching people about the kingdom of God. Parents wanted their children to experience Jesus' grace and mercy. They sought His touch for their little ones. They recognized a goodness and power within Jesus. Loving parents desired the impartation of His blessing upon their children. The Passion Translation describes the scene: *"The parents kept bringing their little children to Jesus so that he would lay his hands on them and bless them. But the disciples kept rebuking and scolding the people for doing it."* (Mark 10:13)

---
1 *e-Sword X* notes, Philippians 2:1-11

Listen to the correction of Jesus and His declaration of truth:

> *But when Jesus saw this, He was indignant and He said to them, "Allow the children to come to Me; do not forbid them; for the kingdom of God belongs to such as these. I assure you and most solemnly say to you, whoever does not receive and welcome the kingdom of God like a child will not enter it at all." And He took the children [one by one] in His arms and blessed them [with kind, encouraging words], placing His hands on them.* (Mark 10:14-16 AMP)

Wow! I can picture Jesus embracing a child with an all-encompassing hug, resting His right hand upon their head, then speaking, yes, depositing within that child the power of His truth and goodness into their lives, their personalities, their future. It's no wonder that parents were doggedly determined to get to Jesus. They longed for what He offered, as a deer pants for the water, so their souls were longing for Him.

Do you have children, grandchildren, nephews, or nieces? What happens within your heart when someone expresses kindness, generosity, provision, and love to them?

I expect that your heart becomes tender and grateful toward the giver. If you look behind the scenes, you will see God at work on their behalf! God's hand is not so short that He can't bless and supply the needs of your loved ones! He works through others to accomplish His lovingkindness. Will you make yourself available to Him to accomplish good works through you? Will you allow His words of grace and mercy to flow through you?

Shall we not allow Jesus' mindset to become our motivation? Jesus had a longing within His heart, too. He deeply desired that everyone, young and old, understand and experience the kingdom of God within and through their lives. His mindset was operating at FULL capacity as *"he humbled himself by becoming obedient to the point of death, even death on a cross."* (Philippians 2:8 TPT)

The writer of Hebrews helps us grasp the magnitude of Jesus' devotion and inward drive to accomplish the eternal plan for redemption. The Amplified™ Bible provides a depth of understanding to those words:

> *[Looking away from all that will distract us and] focusing our eyes on Jesus, who is the Author and Perfecter of faith [the first incentive for our belief and the One who brings our faith to maturity], who for the joy [of accomplishing the goal] set before Him endured the cross, disregarding the shame, and sat down at the right hand of the throne of God [revealing His deity, His authority, and the completion of His work].* (Hebrews 12:2)

Jesus focused on the joy of providing the Atonement for our sins so that we could become His beloved. His mindset was so complete that He suffered all the way to the Cross. That's why He told His disciples to allow the little children to approach Him. He longed for them to become His. Those young ones were the **next generation** that would experience, carry, and declare His blessings to others!

From Jesus' perspective, children should not be marginalized, but highly valued. Jesus treasured their purity and innocence. Their hearts had not become hardened by religious spirits, unforgiveness, anger, and resentment. As He held each child, He spoke, and they heard the heart of the Father's plan for their lives through the Son's words.

Fathers, mothers, grandparents, do your children and grandchildren hear the heart of their Heavenly Father's plan for their lives through the words of His Son, Jesus?

"So faith comes from hearing, and hearing through the word of Christ." Romans 10:17

Shall we not share the word of Christ and the heart of the Father? Shall we not activate His word? Shall we not speak blessing declarations over the lives of our children (young and older), over our grandchildren, nephews, and nieces? What's hindering us?

If we have children who are adults, do they not long, yes, need our words of truth, hope, love, and affirmation? Do they not need to hear the heart of God through our blessing declarations? They celebrate birthdays, anniversaries, job promotions, job changes, etc. Celebrate those events with a blessing declaration.

Here's an example to honor an anniversary:

> Anthony and Cassidy,
>
> As you celebrate twenty years of marriage, may your hearts be filled with gratitude, overflowing with an excited expectation.
>
> May you look to the future with a true and deep confidence of God's love for you and your family.
>
> May He share with you His intimacies and mysteries of His Kingdom being advanced in and through your lives!
>
> In Jesus' Name. Amen.

A scriptural basis for each part of this Anniversary Blessing Declaration:

1. Ephesians 5:20; Psalm 118:1; 1 Thessalonians 5:18; 1 Corinthians 15:57
2. Philippians 1:6; Proverbs 3:26; Ephesians 3:12; Hebrews 10:22-23; 1 Thessalonians 5:24; Psalm 57:2; Psalm 138:8
3. 1 Corinthians 2:6-16; John 15:15; Luke 10:8; Matthew 13:11

Please read Matthew 13:11 in The Passion Translation: *"He [Jesus] explained, 'You've been given the intimate experience of insight into the hidden truths and mysteries of the realm of heaven's kingdom, but they have not.'"* (brackets added)

Jesus desires that we hear, receive, and respond to His intimate relationship and insight into the kingdom of God. Did you notice that there are others who are not entrusted with these mysteries and hidden truths: "You've been given…but they have not."

Devious, perverse people are an abomination to the Lord. Yet, read in Proverbs 3:32 how He treats those who love Him: *"…his secret is with the righteous."* KJV

"…the upright are in his confidence."

"…finds friendship with God and will hear his intimate secrets." TPT

"…He is intimate with the upright." NAS

It is by and through the Spirit of God that we hear, receive, and are empowered to respond to His secret counsel. What a gift! What a privilege!

Consider Paul's explanation of God's hidden counsel as described by The Message translation: "God's wisdom is something mysterious that goes deep into the interior of his purposes. You don't find it lying around on the surface. It's not the latest message, but more like the oldest—what God determined as the way to bring out his best in us, long before we ever arrived on the scene......But you've seen and heard it because God by his Spirit has brought it all out into the open before you......God offers a full report on the gifts of life and salvation that he is giving us....we learned it from God, who taught us person-to-person through Jesus, and we're passing it on to you in the same firsthand, personal way....God's Spirit and our spirits in open communion. Spiritually alive, we have access to everything God's Spirit is doing..." (excerpts from 1 Corinthians 2:6-16, The Message)

You may need to read the above excerpt from *The Message* a few times to allow Holy Spirit to quicken its truth within your heart. There is a Rhema word for each of us. As I read it another time, the truth that "God's wisdom is...what God determined as the way to bring out his best in us" joined with "you've seen and heard it because God by his Spirit brought it all out into the open before you" almost jumped off the page for me.

Read it one more time. What did God's Spirit make come alive in your heart?

_____

_____

_____

Consider the parents who brought their children to Jesus for Him to touch them with His heart, His words of life and truth, His blessings. These loving parents wanted the **next generation** to experience God through a "person-to-person" relationship with Jesus.

God, our Abba Father, deeply desires to "bring out his best" in each person. As we spend sweet communion time with the Holy Trinity, our Three-in-One God, we will hear what the Spirit is saying for ourselves and others. Our God will share the depths of His wisdom which we can speak, declare over and deposit into others as the Spirit leads us.

Our blessing declarations will encourage others to love our heavenly Father and His Son, Jesus. We have the privilege of sharing a partnership with our Abba Father, our King Jesus, our Helper Holy Spirit. Allow our faith to be strengthened by hearing the words of Christ:

> *If you love me, you will keep my commandments. And I will ask the Father, and he will give you another Helper, to be with you forever, even the Spirit of truth, whom the world cannot receive, because it neither sees him nor knows him. You know him, for he dwells with you and will be in you.* (John 14:15-17)

Continue reading John 14:23 & 26:

> *If anyone loves me, he will keep my word, and my Father will love him, and we will come to him and make our home with him."* (26) *"But the Helper, the Holy Spirit, whom the Father will send in my name, he will teach you all things and bring to your remembrance all that I have said to you.*

Co-laboring with Holy Spirit is essential. Being one with the Godhead in our labors is of the utmost importance. Walking in sync with God is vital. Activating His angels by declaring God's word is powerful.

As a segue into the next chapter, I would encourage you to watch *"The Boys in the Boat"* movie. The young men "in the boat" were rowing to obtain the highest goal in their competition: the Olympic Gold Medal in 1936. Their rowing was in sync with each other.

How did they reach that crescendo in their lives? In the midst of the Great Depression, these young men and their coaches looked beyond their circumstances and focused their attention forward. They grabbed a vision of something that seemed impossible. They experienced continued opposition and internal conflict. Yet, they pressed on to the high calling of that prize: an Olympic Gold Medal.

Paul's letter to the believers in Philippi references another "high calling."

"I press on toward the goal for the prize of the upward call of God in Christ Jesus." (Philippians 3:14)

The Amplified™ Bible Classic Edition provides an additional perspective to Paul's message: *"I press on toward the goal to win the [supreme and heavenly] prize to which God in Christ Jesus is calling us upward."*

There is a direct correlation between the young men in the "Junior" team's boat to Paul's message: they were "called," that is, invited. As you watch this phenomenal movie, notice how some members came very close to losing their privilege and position on the team. Notice the internal and external pressures against this team's unity.

As the movie ended, the principal character shared great insight with his grandson when the young boy asked if he liked rowing with a team of eight. The aged Olympian deposited a kingdom dynamic into his inquisitive grandson: "we weren't eight, we were one."

We must press on toward that high calling: being one with the Holy Trinity.

Join me in speaking, hearing, and receiving this blessing declaration for ourselves:

May you, _____
(add your name), *"walk in a manner worthy of the calling to which you have been called, with all humility and gentleness, with patience, bearing with one another in love, eager to maintain the unity of the Spirit in the bond of peace."* (Ephesians 4:1-3)

May the Father grant you, _____,
"to be strengthened with power through his Spirit in your inner being," (Ephesians 3:16)

"Then, by constantly using your faith, the life of Christ will be released deep inside you, and the resting place of his love will become the very source and root of your life." (Ephesians 3:17 TPT)

May you, _____, *"have strength to comprehend with all the saints what is the breadth and length and height and depth, and to know the love of Christ that surpasses knowledge, that you may be filled with all the fullness of God."* In Jesus' Name. Amen. (Ephesians 3:18-19)

Intersecting the When of God's Timing:

"To every thing there is a season, and a time to every purpose under the heaven....A time to rend, and a time to sew; a time to keep silence, and a time to speak." (Ecclesiastes 3:1,7 KJV)

There is a "right now" time for every good work, pleasure, and purpose of God. There is a "right now" time to speak blessing declarations.

"For it is God who works in you, both to will and to work for his good pleasure." (Philippians 2:13)

Jesus continually submitted Himself to the Father's directive and timing. He encountered the Samaritan woman at Jacob's well during the heat of the day. He was weary and thirsty, yet He availed Himself to every good work, pleasure, and purpose of His Father.

Jesus' submission allowed for many Samaritans to believe in Him. Their conversion came through one "right now" time when Jesus spoke with the woman. (John 4:1-43)

What must you do to prepare your heart and spiritual ears to "hear what the Spirit is saying?"

_____

_____

Make a note of discovering God's "right time" which created additional opportunities for others to hear about Jesus.

_____

_____

How did you recognize the "when" of God's "right now" timing? Describe it.

_____

_____

Chapter 4

Where Did Jesus Speak?

Jesus spoke where grace and truth were needed. He spoke where every good and perfect gift of life would deposit His truth. Jesus spoke where His pure light would overpower the darkness of sin. He spoke where the Father of lights would illuminate hearts that had been darkened with confusion, disappointment, and despair. He spoke where transformation was needed, even in the presence of religious spirits.

In the previous chapter we read how Jesus confronted those religious spirits controlling and operating through the Pharisees:

"You brood of vipers! How can you speak good, when you are evil? For out of the abundance of the heart the mouth speaks." (Matthew 12:34)

> *He also told this parable to some who trusted in themselves that they were righteous, and treated others with contempt: Two men went up into the temple to pray, one a Pharisee and the other a tax collector. The Pharisee, standing by himself, prayed thus: "God, I thank you that I am not like other men, extortioners, unjust, adulterers, or even like this tax collector. I fast twice a week; I give tithes of all that I get." But the tax collector, standing far off, would not even lift up his eyes to heaven, but beat his breast, saying, "God, be merciful to me, a sinner!" I tell you, this man went down to his house justified, rather than the other. For everyone who exalts himself will be humbled, but the one who humbles himself will be exalted.* (Luke 18:9-14)

The Spoken Blessing II: Influencing Generations

The external "righteousness" of the proud religious leaders was being identified and confronted by Jesus. These men *"...substituted the outward actions for the correct inner attitudes and true devotion to God."*[1]

> "The Pharisee was puffed up with pride and self-righteousness. They ignore their sinful nature (i.e., their condition of opposition to and separation from God), their own unworthiness and their constant need for God's help and mercy. Because of their exceptional commitment and works that seem to be good, they do not think they need to repent and ask for God's forgiveness.[2]

It is into those same settings, lives, and hearts that Jesus sends us. We are to speak His word of truth, propelling His light to break forth over people as the morning dawn.

Can hardened and bound hearts be set free? Were the words of Christ able to break the chains of religious spirits controlling those men?

Read the answer found in John 3:1 : *"Now there was a man of the Pharisees named Nicodemus, a ruler of the Jews."*

The Passion Translation offers this: *"Now there was a prominent religious leader among the Jews named Nicodemus, who was part of the sect called the Pharisees and a member of the Jewish ruling council* [the Sanhedrin].*"* (brackets added)

Nicodemus chose to meet with Jesus privately: *"This man came to Jesus by night and said to him,...."* (John 3:1).

Before we hear the words of Nicodemus, should we consider the reason for privately meeting with Jesus at night? Dr. Herbert Lockyer offered one perspective within his *All the Men of the Bible*:

> We feel that he came by night because it was the best time for both Jesus and himself to have a quiet, uninterrupted conversation about spiritual matters." "Nicodemus had been occupied all day with his teaching duties, and Jesus had been active in His out-of-door ministry. Now both could relax and talk through the night. It may be that Nicodemus had such a heart hunger that he

---

1   *FireBible*™, p. 1524, note on Matthew 5:20
2   *FireBible*™, pp. 1698-99, note on Luke 18:9-14

could not wait until morning, and so came running to Jesus as soon as he could. There had been no direct voice from God in Israel for a long time, and here was One whose message carried the stamp of divine authority. So Nicodemus, the cautious enquirer, but a man of spiritual perception (John 3:2), sought out Christ, and listened to one of His remarkable conversational sermons.[1]

Let's return to the passage in the third chapter of John to hear the words of Nicodemus:

> *Rabbi, we know that you are a teacher come from God, for no one can do these signs that you do unless God is with him." Jesus answered him, "Truly, truly, I say to you, unless one is born again he cannot see the kingdom of God." Nicodemus said to him, "How can a man be born when he is old? Can he enter a second time into his mother's womb and be born?" Jesus answered, "Truly, truly, I say to you, unless one is born of water and the Spirit, he cannot enter the kingdom of God.* (John 3:2-5)

The heart of this religious leader was searching for answers; he earnestly wanted to know the essence of the kingdom of God. *"Nicodemus said to him, 'How can these things be?'"* (John 3:9) Jesus recognized a heart ready for truth and transformation. It was within this one-on-one conversation that Jesus explained the Father's love and gift:

> *For God so loved the world, that he gave his only Son, that whoever believes in him should not perish but have eternal life. For God did not send his Son into the world to condemn the world, but in order that the world might be saved through him.* (John 3:16-17)

When we consider the powerful message that Jesus delivered and shared within this intimate conversation with a religious leader, we might ask, "Did Nicodemus believe in Jesus as the Messiah? Did he believe that Jesus was truly the Son of God, sent to save him?"

John continued to reveal the story of this influential Pharisee by including the heated discussion among Nicodemus' fellow religious leaders who had sent officers to arrest Jesus. It is described in John 7:32. When these officers returned empty-handed, the Pharisees and chief priests an-

---

1   Lockyer, p. 259

grily confronted the soldiers: *"Why did you not bring him?"* Listen to the officers' words: *"No one ever spoke like this man!"* (John 7:45,46)

How many times had these temple guards listened and watched this Galilean speak to the crowds? On how many occasions had Nicodemus walked by those same crowds who surrounded Jesus? Had this religious leader witnessed their facial expressions and heard the words of the common people yearning for simple truths for daily living? How many descriptions of the kingdom of God had this Pharisee heard from the Master Teacher's mouth? You see, Nicodemus was a teacher; he was also a member of the governing body, the Sanhedrin. He recognized the authority and influence he wielded within his people. So, why did he search out this Speaker of truth? Why did he interrupt his fellow Pharisees to defuse their explosive hatred of Jesus? Possibly it is for the same reason that the officers did not arrest Jesus as they were directed by the chief priests and Pharisees.

The Passion Translation provides insight into John's passage:

> *Just then, Nicodemus, who had secretly spent time with Jesus, spoke up, for he was a respected voice among them. He cautioned them, saying, "Does our law decide a man's guilt before we first hear him and allow him to defend himself?" They argued, "Oh, so now you're an advocate for this Galilean! Search the Scriptures, Nicodemus, and you'll see that there's no mention of a prophet coming out of Galilee!" So with that their debate ended.* (John 7:50-52)

It is apparent that Nicodemus's words interjected a level of examination that caused the heated, hate-filled atmosphere to dissipate, for a time. Consider the power of our words!

John continued his narrative of this religious leader whose heart had been tenderized by spending time with Jesus and had been transformed by His words of truth. The scene was this: as Jesus hung on the cross, He said, *"'It is finished,' and he bowed his head and gave up his spirit."* (John 19:30)

> *After these things Joseph of Arimathea, who was a disciple of Jesus, but secretly for fear of the Jews, asked Pilate that he might take away the body of Jesus, and Pilate gave him permission. So he came and took away his body.* (John 19:38)

Luke, in his gospel writing, recalled Joseph's devotion and actions:

> *Now there was a man named Joseph, from the Jewish town of Arimathea. He was a member of the [Sanhedrin] council, a good and righteous man, who had not consented to their decision and action; and he was looking for the kingdom of God. This man went to Pilate and asked for the body of Jesus. Then he took it down and wrapped it in a linen shroud and laid him in a tomb cut in stone, where no one had ever yet been laid.* (Luke 23:50-53, brackets added)

John continued his narrative:

"Nicodemus also, who earlier had come to Jesus by night, came bringing a mixture of myrrh and aloes, about seventy-five pounds in weight."

(John 19:39)

The Amplified™ Bible offers this: *"Nicodemus, who had first come to Him at night, also came bringing a mixture of myrrh and aloes, [weighing] about a hundred [Roman] pounds."* (John 19:39 AMP)

"Can two walk together, except they be agreed?" (Amos 3:3 KJV)

Joseph of Arimathea and Nicodemus walked in harmony within their hearts to honor and lovingly care for Jesus' body. Neither man had consented to the decision and action of the council. *(See page 131 for resources and additional information)

> *So they took Jesus' body and bound it in linen wrappings with the fragrant spices, as is the burial custom of the Jews. Now there was a garden at the place where He was crucified, and in the garden a new tomb [cut out of solid rock] in which no one had yet been laid.*
> (John 19:40,41 AMP)

As Joseph honored Jesus by providing a burial place in his personal tomb, he participated in fulfilling the prophecy spoken and released by Isaiah: *"And they made his grave with the wicked and with a rich man in his death, although he had done no violence, and there was no deceit in his mouth."* (Isaiah 53:9)

Joseph of Arimathea, along with Nicodemus, fulfilled the word of God. Joseph's preparation of this tomb worked in partnership with Nicodemus's contribution of seventy-five pounds of myrrh and aloes (seventy-five represents separation, cleansing and purification). In honoring their Yeshua, they accomplished God's word released centuries before their time on earth. When God releases His word, He makes certain it succeeds. Again, we discover that His prophet, Isaiah, explained this facet of God's nature: *"So shall my word be that goeth forth out of my mouth: it shall not return unto me void, but it shall accomplish that which I please, and it shall prosper in the thing whereto I sent it."* (Isaiah 55:11 KJV)[1]

As you recall, Jesus IS the Word that became flesh. Out of God's love for a dying, sin-filled world, He sent His Son, the Word. As we read earlier, Isaiah spoke of the coming Messiah, describing Him in this way:

> *Yet it pleased the LORD to bruise him; he hath put him to grief: when thou shalt make his soul an offering for sin, he shall see his seed, he shall prolong his days, and the pleasure of the LORD shall prosper in his hand.* (Isaiah 53:10 KJV)

We are His seed. We are the harvest of Jesus' righteousness being fulfilled, the spoken word of God released and accomplished!

You and I have similar assignments to fulfill, to co-labor with the heart of God and with the words of Christ:

"You are the light of the world…you are the salt.…you shall do greater things than these."

We fulfill prophecy when we act upon the words of Christ wherever we are, wherever we shine His light of truth that overpowers darkness.

You and I are delegated instruments of God's truth, His peace, His light: *"For it is God who works in you, both to will and to work for his good pleasure."* (Philippians 2:13)

Do you recall our questions: "Did Nicodemus believe in Jesus as the Messiah? Did he believe that Jesus was truly the Son of God, sent to save him?"

Consider the privilege of being in the presence of the Lamb who was slain to cover all sin. As a teacher, Nicodemus would have taught about the Passover lamb's blood applied to the lintels and doorposts of the He-

---

1   Kevin J. Conner, *Interpreting the Symbols and Types*, p. 167

brews' houses in Egypt. In "real time" for Nicodemus, the Passover lamb had been slain in the Temple, and God's Lamb on Calvary.

Consider the honor of anointing Jesus' body with myrrh and aloes. During this extensive labor of love, it is very probable that Nicodemus recalled the words of Isaiah's prophecy: *"He was despised and rejected by men, a man of sorrows and acquainted with grief; and as one from whom men hide their faces…"* (53:3)

More strips of linen, more aloes, more myrrh carefully rubbed into the stricken, smitten body of the Master Teacher. **(See page 131 for resource and additional information) We can only imagine that both Joseph of Arimathea and Nicodemus did not speak much, but their hearts and minds were echoing the word of God that both knew very well. Were the prophet's words of the coming Messiah continuing to speak volumes to these sorrow-filled men:

> *Surely, he has borne our griefs and carried our sorrows; yet we esteemed him stricken, smitten by God, and afflicted. But he was pierced for our transgressions; he was crushed for our iniquities; upon him was the chastisement that brought us peace, and with his wounds we are healed. All we like sheep have gone astray; we have turned—every one—to his own way; and the LORD has laid on him the iniquity of us all."* (Isaiah 53:4-6)

Did the words of Jesus invade Nicodemus' mental and emotional anguish as he remembered the night he had spent with the Rabbi?

> *For God so loved the world, that he gave his only Son, that whoever believes in him should not perish but have eternal life. For God did not send his Son into the world to condemn the world, but in order that the world might be saved through him.* (John 3:16,17)

Could being in the presence of and coming in contact with the body, the bones of this dead Man bring forth new life within Nicodemus and Joseph? Consider the power of the bones of Elisha when a corpse was hurriedly tossed into his tomb and upon his dead body:

> *So Elisha died, and they buried him. Now bands of Moabites used to invade the land in the spring of the year. And it came to pass, as they were burying a man, that, behold, they spied a band of men; and*

they cast the man into the sepulchre of Elisha: and when the man was let down, and touched the bones of Elisha, he revived, and stood up on his feet. (2 Kings 13:20,21 KJV)

Elisha, whose name means—God is Savior, was a type of Christ.[1]

I truly believe that Nicodemus' and Joseph's spirits were revived within the tomb of Jesus.

I believe that as they completed their ministry of honor and love for Jesus, their old lives were left in that tomb and their new lives were in their Savior, and He in them. I firmly believe that as these two men exited that tomb, they were new creatures: *"Therefore if any man be in Christ, he is a new creature: old things are passed away; behold, all things are become new."* (2 Corinthians 5:17 KJV)

Let's recall the definition of the word "in:" Strong's Concordance, G1722—en: A primary preposition denoting (fixed) position (in place, time or state), and (by implication) instrumentality (medially or constructively), that is, a relation of rest." Take note: a "fixed position" and "a place of rest" in Jesus.

What is the answer to our questions? Yes, Nicodemus, a religious leader, came to believe in Jesus as the Son of God sent to save him. This provides an encouragement for us. We walk by faith in what Jesus, the Word, can do within a person's heart. We must continue to speak and release blessing declarations over people and into their hearts, for even a religiously bound heart can be transformed by God's word. *"For the word of God is living and active…"* (Hebrews 4:12)

Paul reminds us that: *"So faith comes from hearing, and hearing through the word of Christ."* (Romans 10:17)

You and I have the privilege and responsibility to speak and release the truth of God's kingdom to others. You and I can provide opportunities for people to hear about Jesus as we deposit His words into and over their lives. Yes, there may be a need for correcting old mindsets and worldviews that do not align with the words of Christ. The Rabbi confronted Nicodemus during their late-night meeting: *"Are you the teacher of Israel and yet you do not understand these things?"* (John 3:10)

---

1 Lockyer, *All the Men of the Bible*, p. 105

Jesus did not shrink back from challenging a highly trained teacher of the Law and the Prophets because He came to fulfill and complete them. (Matthew 5:17)

Jesus spoke **where** His light of truth was needed. As recorded in John's writings, Jesus concluded His conversation with Nicodemus by encouraging him: *"But whoever does what is true comes to the light, so that it may be clearly seen that his works have been carried out in God."* (John 3:21)

Jesus corrected a stale, restrictive mindset, then served this searching teacher a healthy portion of hope and encouragement. Jesus called Nicodemus into His marvelous light.

Jesus came to serve, not to be served.

You and I can challenge and call others out of a "dark place" emotionally, mentally, and spiritually into the light of truth based on the knowledge of God. Fear and trepidation of the future can paralyze people from moving into their kingdom purposes and destiny. We have opportunities to redirect where they are headed. As we carefully listen to what they are speaking over themselves or about a situation, we can provide a warning: "…don't go down that road…" We are cautioning them to guard their minds and emotions from following an unhealthy path. We can serve others healthy words of truth: *"…the tongue of the wise brings healing."* (Proverbs 12:18)

"Gracious words are like a honeycomb, sweetness to the soul and health to the body." (Proverbs 16:24)

"Nothing is more appealing than speaking beautiful, life-giving words. For they release sweetness to our souls and inner healing to our spirits."
(Proverbs 16:24 TPT)

The apostle Paul recognized the lure of "doom and gloom," self-defeating thinking when he instructed:

> *For the weapons of our warfare are not of the flesh but have divine power to destroy strongholds. We destroy arguments and every lofty opinion raised against the knowledge of God, and take every thought captive to obey Christ.* (2 Corinthians 10:4,5)

Now read the same verses in The Passion Translation:

We can demolish every deceptive fantasy that opposes God and break through every arrogant attitude that is raised up in defiance of the true knowledge of God. We capture, like prisoners of war, every thought and insist that it bow in obedience to the Anointed One.

As we listen to the "deceptive fantasy" that has become a stronghold dominating others' thoughts, we can help them break free and destroy those lies that oppose God's word.

We must listen, not with a condemning heart, but with a heart filled with the compassion of Christ, the Anointed One, that all should come to the knowledge of our Holy God. We must correct where correction and liberation are needed. Then we speak and release blessing declarations, pouring over them the refreshing water of the word of God. As our Father God loves His creation, He desires that His mercies flow into and over people.

Where should we be within our relationship with God to speak and release blessing declarations?

Please read 1 John 4:16 in the English Standard Version and The Amplified™ Bible:

"So we have come to know and to believe the love that God has for us. God is love, and whoever abides in love abides in God, and God abides in him."

We have come to know [by personal observation and experience], and have believed [with deep, consistent faith] the love which God has for us. God is love, and the one who abides in love abides in God, and God abides continually in him. (AMP)

May I ask a few penetrating questions?

1. Have you come to know and to believe that God loves you?

    a. *"In this is love, not that we loved God, but that He loved us and sent His Son to be the propitiation [that is, the atoning sacrifice, and the satisfying offering] for our sins [fulfilling God's requirement for justice against sin and placating His wrath]."* (1 John 4:10 AMP)

b. *"See what kind of love the Father has given to us, that we should be called children of God; and so we are. The reason why the world does not know us is that it did not know him."* (1 John 3:1)

2. Do you have a personal experience with God's love?

   a. *"But God clearly shows and proves His own love for us, by the fact that while we were still sinners, Christ died for us."*
   (Romans 5:8 AMP)

   b. *"As the Father has loved me, so have I loved you. Abide in my love."* (John 15:9)

   c. *"Just as the Father has loved Me, I also have loved you; remain in My love.* (John 15:9 NASB)

   Are you allowing God's love to remain in your heart? Are you remaining in Jesus' love?

   d. Please receive this blessing declaration for your life which is based on Ephesians 3:16-19:

   May the Father grant you to be strengthened with power through His Spirit in your inner being, so that Christ may dwell in your hearts through faith—that you, being rooted and grounded in love, may have strength to comprehend with all the saints what is the breadth and length and height and depth, and to know the love of Christ that surpasses knowledge, that you may be filled with all the fullness of God. In Jesus' Name. Amen.

3. Do you "trust in the love" God has for you?

   a. *"And I am sure of this, that he who began a good work in you will bring it to completion at the day of Jesus Christ."* (Philippians 1:6)

   b. May I provide this example of sowing the seed of trusting God into the heart of our daughter, Elizabeth? Every morning as I drove her to middle school, I spoke and released a specific blessing declaration over her. Let me emphasize "every morning." I even asked the Lord about my repetitiveness. He confirmed that I was to release that specific word over her, again and again. Please consider that she was a young teenager trying to navigate life at school and at home. She was surrounded by three brothers, two older, one younger. Her middle school atmosphere was heavily weighted with fellow teenagers trying to understand their purpose in life. Elizabeth needed to hear about God's faithfulness.

I used the wording found in the King James Version of Philippians 1:6: *"Being confident of this very thing, that he which hath begun a good work in you will perform it until the day of Jesus Christ."*

My blessing declaration sounded like this: "May you, Elizabeth, be confident of this very thing: that He who has begun a good work in you will perfect and complete it until the day of Jesus Christ. In Jesus' Name. Amen."

God's word of truth took root and grew within her heart. Now, as a wife and a mother of five, she trusts God to accomplish His loving and mighty deeds in and through her life. She bears witness of the power and fruitfulness of His word. Seeds of truth and trust were sown; God caused a great harvest.

4. Are you "living in close fellowship with the Son and with the Father?"

   a. *"So you must be sure to keep the message burning in your hearts; that is, the message of life you heard from the beginning. If you do, you will always be living in close fellowship with the Son and with the Father."* (1 John 2:24 TPT)

   b. *"And this is the promise that he made to us—eternal life."* (1 John 2:25)

   c. *"SEE WHAT [an incredible] quality of love the Father has given (shown, bestowed on) us, that we should [be permitted to] be named and called and counted the children of God! And so we are! The reason that the world does not know (recognize, acknowledge) us is that it does not know (recognize, acknowledge) Him."* (1 John 3:1 AMPC)

   d. *"Jesus answered him, 'If anyone loves me, he will keep my word, and my Father will love him, and we will come to him and make our home with him.'"* (John 14:23)

5. Does God live in and through you?

    a. *"Jesus answered, If a person [really] loves Me, he will keep My word [obey My teaching]; and My Father will love him, and We will come to him and make Our home (abode, special dwelling place) with him."* (John 14:23 AMPC) Keep, protect and preserve His teaching in your heart.

    b. *"Truly, truly, I say to you, whoever believes in me will also do the works that I do; and greater works than these will he do, because I am going to the Father."* (John 14:12)

    c. *"I assure you and most solemnly say to you, anyone who believes in Me [as Savior] will also do the things that I do; and he will do even greater things than these [in extent and outreach], because I am going to the Father."* (John 14:12 AMP)

6. Do you believe that Jesus Christ is the only begotten Son of God and that God raised Him from the dead?

    a. *"… if you confess with your mouth that Jesus is Lord and believe in your heart that God raised him from the dead, you will be saved. For with the heart one believes and is justified, and with the mouth one confesses and is saved."* (Romans 10:9,10)

    Is this what you believe and confess?

    b. *"For 'everyone who calls on the name of the Lord will be saved.'"* (Romans 10:13)

7. How will you express your devotion and love to Jesus?

    a. *"If you love me, you will keep my commandments."* (John 14:15)

    b. *"As the Father has loved me, so have I loved you. Abide in my love."* (John 15:9)

    "The only faith-filled response to Christ's love is to obey his commandments. It is his love that provided the opportunity for our spiritual salvation and a personal relationship with Christ. Our obedience is a large part of maintaining that relationship and fulfilling God's purposes for our lives (see

14:15,21,23). Obedience and love must always go together in our relationship with God…"[1]

c. *"And this is love, that we walk according to his commandments; this is the commandment, just as you have heard from the beginning, so that you should walk in it."* (2 John 6)

d. *"whoever says he abides in him ought to walk in the same way in which he walked."* (1 John 2:6)

"Following Jesus' example is not meant to be optional for Christians; it is to be a way of life…that boldly identifies with Christ… and reflects his character. This is not entirely possible without spending time in God's Word because that is the one place where we actually see what Jesus would do. By studying God's Word for ourselves and praying that God would help us apply it to our lives, we invite the Holy Spirit to guide us in Jesus' steps and develop his character in us…"[2]

e. *"whoever says he lives in Christ [that is, whoever says he has accepted Him as God and Savior] ought [as a moral obligation] to walk and conduct himself just as He walked and conducted Himself."*

(1 John 2:6 AMP)

8. Where does Jesus lead you? Are you prepared to follow as the Spirit leads?

   a. *"And Jesus answered them, 'Have faith in God.'"* (Mark 11:22)

   b. *"Truly, I say to you, whoever says to this mountain, 'Be taken up and thrown into the sea,' and does not doubt in his heart, but believes that what he says will come to pass, it will be done for him."*

(Mark 11:23)

A "mountain" can be something that has risen or reared up in our thoughts or beliefs. We must cast down those vain imaginations that come against the knowledge of God. When we don't waver in, nor doubt our authority to evict those mountainous regions in our thinking and entrust our spiritual well-being to

---

[1] *FireBible*™, notes on John 15:9-10, p. 1765
[2] *FireBible*™, p. 2211, note on 1 John 2:6

Jesus Christ, then those lofty lies must leave. Jesus responds to our faith-filled declarations and our freedom comes to pass.

c. *"Therefore I tell you, whatever you ask in prayer, believe that you have received it, and it will be yours."* (Mark 11:24)

d. *"Whatever you ask in my name, this I will do, that the Father may be glorified in the Son."* (John 14:13)

e. *"If you ask Me anything in My name [as My representative], I will do it."* (John 14:14 AMP) These scriptures do not support the "name and claim it" idea. Read the following relational condition that must exist:

f. *"If you abide in me, and my words abide in you, ask whatever you wish, and it will be done for you."* (John 15:7)

g. *"But if you live in life-union with me and if my words live powerfully within you—then you can ask whatever you desire and it will be done."* (John 15:7 TPT)

Living in "life-union" with Jesus transforms your life to the point where you can speak and release blessing declarations over and into others.

An example of a "mountainous region" in someone's thinking:

To be accepted into a Physician Assistant Master's Degree program, our second son, Peyton, had to obtain a certain score on the GRE (Graduate Record Exam). He dedicated weeks in preparation. Along his journey of studying, Peyton began mentally and emotionally accepting a lofty lie, a mountainous region of defeat and not success.

Exam Day arrived.

As he was leaving, I followed him to his car. As he walked, he talked, identifying that mountainous region of trepidation. Peyton spoke and released authority for this one exam to control his future. I quickly negated that belief and released a blessing declaration over him. I rejected that mindset, replacing it with the word of God. In doing this, the authority and power of God was glorified, then magnified within our son's expectations. Peyton would succeed and not fail. His eyes were redirected to God's plan for his life: **to prosper**.

As a teenager, Peyton had received prophetic words foretelling God's plan for him: "World Changer." At different times, guest speakers visited our church in Tallahassee. Independent of each other, yet following the leading of Holy Spirit, these speakers revealed and released God's plan: Peyton would be used as an instrument for **change** in people's lives, i.e., their **worlds**. As he stepped into the role and responsibility of being a PA (Physician Assistant) in the Emergency Room of Tallahassee's largest hospital, God deposited into Peyton the ability to detect and discern underlying causes for illnesses and conditions. Recommendations and diagnoses that he presented changed the future for his patients. God was fulfilling His plans, giving a future and a hope not only to Peyton but to countless others.

I asked a question earlier: "Where" should we be within our relationship with God to speak and release blessing declarations? Your thoughts?

_____

_____

_____

Consider where Jesus was when He explained the "life-union" with Him as we read in The Passion Translation of John 15:7. Reading the verses prior to that, we discover Jesus was talking with His eleven disciples following their last meal shared before the Cross. As they ate in an upper room of a dwelling, Jesus spoke of future events. Then, He directed His friends: *"...Rise, let us go from here."* (John 14:31)

Where would Jesus lead His disciples?

Matthew, one of the disciples, identified Jesus' intended destination: *"And when they had sung a hymn, they went out to the Mount of Olives."* (Matthew 26:30)

As Mark wrote his historical account of that night, he included this: *"And when they had sung a hymn, they went out to the Mount of Olives...And they went to a place called Gethsemane...."* (Mark 14:26,32)

In Luke's account of Jesus' life, ministry, death, and resurrection, he provided an additional confirmation of their destination: *"And he came out* and went, as was his custom, to the Mount of Olives, and the disciples followed him." (Luke 22:39)

"As was His custom" indicates that Jesus' disciples were familiar with where He was headed.

They knew that Jesus frequented the Garden of Gethsemane for prayer. In the natural sense, His companions could anticipate their destination. In the supernatural, spiritual realm, did they foresee Jesus revealing Himself: *"I am the true vine…"*?

I have no doubt that when these eleven men heard their Rabbi's words, they pushed closer to Him so as not to miss His message. These followers had heard Jesus reveal Himself to unbelieving Jews: *"Jesus said to them, 'Truly, truly, I say to you, before Abraham was, I am.'"* (John 8:58)

The revealing of His true essence was not well-received by the religious folk. *"So they picked up stones to throw at him, but Jesus hid himself and went out of the temple."* (John 8:59) Witnessing rocks poised to be hurled at their Teacher left them with a strong and memorable image!

These eleven men knew the historical account of the call of Moses to deliver God's people out of the bondage and control of the Egyptian pharaoh. God revealed Himself to Moses as He spoke out of the burning bush. During their exchange, Moses asked for reassurance as to the authority of the One who was sending him back to Egypt.

> *Then Moses said to God, "If I come to the people of Israel and say to them, 'The God of your fathers has sent me to you,' and they ask me, 'What is his name?' what shall I say to them?" God said to Moses, "I AM WHO I AM." And he said, "Say this to the people of Israel: 'I AM has sent me to you. This is my name forever, and thus I am to be remembered throughout all generations.'"*
> (Exodus 3:13-15)

The Great I AM is to be remembered throughout all generations. Just as God revealed Himself to Moses as the Self-Existing One, Jesus confirmed His eternal name: I AM.

"It is in Jesus that all Jehovah promised to be to his people finds full realization."[1]

---
1 Herbert Lockyer, D.D.: *All the Divine Names and Titles in the Bible*, p. 172

Then Jesus revealed another facet of His eternal nature: the True Vine as opposed to the vine of Israel who had detached herself from the Vine of Life and had become unfruitful.

Let's rejoin the eleven disciples as they listened to their Master Teacher's instruction:

"Abide in me, and I in you. As the branch cannot bear fruit by itself, unless it abides in the vine, neither can you, unless you abide in me." (John 15:4)

The Passion Translation offers this:

So you must remain in life-union with me, for I remain in life-union with you. For as a branch severed from the vine will not bear fruit, so your life will be fruitless unless you live your life intimately joined to mine. (John 15:4 TPT)

This describes where we must remain—in "life-union" with Jesus. Being joined with Jesus produces powerful results: *"I am the vine; you are the branches. Whoever abides in me and I in him, he it is that bears much fruit, for apart from me you can do nothing."* (John 15:5)

"I am the sprouting vine and you're my branches. As you live in union with me as your source, fruitfulness will stream from within you—but when you live separated from me you are powerless." (John 15:5 TPT)

This kingdom of God principle leads us where we need to be in life-union with Jesus, bearing much fruit, thus proving to be His disciples. In that way we glorify the Father.

"If you abide in me, and my words abide in you, ask whatever you wish, and it will be done for you. By this my Father is glorified, that you bear much fruit and so prove to be my disciples." (John 15:7,8)

Read The Passion Translation for verse 8: *"When your lives bear abundant fruit, you demonstrate that you are my mature disciples who glorify my Father!"*

You and I are invited to walk in step with the Word, that is, Jesus. Notice the capital W. Notice the use of the capital W in John 1:1: *"In the beginning was the Word, and the Word was with God, and the Word was God."*

Spend time reading God's word to know the Word; the I AM. Listen to His Spirit.

Holy Spirit, the Spirit of Jesus, fills to overflowing those believers who are submitted and committed to being a conduit of the Father's love, mercy, and grace. We are the heart, hands, and feet of Jesus wherever we minister to others in His Name and for His sake.

Consider these kingdom principles as you and I move forward in serving God and others.

1. We can serve God and others as we:

    a. maintain an intimate relationship with Jesus.

    b. receive His directive and engage His authority to speak and act for His sake, to the glory of His Father. Recall that Jesus commissioned the first twelve disciples: *"And he called to him his twelve disciples and gave them authority over unclean spirits, to cast them out, and to heal every disease and every affliction."* (Matthew 10:1)

    As Jesus prepared to return to Heaven, He released His directive:

    And Jesus came and said to them, "All authority in heaven and on earth has been given to me. Go therefore and make disciples of all nations, baptizing them in the name of the Father and of the Son and of the Holy Spirit, teaching them to observe all that I have commanded you. And behold, I am with you always, to the end of the age." (Matthew 28:18-20)

    Generations of disciples later, you and I are to carry Jesus' directive to proclaim God's kingdom here in earth as it is in Heaven. Commissioned with His authority, His delegated influence, and jurisdiction, and empowered by His Holy Spirit, we speak and release the power to break the control of illness and evil over people's lives. We show the compassion of Christ to others and express our devotion to God.

    c. operate from and with a heavenly perspective as Paul identified: *"even when we were dead in our trespasses, made us alive together with Christ—by grace you have been saved—and raised us up with him and seated us with him in the heavenly places in Christ Jesus,"* (Ephesians 2:5-6)

2. We fulfill our kingdom destinies as we walk in life-union with Jesus:

   a. *"For we are his workmanship, created in Christ Jesus for good works, which God prepared beforehand, that we should walk in them."* (Ephesians 2:10)

   b. *You did not choose me, but I chose you and appointed you that you should go and bear fruit and that your fruit should abide, so that whatever you ask the Father in my name, he may give it to you.* (John 15:16)

   3. Consider, then describe how you are walking in life-union with Jesus.

What does your union with Jesus look like on a daily basis?

_____

_____

_____

Identify where the Spirit of Christ has led you in walking out your obedience and love toward Jesus.

Within your family:

_____

_____

_____

Within your place of employment:

_____

_____

_____

Where Did Jesus Speak?

Among the Body of Christ:

_____

_____

_____

Throughout your community:

_____

_____

_____

May I share a powerful picture of the Father's love expressed toward His beloved?

Several years ago, the women's group of our church hosted a luncheon. In preparing the tables for this gathering, I placed a blessing scroll at each place setting. During this ladies' luncheon, a time was designated for each participant to read aloud their blessing. One participant's blessing referred to being a "Barnabas" as he served as an encourager within the Body of Christ. This lady was noticeably touched by this blessing. She explained how many of her friends described her as being their "Barnabas" as she continually encouraged and uplifted them.

As women continued to read their blessing scroll, one attendee paused and noted that she had received a blessing written in Spanish. [A side note: I have had a few blessing sets translated into different languages. I was aware that we were expecting Spanish-speaking guests; therefore, I had included those Spanish blessing scrolls on a table.] This English-speaking guest allowed someone to translate the Spanish blessing into English. Another guest handed this lady a second blessing which had been written in English. As this guest unrolled the second scroll, she was stunned. It was the exact blessing she had been given in Spanish. [A side note: each blessing set contains a variety of Scripture-based blessings. This was not a "coincidence," nor orchestrated by any of us.] This beloved believer received the Father's confirmation of His love and attention toward her.

Would you spend another moment with me as I walk within the marketplace of our community? May I take you to our local bank? Stand with me and observe a teller's cubicle. What do you notice? What is taped around her, on the half-walls of her station? Yes, those are the blessing scrolls I have shared with her over the years. Remember, the blessing scrolls contain the living word of God. As I recalled this image, Holy Spirit spoke to me. He explained that what is in the natural setting of this lady's workplace exists within her heart. This is a picture of God's word richly dwelling within her. That's what we can offer others in the marketplace of our lives—God's word. We can speak and release His powerful, transformative truth through blessing declarations. The visible collection of blessing scrolls is symbolic of the multiple opportunities the Lord sets before us to cover and encompass others with His living and abiding word.

Let's drive down the street and take a right. Would you walk into our post office with me? These employees have always treated me kindly and have graciously received blessing scrolls. There's a place in their hearts for God's word. Everyone needs a cup of cool water! Would you go one more mile with me? (Matthew 5:41) Let's visit another place of business. Many local residents shop at this store whose goods are economically priced. As you and I walk up and down the aisles, we encounter various shoppers, all needing God's word. You and I can ask God for Divine Appointments to comfort and encourage individuals who are moving through a difficult place in their lives. We can bless sales associates as we pay for our items. As I make a habit of sharing the blessing scrolls with salesclerks, they remember them, smile when I offer a scroll, then thank me. Not one associate has refused them. On one of the electronic card readers, a blessing scroll is taped! What grabbed my heart so deeply was that God's truth, His living word was being honored and placed before hundreds of people as they pay for their items. God knows all things. He knows who has been touched when they read that blessing scroll. Our communities are ripe for God's life-depositing word. You and I have God's word in our hearts and in our mouths. Let's speak and declare it to others.

My Blessing Declaration for you:

> May God's hand of favor bless your going out and your coming in.
>
> May you be blessed in the city and in the field.
>
> May you be the head and not the tail. May you be the lender and not the borrower.
>
> May you walk in a way that is worthy of His calling on your life.
>
> May whatever you do bring God glory and honor.
>
> May you walk in His way.
>
> In Jesus' Name. Amen.

Resource for page 113:

*Craig S. Keener: *The IVP Bible Background Commentary-New Testament* (page 252) provides a historical background for "The Decree of the Sanhedrin."

> Luke 22:66: Leading priests,' 'elders' and 'scribes' were the three groups represented on the Sanhedrin, the ruling religious court of Israel. The full Sanhedrin, with seventy-one members, normally assembled in a meeting hall in the temple called the Chamber of Hewn Stone, where they sat in a semicircle with the high priest in the center. Although the body acted as a whole, not all its members concurred (23:51); writers would often make a general statement about a group without listing explicit exceptions (cf. Jer 26:16, 24).

Resource for page 115:

**Craig S. Keener: *The IVP Bible Background Commentary-New Testament* provides a historical background for Jesus' burial as mentioned in John 19:38-42.

> 19:38: Crucifixion victims were usually thrown into a common grave for criminals and were not to be mourned publicly after their death..." "But exceptions seem to be made at times if family or powerful *patrons interceded for the body. Burying the dead was a crucial and pious duty in Judaism, and an important

act of love; being unburied was too horrible to be permitted even for criminals. To accomplish his task before sundown and the advent of the sabbath, Joseph of Arimathea has to hurry.

19:39: Nicodemus's mixture…is a lavish expression of devotion….Myrrh was used for embalming the dead, and aloes for perfume.

19:40: John mentions the Jewish custom; Jewish people did not burn dead heroes, as Greeks and Romans did, or mutilate them for embalming, as Egyptians did. Bodies were wrapped in shrouds, sometimes expensive ones, especially prepared for burials. Jewish sources are emphatic that none of these actions may be undertaken unless the person is clearly dead; thus those burying Jesus have no doubt that he is dead. Here strips of linen rather than a full shroud are used, perhaps because of the imminent approach of the sabbath at sundown.

19:41: To be buried in a tomb not yet used was no doubt a special honor and would make the tomb difficult to confuse with others in the vicinity.

19:42: The sabbath (or in this case, the coming of Passover—18:28) interrupted all other activities. Joseph and Nicodemus did not need to "lay" Jesus there very carefully; this would have been only a preliminary burial even had the sabbath not approached, to be completed a year later, after the flesh had rotted off the bones. (pp. 314-315)

Considering Where You Are and Where You Need to Be:

1. Have you come to know and to believe that God loves you?

   _____
   _____
   _____

2. Where are you in experiencing God's intimate love?

   _____
   _____
   _____

3. Have you believed in Jesus for your salvation and received His forgiveness?

   _____
   _____
   _____

4. Are you reading God's word daily?

   _____
   _____
   _____

5. Are you praying daily?

   _____
   _____
   _____

6. Where are you in your obedience to Holy Spirit's leading?

   _____

   _____

   _____

7. Where are you asking Jesus to send you?

   _____

   _____

   _____

8. Where have you sown the seed of God's word through speaking blessing declarations?

   _____

   _____

   _____

Chapter 5

Why Should We Speak Blessing Declarations?

As you and I have chosen to become and remain followers of Jesus Christ, we are given the ability to follow His ways of speaking blessing declarations over others and into the earthly and heavenly realms. Blessing declarations engage the life-creating word of God with people and over their circumstances. As God's word richly dwells within us, Holy Spirit, the Spirit of Truth, will remind us of the spoken words of Christ to release at the appropriate time. In doing this, the word of truth will dispel darkness by infusing the light of truth. God's kingdom will be advanced, here in earth as it is in heaven. (John 14:17,26; Matthew 6:10)

The psalmist declared: *"Thy word is a lamp unto my feet, and a light unto my path."* (Psalm 119:105 KJV)

Those who love God recognize that His word "...contains the spiritual principles that will help us avoid many sorrows, pitfalls and tragedies brought on by wrong decisions and choices. For this reason, we must treasure its wisdom and apply it in all of life's situations...It will never fail to guide us in the right decision."[1]

---

1   *FireBible*™, p. 919, note on 119:105

Did you notice the *FireBible's*™ explanation for treasuring and applying God's word to our lives: "For this reason…it will never fail to guide us in the right decision."

God's word is 100% accurate all the time; 100% trustworthy in all situations.

This is a great answer to: "Why Should We Speak Blessing Declarations?"

"So faith comes from hearing, and hearing through the word of Christ." (Romans 10:17)

Blessing declarations offer others the opportunity to hear the word of God "fitly spoken at the right time." The blessing declarations can be perceived as Solomon described:

"A word fitly spoken is like apples of gold in a setting of silver."
(Proverbs 25:11)

Solomon continued to share his wisdom as he reminded the reader that a timely, gracious message from a faith-filled believer can refresh the soul of the hearer. (Proverbs 25:13)

Elizabeth and Kyle have placed a container of blessing scrolls in the center of their dining table. Anyone can take a scroll at any time. Noah, their son, shared this:

> Whenever you're having a hard time or something, the Blessing (scroll) is exactly what you need. Then you think…whenever you're having a hard time, you go and get one (a scroll), and, of course, it's the correct one.

Noah has already developed a recognition of the timeliness of God and His all-sufficient grace provided through His word. God's "right time" is indeed beautiful.

When a person hears God's word, they are being offered fruit born by a life submitted to Him. When received, this fruit can refresh the person's thirsty soul and a heart hungry for truth and encouragement. God honors His word spoken in faith and He makes certain that it accomplishes His intent. Angels hearken to the voice of God's word being spoken. (Psalm 103:20)

Why Should We Speak Blessing Declarations?

Prompted by the Spirit of God, the prophet Isaiah declared:

For as the rain and the snow come down from heaven and do not return there but water the earth, making it bring forth and sprout, giving seed to the sower and bread to the eater, so shall my word be that goes out from my mouth; it shall not return to me empty, but it shall accomplish that which I purpose, and shall succeed in the thing for which I sent it. (Isaiah 55:10-11)

God's word is eternal, everlasting. Following the prompting of Holy Spirit, Peter, a disciple of Jesus Christ, wrote:

Since you have been born again, not of perishable seed but of imperishable, through the living and abiding word of God…the word of the Lord remains forever. And this word is the good news that was preached to you. (1 Peter 1:23, 25)

Give careful thought to the description that Holy Spirit inspired Peter to use regarding the word of God: "living and abiding." The word of God is "alive" and active, interactive, capable of producing life within people. The word of God abides, remains, dwells, continues to deposit and create life.

As the word of the Lord remains forever, you and I have the privilege and responsibility to engage and assimilate its power and authority. We must continually incorporate the word of our God in our lives.

Peter added a further description of this word: it is the good news that was preached. Consider the meaning of **preached:** to announce good news ("evangelize") especially the gospel: - declare, bring (declare, show) glad (good) tidings, preach (the gospel).[1]

Blessing declarations announce, speak forth, declare good news, telling others about God's plan, purpose, and love for them; to declare to them His future and hope for them. Hope is not an early morning mist that evaporates as the sun's heat warms the atmosphere. Hope is not empty nor illusive when it is grounded and founded on the truth of God's word.

God upholds and accomplishes His Holy word.

---

1 Strong's Concordance, G2097: preached

We recall John's declaration:

In the beginning was the Word, and the Word was with God, and the Word was God. .... And the Word became flesh and dwelt among us, and we have seen his glory, glory as of the only Son from the Father, full of grace and truth." (John 1:1,14)

Jesus is the living and abiding Word of God. He remains forever. He never leaves nor forsakes us. He abides within every person who has called upon His Name, believing in His redemption for them. He asked the Father to send Holy Spirit to abide and remain within believers.

Let's revisit Jesus' explanation of the Third Person of the Trinity:

If you love me, you will keep my commandments. And I will ask the Father, and he will give you another Helper, to be with you forever, even the Spirit of truth, whom the world cannot receive, because it neither sees him nor knows him. You know him, for he dwells with you and will be in you. I will not leave you as orphans; I will come to you. (John 14:15-18)

Jesus comes to us through the presence of Holy Spirit. Jesus reveals Himself to us through the indwelling and empowering of His Spirit. Who was revealed during Creation?

The eternal Godhead's presence and activity was unveiled. The Holy Trinity was at work. As God spoke, He released the Word, and the Spirit's activity gave shape and form to the Word that was spoken. God's sovereign presence, His living Word, His operative Spirit remain today. Our Triune God is ever-present and always active and interactive.

Once released, the word of God remains and is fulfilled, throughout eternity, within every generation. As we submit ourselves to the leading and guidance of His Spirit, we have the privilege of partnering with Him. Holy Spirit will bring to our minds the words of Christ at the exact moment of need and purpose.

We have the awesome responsibility of "grabbing hold" of that **Rhema** word and declaring it over people and into the atmosphere, the conditions surrounding and affecting them.

Why Should We Speak Blessing Declarations?

Let's pause for a moment to understand the term: **rhema.** Wikipedia offers this explanation:

> Rhema (ῥῆμα in Greek) literally means an 'utterance' or 'thing said' in Greek....It is a word that signifies the action of utterance. Plato, a Greek philosopher, associated **rhema** with action. In Christianity, the Greek word **rhema** is useful to distinguish between two meanings of **word**. While both **rhema** and **logos** are translated as **word** in English, in the original Greek there was a substantial distinction.
>
> Some modern usage distinguishes **rhema** from **logos** in Christian theology, with **rhema** at times called 'spoken word',...referring to the revelation received by disciples when the Holy Spirit 'speaks' to them....In this usage, 'Logos' refers to Christ. (emphasis added)[1]

That **Rhema** word becomes effective when activated to deliver others out of darkness into His marvelous light. Holy Spirit, the Spirit of Christ, the Third Person of the Godhead, knows every detail of a person's life and their circumstances. We do not; He does. As we remain submitted to Him and committed to being a conduit of the Father's love, mercy, and grace, Holy Spirit will prompt us to pray and to speak a word that fits the need, a word rightly spoken. We are the heart, hands, and feet of Jesus as we minister to others in His Name and for His sake. This is another reason for "why we should speak…"

Those who hear and grab hold of that blessing declaration do so by faith.

Over the years, I have offered workshops about speaking and releasing blessing declarations. During these sessions, I have shared stories about our children when they were young. At times their energy levels needed to be taken beyond the confinement of our house. As I sent them outside to play, I followed them with a bottle of "bubbles" in my hand. This bottle contained a plastic wand designed with a circle at one end. As soon as I withdrew the wand from the soapy "bubble" solution, I gently blew through the circle. Bubbles began to float above their heads as the game of "catch me if you can" began. Excitedly our children ran and jumped trying to catch one, then two, then three iridescent spheres. When their

---

[1] https://en.wikipedia.org/wiki/Rhema

small hands touched these floating globes, they popped, leaving a bit of "bubble" solution on their skin.

If those bubbles of fun eluded their outstretched hands, we watched them slowly rotate in the breeze, allowing us to glimpse the various colors of the rainbow! On many occasions the "bubble" fun ended when the bottle was emptied. Yet our lively conversation continued as we talked about the beauty of the bubbles, the "big one that got away," how many were "caught," and on and on. Later that evening, Daddy heard their exciting stories.

As I shared this experience with the workshop attendees, I blew "bubbles" over them. Some people reached out to grab a bubble, while others simply watched them float overhead. Some attendees engaged with childlike pleasure; others allowed those shimmering orbs to pass by, gazing at them from a distance.

Consider this analogy of speaking and releasing blessing declarations, proclaiming the word of truth over someone:

The container of soapy solution could be compared to us, God's vessel. The bubble solution could be likened to God's word richly dwelling within us. As Holy Spirit reminds us of the words of Christ, we withdraw the wand, the sword of the Spirit, and allow His Spirit (pneuma—breath) to flow through us as we speak and release the "bubbles" of truth and life. As we release the word of God, we wield its power and authority, and the atmospheric conditions change.

Discover the beauty, power, and authority of God's word within this blessing declaration:

> *May the God of our Lord Jesus Christ, the Father of glory, give you the Spirit of wisdom and of revelation in the knowledge of Him. May the eyes of your heart be enlightened, that you may know what is the hope to which He has called you. May you know the riches of His glorious inheritance in the saints. May you know and experience the immeasurable greatness of His power toward us who believe, according to the working of His great might. In Jesus' Name. Amen.* (Ephesians 1:17-19)

May I encourage you to locate and reread those verses within your favorite Bible. Then ask yourself: "Do I want God to accomplish all of this within my life?" If your answer is a resounding "YES," then grab hold of it and accept His word of truth and life for yourself.

In doing this, you are expressing your faith in God and in His living Word, Jesus.

The writer of Hebrews explained to Christ's followers that some had heard the word of God, yet it did not profit them due to their lack of faith. He wrote: *"For good news came to us just as to them, but the message they heard did not benefit them, because they were not united by faith with those who listened."* (Hebrews 4:2)

The word "benefit" carries the idea of being useful, giving someone an advantage, helping make a person better, providing a way to prevail, adding profit to their life. Those who heard but did not allow God's word to prevail in their lives did not assimilate His truth and His life within their hearts. While they listened to God's word being spoken and released, they were not persuaded to its truthfulness, nor did they accept the opportunity to believe in Jesus for their salvation. These "hearers" rejected the Living Word, Jesus.

For the Good News of Jesus Christ was and is and shall be the solution for mankind's sin.

Mark 5:24 begins the account of a desperate woman in need of healing. She allowed what she heard about Jesus to prevail within her heart, resulting in faith in Him, His love and truth. The benefit she received from what she heard allowed this desperate woman to believe in Jesus' willingness and desire to heal her. The cultural restrictions of separation and isolation placed upon her "uncleanness" did not keep this woman from stretching out her hand to grab hold of His tassel. What she heard about Jesus gave her hope. Even today, people desperately need hope and His wholeness. Remember: faith comes by hearing, hearing by the word of Christ. We must speak of Him.

(Please refer to Leviticus 15:19, 25 to read the restrictions placed upon women who have an issue of blood. Also read in Numbers 15:37-41 about the tassels on a prayer shawl.)

The Spoken Blessing II: Influencing Generations

The tassel on Jesus' prayer shawl was called a "tzitzit." A tzitzit was attached to the four corners of a Jewish man's tallit, his prayer shawl. The tzitzit served as a visual reminder of the LORD's instruction to keep His commandments and to remember one's commitment to Him as their one, true God.

As you read this narrative in Mark 5, take note that Jesus was on His way to help Jairus, a ruler of the synagogue, whose twelve-year-old daughter was dying. The desperate woman saw and seized her opportunity to reach out and grab hold of Jesus. What is so powerful and noteworthy is that Jesus responded to her touch and her faith. She sought Him and found Him. (Proverbs 8:17)

Recall God's word of truth as explained in The Amplified™ Bible:

> *But without faith it is impossible to [walk with God and] please Him, for whoever comes [near] to God must [necessarily] believe that God exists and that He rewards those who [earnestly and diligently] seek Him.* (Hebrews 11:6 AMP)

Read the account of Jesus and this desperate woman in Mark 5, beginning in verse 24:

> *And he [Jesus] went with him [Jairus]. And a great crowd followed him and thronged about him. (25) And there was a woman who had had a discharge of blood for twelve years, (26) and who had suffered much under many physicians, and had spent all that she had, and was no better but rather grew worse. (27) She had heard the reports about Jesus and came up behind him in the crowd and touched his garment. (28) For she said, 'If I touch even his garments, I will be made well.* (brackets added)

Take note of this woman's words of faith. She believed that simply contacting Jesus, in some way, would heal her. She believed it, then spoke it, and acted upon her faith. And it was done.

> *(29) And immediately the flow of blood dried up, and she felt in her body that she was healed of her disease. (30) And Jesus, perceiving in himself that power had gone out from him, immediately turned about in the crowd and said, "Who touched my garments?"*

Why Should We Speak Blessing Declarations?

Take note: Jesus recognized that miraculous power had proceeded forth from Himself.

> *(31) And his disciples said to him, "You see the crowd pressing around you, and yet you say, "Who touched me?" (32) And he looked around to see who had done it. (33) But the woman, knowing what had happened to her, came in fear and trembling and fell down before him and told him the whole truth. (34) And he said to her, "Daughter, your faith has made you well; go in peace, and be healed of your disease."*

Virtue, miraculous power, flowed out of Jesus into a vessel prepared by faith. Verses 27 and 28 identify this woman's heart, soul, and mind were prepared for the redemptive and restorative work of Jesus. Her words released her faith. Her faith in Jesus had saved her; made her well. Her faith had saved, delivered, preserved her (G4982). Jesus spoke and released His peace, His quietness, His rest, His prosperity. Jesus declared that she would be healthy, well, and sound in her body.[1]

This notable woman had heard words about Jesus and believed the words she had heard. Then she spoke forth faith in His power to make her whole. The word she used was sozo (G4982 in Strong's Concordance). Jesus repeated her word when He declared: *"Daughter, thy faith hath made thee whole;..."* Whole (G4982) was used by Jesus. He communicated to this believer that she received that which she believed and spoke. This speaks volumes!

As you and I speak and release blessing declarations based on His truth, we pave the way for faith to be birthed and developed within the hearers. His life-depositing, healing strength can flow through us as we speak and release our faith in Christ, declaring the wholeness found in Him.

The Spirit of God moved in and through the prophet Isaiah and he declared the word of God to the house of Jacob:

> *Remember this and stand firm, recall it to mind, ... for I am God, and there is none like me, declaring the end from the beginning and from ancient times things not yet done, saying, "My counsel shall stand, and I will accomplish all my purpose." (Isaiah 46:8-10)*

---

1   Strong's Concordance for well, peace, healed as used in verse 34

We can use Strong's Concordance to better understand what the LORD was declaring about Himself. "My counsel shall stand" could be understood as: My plan, My purpose, My advice shall be accomplished, confirmed, decreed, performed, established, strengthened and shall be successful. "I will accomplish all my purpose" could be expressed as: I will make, advance, appoint, bring forth, execute, exercise, govern, procure, and provide the whole of My desire, My valuable thing, My great desire.

God's purpose has existed with Him in eternity. Isaiah recognized the eternal nature of the coming Messiah and His work: "…the will of the LORD shall prosper (H6743) in his hand." (Isaiah 53:10, brackets and number added)

Strong's Concordance, H6743: shall prosper means *"…to push forward… break out, come (mightily), go over, be good, be meet, be profitable, (cause to, effect, make to, send) prosper…."*

Knowing that Jesus Christ is the Messiah, and using Strong's Concordance, we could recognize Jesus' work as applying His Spirit-filled, power-filled hands to "push forward", and to "make profitable" the desire, delight, and purpose of the LORD. Jesus truly accomplished the counsel and governance of God.

Did you notice that Jairus' daughter was twelve years old and that the woman with the issue of blood had suffered for twelve years? The number **twelve** is a symbol for divine government.[1]

Jesus had been preaching and presenting that the kingdom of God was at hand, very present and real. A kingdom has a governance to be disseminated and enforced. He was dispersing the divine government of His Father's kingdom in earth as it exists in heaven.

Jesus, the Messiah, revealed God, the Father, to those around Him, as God's word does for us. The will of the LORD was pushed forward through His hands. When asked if He was the Christ, Jesus responded plainly: *"I told you, and you do not believe. The works that I do in my Father's name bear witness of me, but you do not believe…"* (John 10:24-25)

He continued to present the facts: *"I and the Father are one."* (John 10:30)

---

1 Kevin J. Conner: *Interpreting the Symbols and Types*, page 176

Even Jesus' closest disciples failed to see the Father in Jesus. John recorded a conversation between Jesus and His disciples:

> *Philip said to him, "Lord, show us the Father, and it is enough for us." Jesus said to him, "Have I been with you so long, and you still do not know me, Philip? Whoever has seen me has seen the Father....Do you not believe that I am in the Father and the Father is in me? The words that I say to you I do not speak on my own authority, but the Father who dwells in me does his works."* (John 14:8-10)

One of the purposes of Jesus' coming to earth was to reveal the Father. In like manner, our lives, words, and blessings can show others the love, character, and nature of God. Jesus declared this over His disciples: *"Truly, truly, I say to you, whoever believes in me will also do the works that I do; and greater works than these will he do, because I am going to the Father."* (John 14:12) As Jesus revealed the Father, so should we.

Please read His declaration from The Amplified™ Bible:

> *I assure you and most solemnly say to you, anyone who believes in Me [as Savior] will also do the things that I do; and he will do even greater things than these [in extent and outreach], because I am going to the Father.* (John 14:12 AMP)

As Jesus prayed to His heavenly Father, He confirmed the completion of His work on earth.

We can read Jesus' prayer in John 17, beginning with verse 1:

> *Father, the hour has come; glorify your Son that the Son may glorify you.... (4) I glorified you on earth, having accomplished the work that you gave me to do.... (6) I have manifested your name to the people whom you gave me out of the world. Yours they were, and you gave them to me, and they have kept your word.... (17) Sanctify them in the truth; your word is truth. (18) As you sent me into the world, so I have sent them into the world. (19) And for their sake I consecrate myself, that they also may be sanctified in truth. (20) I do not ask for these only, but also for those who will believe in me through their word, (21) that they may all be one, just as you, Father, are in me, and I in you, that they also may be in us, so that the world may believe that you have sent me.... (22) The glory that*

> *you have given me I have given to them, that they may be one even as we are one.... (26) I made known to them your name, and I will continue to make it known, that the love with which you have loved me may be in them, and I in them.*

The work that Jesus accomplished included His manifesting, that is, His making apparent the Father's name, character, and authority to others. Jesus asked His Father to set His disciples apart from the world by and through the word of His truth. Then, Jesus acknowledged to His Father that He was sending forth these disciples on a mission. Jesus identified the requirement of His service to the Father: being sanctified, that is, being purified and consecrated for discipling others. Jesus revealed that future generations of believers would come forth from the word shared by His current disciples. (John 17:20)

You and I are included in those future generations. You and I have the privilege of continuing His work of showing the love of the Father to others, that they may be one as we are one with Him.

This is one of the "whys" of speaking and releasing blessing declarations.

Let's recall a passage we read earlier in Isaiah 55:10-11:

> *For as the rain and the snow come down from heaven and do not return there but water the earth, making it bring forth and sprout, giving seed to the sower and bread to the eater, so shall my word be that goes out from my mouth; it shall not return to me empty, but it shall accomplish that which I purpose, and shall succeed in the thing for which I sent it.*

Through the mouth of His obedient prophet, Isaiah, the LORD provided an analogy explaining the power and effectiveness of His word when spoken. In verse 10 of Isaiah 55, the LORD referenced a seed bringing forth the next generation of its plant for the purpose for which it was created: life, food, provision, sustenance. The plants in our world were created during the original Creation described in Genesis 1. Hundreds of generations of seeds and plants have followed the original Word of life God released during Creation.

In verse 11 of Isaiah 55, the LORD compares the effectiveness of His spoken word to a seed which fulfills its created purpose. His life-depositing word shall accomplish and shall succeed in all that He intended. God's word is eternal and life-producing. It is a seed.

We have the privilege and responsibility to take His word of truth, sow it into the lives of others, and see His truth bring forth a harvest of righteousness. The God of Creation has entrusted us with a partnership of declaring and releasing His life-sustaining word through blessing declarations from generation to generation. As I write this book, I know families who have five generations living. FIVE generations of advancing the kingdom of God and harvesting righteousness are in operation and producing His life. Five is the number for grace. You and I are living in the time of great grace. You and I can sow grace into familial, spiritual, and relational generations.

"And a harvest of righteousness is sown in peace by those who make peace." (James 3:18)

- What precedes a harvest? Seeds sown. What types of seeds are we sowing into others?
- What do others hear when we speak? Do we bless or curse? Are our words sweet or bitter?
- Do our words build up or tear down others? James presented these glaring differences.
- We must ask ourselves those hard, self-examining questions.

James set the standard very high for our conversation and behavior.

Listen to this follower of Jesus: *"Who is wise and understanding among you? By his good conduct let him show his works in the meekness of wisdom."* (James 3:13)

James continued in verse 17: *"But the wisdom from above is first pure, then peaceable, gentle, open to reason, full of mercy and good fruits, impartial and sincere."*

Therefore, James identified that we must seek, pursue, and embrace God's wisdom, His perspective, His nature which is pure. God shows us His way to pursue peace and sanctification, without which no one will see the Lord. (Hebrews 12:14 ASV) There is a blessing for us as we speak and release the peace of God: we shall be called sons of God.

The Spoken Blessing II: Influencing Generations

We are His own.

"Blessed are the peacemakers, for they shall be called sons of God."
(Matthew 5:9)

Great wisdom was shared by the writer of Proverbs: *"Evil people may get a short-term gain, but to sow seeds of righteousness will bring a true and lasting reward."* (11:18 TPT)

"Seeds of righteousness" are sown for the benefit of the generations living around us and for those who are yet to be born. As a seed, God's word will germinate within them.

May I share a third generation recipient of our speaking blessing declarations over our children? Within my first book: *The Spoken Blessing—A Spiritual Posture*, I identified how our family had hit "rock bottom" within our relationships and attitudes toward each other.

Our children were young and did not understand the turmoil. Cal and I prayed and prayed. We needed help. We recognized that our attitudes did not reflect the love, patience, kindness, nor forgiveness of Christ. Those around us may not have been cognizant of the strife that existed. But our loving heavenly Father knew; He heard our cries for help. His answer came through an obedient pastor from Brunswick, Georgia, Dr. Bill Ligon.

During a Sunday night's message, our guest speaker, Dr. Ligon, threw a life-ring to our emotionally sinking family. He presented God's word in such a way that the power of speaking blessings over family members was simple to understand and to implement.

Cal and I immediately began examining our hearts, casting out negative, condemning words and replacing them with God's words of truth and encouragement. Our second son, Peyton, was around 8 (8 is the number for new beginnings). He hated school and felt very defeated. His parents needed an "about face" in their attitudes toward him. Speaking blessings over him instead of "word curses" or maledictions was imperative. Changes began. It took commitment and perseverance, but the power of God's word prevailed. Lives and futures were changed for the better. Our children became the second generation of our blessing declarations.[1]

---

1 Kevin J. Conner, page 140

Why Should We Speak Blessing Declarations?

Fast forward to the next generation: Peyton and his beautiful wife, Amy, have four precious children. Recently one of them began disconnecting himself from the immediate activities surrounding him. He began to immerse himself in his electronic devices and became "oblivious" to others within his family. At first it was a bit humorous. The term "oblivious" was used to describe his "disconnect." This son embraced that term and began speaking it over himself. "Oblivious" became his identity, also his excuse.

Suddenly, Holy Spirit's light of truth revealed what was happening. His penetrating light showed Peyton that those "word curses" were fueling a self-fulfilling prophecy, forecasting a very negative future. Peyton and Amy agreed that attitudes, words, and behavior needed to change. The future of their son was being redirected for the good, for his benefit!

Our sweet grandson is the third generation of our blessing declarations. His identity is no longer defined by those maledictions, but by who God says he is! Our son and our grandson are living testimonies of the power of speaking and releasing God's word of truth over and into lives.

Life, not death; freedom, not bondage are our grandson's future and hope in God.

The Apostle Paul identified his reward—to witness his spiritual children living in the way of truth, being submitted to and loving Jesus, walking in the path of righteousness.

Paul is encouraged by the believers' faith as his spiritual son brings him word:

> *"But now that Timothy has come to us from you, and has brought us the good news of your faith and love and reported that you always remember us kindly and long to see us, as we long to see you."*
> (1 Thessalonians 3:6)

These believers were the next generation of Christians, Christ's followers.

Paul continued to describe his reward in verse 7:

> *For this reason, brothers, in all our distress and affliction we have been comforted about you through your faith."* (8) *"For now we live,*

if you are standing fast in the Lord." (9) "For what thanksgiving can we return to God for you, for all the joy that we feel for your sake before our God,

The Amplified™ Bible expresses Paul's words in verses 8–9 in this way:

Because now we really live [in spite of everything], if you stand firm in the Lord. (9) For what [adequate] thanks can we offer to God for you in return for all the joy and delight we have before our God on your account?

Take note of what Paul did on behalf of those Thessalonian believers: *"As we pray most earnestly night and day that we may see you face to face and supply what is lacking in your faith?"* (1 Thessalonians 3:10)

Let's follow Paul's example of praying for others in preparation for future opportunities to teach, impart, speak the words of truth and life. <u>Prayer is an important preparation</u> for speaking and releasing blessing declarations. Submitting to God's all-knowingness allows us to supply the needs of others. He knows the depth of their needs and how we can be used by Him to help perfect and mature others in their faith. We can gain great comfort as we witness others standing firm in their faith in Christ.

Paul's message continued:

Now may our God and Father himself, and our Lord Jesus, direct our way to you, and may the Lord make you increase and abound in love for one another and for all, as we do for you, so that he may establish your hearts blameless in holiness before our God and Father, at the coming of our Lord Jesus with all his saints"

(1 Thessalonians 3:11-13)

The writer of Hebrews identifies another purpose and reason for our speaking and releasing God's word of truth: *"Therefore, holy brothers, you who share in a heavenly calling, consider Jesus, the apostle and high priest of our confession,"* (Hebrews 3:1)

You and I "share in a heavenly calling" and must follow the example and ministry of Jesus as He imparted truth into people and over situations. Jesus advanced the kingdom of God as He released God's kingdom way of thinking and living: *"You are the salt of the earth…"*

Why Should We Speak Blessing Declarations?

The *FireBible*™ provides an explanation and application of Jesus' metaphor in Matthew 5:13:

> Salt seasons and flavors food, just as Christians should enhance and favorably influence the people and society around them. Salt is a preservative, just as Christians and the church should resist moral corruption and decay, preserving a godly influence on the culture. In addition, salt has healing properties, just as Christ's followers must help bring healing to people who are hurting physically, emotionally and spiritually. Salt also creates thirst, just as Christians—through their good example—should create spiritual thirst or desire in others to know more about God.[1]

Jesus continued using metaphors as He revealed the light and truth of God's kingdom coming to earth:

> *You are the light of the world. A city set on a hill cannot be hidden. Nor do people light a lamp and put it under a basket, but on a stand, and it gives light to all in the house. In the same way, let your light shine before others, so that they may see your good works and give glory to your Father who is in heaven.* (Matthew 5:14-16)

The Amplified™ Bible offers verse 16 in this way: *"Let your light shine before men in such a way that they may see your good deeds and moral excellence, and [recognize and honor and] glorify your Father who is in heaven."* (Matthew 5:16)

Our being "salt" and "light" will give glory to our heavenly Father. In accomplishing that, we are following the heart and life of Jesus. Jesus' focus was on His Father and in doing His will. Jesus recognized that people's lives and circumstances needed to change drastically to accomplish God's kingdom authority, His jurisdiction, and governance on the earth. Supernatural transformation needed to occur within their lives to accomplish God's original design: "be fruitful and multiply" His character and image across the earth.

Not only was there a need for a colossal change within the mindsets of those around Jesus, but also in the surrounding atmosphere. In the gospel according to John, he related Jesus' declaration about the Good

---

1   *FireBible*™, p. 1522, note on Matthew 5:13

Shepherd: *"The thief comes only to steal and kill and destroy. I came that they may have life and have it abundantly. I am the good shepherd. The good shepherd lays down his life for the sheep."* (John 10:10,11)

Please read these verses from The Amplified™ Bible:

> *The thief comes only in order to steal and kill and destroy. I came that they may have and enjoy life, and have it in abundance [to the full, till it overflows]. I am the Good Shepherd. The Good Shepherd lays down His [own] life for the sheep.* (John 10:10,11)

Jesus clearly exposed the enemy and his work. Jesus contrasted the destructive works of Satan to Himself, His sacrificial life and His gift. Jesus described the opposing kingdoms: dark versus light; evil versus good; lack versus abundance; death versus life.

Peter, the apostle, knew from personal experience the opposition of the enemy. Jesus revealed the devil's strategy: *"Simon, Simon, behold, Satan demanded to have you, that he might sift you like wheat, but I have prayed for you that your faith may not fail. And when you have turned again, strengthen your brothers."* (Luke 22:31,32)

Let's read these two verses from The Amplified™ Bible:

> *Simon, Simon (Peter), listen! Satan has demanded permission to sift [all of] you like grain; but I have prayed [especially] for you [Peter], that your faith [and confidence in Me] may not fail; and you, once you have turned back again [to Me], strengthen and support your brothers [in the faith].* (Luke 22:31,32)

Recognizing the atmospheric pressure that existed in the spiritual realm, Peter sounded the alarm for the brethren: *"Be sober-minded; be watchful. Your adversary the devil prowls around like a roaring lion, seeking someone to devour."* (1 Peter 5:8)

"Be sober [well balanced and self-disciplined], be alert and cautious at all times. That enemy of yours, the devil, prowls around like a roaring lion [fiercely hungry], seeking someone to devour." (1 Peter 5:8 AMP)

You and I can listen to people and see the circumstances surrounding them. We can recognize similar atmospheric pressures created by demonic activity trying to sift and destroy people's faith. There have been occasions in talking or texting with someone that I hear words of defeat and unbelief in the power of God. They allow past and present difficulties to control their attitudes toward life and their future. They permit their trials to loom over their lives as a dark, ominous cloud—demonic atmospheric pressure. Satan's lies create scenarios of "doom and gloom," failures not victories; despair, not hope.

We can encourage others by redirecting their thoughts and confessions of their mouths to focus on the word of God and not on vain imaginations that come against the knowledge of Him. Unbelief in the authority, power, and love of God is deadly.

The writer of Hebrews released an urgent warning to the believers: *"Take care, brothers, lest there be in any of you an evil, unbelieving heart, leading you to fall away from the living God."* (Hebrews 3:12)

"Take care, brothers and sisters, that there not be in any one of you a wicked, unbelieving heart [which refuses to trust and rely on the Lord, a heart] that turns away from the living God." (Hebrews 3:12 AMP)

You and I are exhorted, strongly urged to search our hearts first. We must make certain that no hurtful, destructive disobedience or faithlessness lurks hidden within our hearts. Unbelief and disobedience to God's word can lead us into withdrawing from His presence.

What did Adam and Eve do after they sinned in the Garden of Eden?

> *And they heard the sound of the LORD God walking in the garden in the cool of the day, and the man and his wife hid themselves from the presence of the LORD God among the trees of the garden.*
> (Genesis 3:8)

Instead of withdrawing, let us draw near to Him in times of need. Confusion in what we believe or have been told about God can cause us to stumble in our walk of faith or shrink away from His presence. May we remember: *"You make known to me the path of life; in your presence there is fullness of joy; at your right hand are pleasures forevermore."* (Psalm 16:11)

The writer of Hebrews encouraged us in this way:

> *Let us then with confidence draw near to the throne of grace, that we may receive mercy and find grace to help in time of need...let us draw near with a true heart in full assurance of faith, with our hearts sprinkled clean from an evil conscience and our bodies washed with pure water.* (Hebrews 4:16; 10:22)

As we experience the all-sufficient grace of God, we can encourage and direct others to do the same. I am confident that the writer of Hebrews had received God's mercy and grace multiple times, which provided a basis for his admonishment. Holy Spirit prompted this writer to share the power and effectiveness of drawing near to God and receiving His forgiveness through faith in His Son, Jesus Christ.

"*But exhort one another every day, as long as it is called 'today,' that none of you may be hardened by the deceitfulness of sin.*" (Hebrews 3:13)

For an example of the hardening of hearts by the "deceitfulness of sin," we can step into the Garden of Eden and listen to the hearts of Adam and Eve once they sinned against God. Both began to play the "blame game."

> *And they heard the sound of the LORD God walking in the garden in the cool of the day, and the man and his wife hid themselves from the presence of the LORD God among the trees of the garden. But the LORD God called to the man and said to him, 'Where are you?' And he said, "I heard the sound of you in the garden, and I was afraid, because I was naked, and I hid myself." He said, "Who told you that you were naked? Have you eaten of the tree of which I commanded you not to eat?" The man said, "The woman whom you gave to be with me, she gave me fruit of the tree, and I ate" Then the LORD God said to the woman, "What is this that you have done?" The woman said, "The serpent deceived me, and I ate."* (Genesis 3:8-13)

How many times do we hide behind excuses and cast the blame on someone or something else, trying to escape correction and admittance of sin?

Let us **purpose** in our hearts to allow Holy Spirit to shine His light of love into the crevices of our minds, our wills, and our emotions. If the Spirit reveals unforgiveness, grief, self-pity, anger, or stubbornness, then repent. Receive His forgiveness.

Why Should We Speak Blessing Declarations?

Let us **permit** our Savior's redeeming love to cover that sin and remember it no more; to forgive as we have been forgiven. Receive His grace.

Let us **plan** our days with goals to help others enter the rest and peace of walking in belief in Jesus Christ and in His redeeming, restorative love. Receive His depth of love.

> *But I have prayed [especially] for you [Peter], that your faith [and confidence in Me] may not fail; and you, once you have turned back again [to Me], strengthen and support your brothers [in the faith].* (Luke 22:32 AMP)

Jesus gave Peter a strong directive to confirm, set fast, and establish the faith of others.[1]

Jesus called Peter to be intentional in his life, to turn resolutely in the direction of seeking occasions to assist the brethren in their faith walk. Jesus recognized that the Tempter looks for opportunities to cause people to falter and fail.

The writer of Hebrews warned his readers about the danger and consequence of unbelief; the result of accepting the lies sown by the enemy of our souls. Let's reread his warning:

"Therefore, while the promise of entering his rest still stands, let us fear lest any of you should seem to have failed to reach it." (Hebrews 4:1)

> *THEREFORE, WHILE the promise of entering His rest still holds and is offered [today], let us be afraid [to distrust it], lest any of you should think he has come too late and has come short of [reaching] it.* (Hebrews 4:1 AMPC)

Let's recall the warning included in verse 2:

> *For good news came to us just as to them, but the message they heard did not benefit them, because they were not united by faith with those who listened." "For indeed we have had the good news [of salvation] preached to us, just as the Israelites also [when the good news of the promised land came to them]; but the message they heard did not benefit them, because it was not united with faith [in God] by those who heard."* (AMP)

---

1 Strong's Concordance, G4741: strengthen

Every person has a choice to make when they hear God's message of truth: to accept or reject it. When the life-depositing word is spoken, the hearer either grabs hold of God's truth OR allows the testimony of Jesus to "float away." Do you recall my account of "blowing bubbles" over our children? Read the following blessing declaration aloud. Join your faith with the life-activating word of truth and grab hold of it for your life. Don't let it float away.

> May you receive, yes, lay hold of the gift from heaven, the gospel of Jesus Christ.
>
> May the Father of lights shower you with His counsel and wisdom through the infilling presence of His Holy Spirit.
>
> May you lean in and listen to Holy Comforter.
>
> May you hear what the Spirit is saying.
>
> May you allow Him to do His work of sanctifying your heart, setting you apart for God's holy calling.
>
> May you recognize and accept your special mission, that is, to be God's ambassador to the world, reconciling others to Him through the Lord Jesus Christ.
>
> In Jesus' Name. Amen.
>
> (John 3:27; James 1:17; John 14:16,17,26; 15:26; John 16:13-15; 2 Corinthians 5:20)

How did you respond to this blessing declaration which was based on God's word of truth?

Our personal relationship with God through faith in Jesus Christ requires an active faith, not a passive belief.[1]

We must entrust every day to God's love, provision, purpose, and plan for us, you and me. We must embrace the truth that God created us for the joy of knowing and loving us, interacting with us every day! If you haven't read and personalized the truth found in Psalm 139, turn to it now. It was written with you in mind. As David wrote this psalm, he concluded with an earnest request:

---

1   *FireBible*™, p. 2143, note on Hebrews 4:11

Why Should We Speak Blessing Declarations?

> *"Search me, O God, and know my heart! Try me and know my thoughts! And see if there be any grievous way in me, and lead me in the way everlasting!"* (Psalm 139:23,24)

> *God, I invite your searching gaze into my heart. Examine me through and through; find out everything that may be hidden within me. Put me to the test and sift through all my anxious cares. See if there is any path of pain I'm walking on, and lead me back to your glorious, everlasting ways—the path that brings me back to you.*
> (Psalm 139:23,24 TPT)

The writer of Hebrews identified the same power and effectiveness of God's involvement in our lives:

> *For the word of God is living and active, sharper than any two-edged sword, piercing to the division of soul and of spirit, of joints and of marrow, and discerning the thoughts and intentions of the heart.* (Hebrews 4:12)

Take a moment and read it from The Amplified™ Bible:

> *For the word of God is living and active and full of power [making it operative, energizing, and effective]. It is sharper than any two-edged sword, penetrating as far as the division of the soul and spirit [the completeness of a person], and of both joints and marrow [the deepest parts of our nature], exposing and judging the very thoughts and intentions of the heart.* (Hebrews 4:12 AMP)

Our God, who created us, desires to commune with us, refining us into His image. Recall God's original plan and purpose for mankind: *"Then God said, 'Let us make man in our image, after our likeness. And let them have dominion over the fish of the sea and over the birds of the heavens and over the livestock and over all the earth and over every creeping thing that creeps on the earth.'"* (Genesis 1:26)

Desiring to commune with Adam and Eve, God called out for them: *"But the LORD God called to the man and said to him, 'Where are you?'"* (Genesis 3:9)

Does this indicate that God truly did not know where they were? No, God is all-knowing; that is, He is omniscient. He was calling them to confront their sin of disobedience and unbelief. He was calling them to confess their choice to believe a lie from the enemy more than His word of truth, love, protection, and provision.

My personal experience with the "question and answer" exchange occurred during a weekend when our grandchildren were visiting us. I noticed one grandson exiting our pantry with his mouth chewing, full of something. My sudden appearance surprised him, for his eyes became quite large and his face began to blush. His mouth continued to chew. From the multi-colored markings around his mouth, I could see that he had discovered my bag of chocolate candies. While those delicious treats did not melt in his hands, they were all over his young, not-so-innocent face. We both knew what he had done, but he was not quite ready to admit it. We had a talk.

John wrote in his power-packed message: *"If we confess our sins, he is faithful and just to forgive us our sins and to cleanse us from all unrighteousness."* (1 John 1:9)

Let's read it from The Amplified™ Bible Classic Edition:

> *If we [freely] admit that we have sinned and confess our sins, He is faithful and just (true to His own nature and promises) and will forgive our sins [dismiss our lawlessness] and [continuously] cleanse us from all unrighteousness [everything not in conformity to His will in purpose, thought, and action]."* (1 John 1:9)

During my own walk of faith in Christ, I have discovered much freedom from the heaviness of sin when I have repented and received the forgiveness of Jesus. It's that freedom we can share with others as we speak and release the word of God over them and their circumstances. Here's an example of a blessing declaration we can speak and release:

> May you invite God to examine your heart, searching for any mindset or attitude that opposes His way of love and truth.
>
> May you allow Him to speak to you, calling you to a place of repentance.
>
> May you entrust your cares and worries to Him, for He cares for you.

Why Should We Speak Blessing Declarations?

May you draw near to God, embracing His lovingkindness which guides you along His path of righteousness for His Name's sake.

May you allow His image to be shaped within you.

In Jesus' Name. Amen.

(Psalm 139:23,24; 1 Peter 5:7; Hebrews 10:22; Colossians 3:10)

Why should we speak and release blessing declarations? We are partners with Jesus Christ.

"And they went out and preached everywhere, while the Lord worked with them and confirmed the message by accompanying signs." (Mark 16:20)

Jesus was the disciples' fellow worker; that is, "the Lord worked with them."

"For we are God's fellow workers. You are God's field, God's building."
(1 Corinthians 3:9)

We are co-laborers with God.

"Working together with him, then, we appeal to you not to receive the grace of God in vain." (2 Corinthians 6:1) We co-operate with God.

> LABORING TOGETHER *[as God's fellow workers] with Him then, we beg of you not to receive the grace of God in vain [that merciful kindness by which God exerts His holy influence on souls and turns them to Christ, keeping and strengthening them--do not receive it to no purpose].* (2 Corinthians 6:1 AMPC)

People of all ages seek to answer the question: "What is my purpose in life? Why was I born?" To discover an answer to those questions, hear the words of Jesus as He prayed to His Father before going to the Cross for you and me:

"I made known to them your name, and I will continue to make it known, that the love with which you have loved me may be in them, and I in them." (John 17:26)

"Human love is a revelation of the divine; an earthen pitcher which God fills with heavenly treasure; a chalice holding the wine of life."[1]

---
1 e-Sword X notes on 1 Corinthians 16:13-24

We love God because of what Jesus did for us:

> *For God so loved the world, that he gave his only Son, that whoever believes in him should not perish but have eternal life. For God did not send his Son into the world to condemn the world, but in order that the world might be saved through him.* (John 3:16,17)

When we are infinitely loved, we want to return that infinite love. We express that love through our lives, through continuing a daily communion with Him. We express the depth of our love for God by sharing with others who He is.[1]

Speak and release blessing declarations to point others to Him and His love for them.

---

[1] https://www.youtube.com/watch?v=5vp9hV8bOjk

Engaging Blessing Declarations within Others:

Who in your life needs to know Jesus? What is occurring in their lives that your blessing declaration could encompass with His hope and truth?

List their names and needs:

_____

_____

_____

_____

Search the Scriptures for applicable truths and words of hope and life.

_____

_____

_____

_____

Using God's word, write a blessing declaration for each person.

May you:

_____

_____

_____

_____

_____

The Spoken Blessing II: Influencing Generations

May you:

_____

_____

_____

_____

May you:

_____

_____

_____

_____

Pray for each person on your list. Begin to speak and release their blessing declaration into the atmosphere. Ask God to show you how and when to share each blessing declaration.

You are loved.

Chapter 6

How Do We Advance God's Kingdom through Blessing Declarations?

In Chapter 1 we discovered that the provision for our continual fellowship with God was through the gift of His Spirit. Jesus explained His plan to ask His Father to send "another Helper" to His disciples.

"And I will ask the Father, and he will give you another Helper, to be with you forever." (John 14:16)

The King James Version uses the term "Comforter." Both terms identify the all-important work and relationship of Holy Spirit to the disciples of Jesus Christ. If you have believed on the Lord Jesus as your Savior, you are one of His disciples and have been given the gift of His Spirit.

The *FireBible*™ provides an excellent note on Holy Spirit. May I share it with you:

> Jesus calls the Holy Spirit 'another Helper,' just as Jesus himself had been for his disciples. The title 'Helper' translates the Greek *parakletos*, meaning literally 'one called alongside to help.' This is a rich word that refers to a wide range of spiritual roles, such as Counselor, Strengthener, Comforter, Helper, Adviser, Advocate, Intercessor, Ally and Friend. The Greek word for 'another' is *allon*, meaning 'another of the same kind,' rather than *heteros*,

meaning 'another of a different kind.' Therefore, the Holy Spirit, like Jesus, is also God and will continue what Christ himself did while on earth.[1]

The Spirit is a personal being who will be by the disciples' side to help and strengthen them (cf. Mark 14:30-31), to teach them the truth and guide the course of their lives (v.26), to strengthen and comfort them in difficult situations (v. 18), to intercede (i.e., to plead a case for them) through prayer (Rom. 8:26-27; cf. 8:34), to be a friend who promotes their best interest (v. 17) and to remain with them forever.[2]

The word *parakletos* is applied to the Lord Jesus in 1 John 2:1. Jesus is our helper and intercessor (i.e., an advocate who pleads our case and represents us) in heaven (cf. Heb. 7:25), while the Holy Spirit is our helper and intercessor on earth (Rom. 8:9,26; 1 Cor. 3:16; 6:19; 2 Cor. 6:16; 2 Tim. 1:14).[3]

As we understand the work and activity of Holy Spirit, we are encouraged to listen to His voice. He is the Voice of God because He is God. He is the Third Person of the Holy Trinity, i.e., the Godhead. He knows the heart and thoughts of God and He shares them with us.

Are we willing to listen and follow His guidance?

Holy Spirit is the Agent of the Godhead who is actively working in and through believers to establish God's kingdom authority, dominion, and love here on earth. He is our Partner, our Confidant, our Teacher, our Counselor, our Sanctifier. He knows the depths of our being—to the uttermost. That is a good thing.

King David cried out to the LORD: *"Create in me a clean heart, O God, and renew a right spirit within me."* (Psalm 51:10) David recognized that his heart needed God's cleansing and restorative work.

Please read it from The Amplified™ Bible: *"Create in me a clean heart, O God, And renew a right and steadfast spirit within me."* David's longed for God to rebuild and establish his life to follow Him.

---

1   *FireBible™*, p. 1763, note on John 14:16
2   ibid
3   ibid

How Do We Advance God's Kingdom through Blessing Declarations?

Verse 11 of Psalm 51 records more of David's plea: *"Cast me not away from your presence, and take not your Holy Spirit from me."* (Psalm 51:11)

Generations ago, King David recognized the importance and necessity of remaining in close communion with God through the work of His Spirit. King David was broken when he was confronted with his sin. He had been living according to his fleshly desires.

"For those who live according to the flesh set their minds on the things of the flesh, but those who live according to the Spirit set their minds on the things of the Spirit." (Romans 8:5)

"You, however, are not in the flesh but in the Spirit, if in fact the Spirit of God dwells in you. Anyone who does not have the Spirit of Christ does not belong to him." (Romans 8:9)

Now read this passage from The Amplified™ Bible:

However, you are not [living] in the flesh [controlled by the sinful nature] but in the Spirit, if in fact the Spirit of God lives in you [directing and guiding you]. But if anyone does not have the Spirit of Christ, he does not belong to Him [and is not a child of God]. (Romans 8:9 AMP)

Advancing God's kingdom requires us to submit ourselves to the sanctifying work of His Holy Spirit. We must listen and obey Him. Our lives depend on Him.

Holy Spirit speaks only TRUTH. You, I, and everyone around us want to know, see, hear, and experience TRUTH. Our entire beings need the grounding and stability of TRUTH.

Holy Spirit is the Spirit of Christ.

As Jesus and His disciples shared their last meal before He headed to the Cross:

"Jesus said to him [Thomas], 'I am the way, and the truth, and the life. No one comes to the Father except through me.'" (John 14:6, brackets added)

Let's recall that moments later Jesus explained:

> *And I will ask the Father, and he will give you another Helper, to be with you forever, even the Spirit of truth, whom the world cannot receive, because it neither sees him nor knows him. You know him, for he dwells with you and will be in you."* (John 14:16,17)

Using every precious minute Jesus had with his disciples, He encouraged them by saying: *"Nevertheless, I tell you the truth: it is to your advantage that I go away, for if I do not go away, the Helper will not come to you. But if I go, I will send him to you."* (John 16:7)

> *When the Spirit of truth comes, he will guide you into all the truth, for he will not speak on his own authority, but whatever he hears he will speak, and he will declare to you the things that are to come. He will glorify me, for he will take what is mine and declare it to you. All that the Father has is mine; therefore I said that he will take what is mine and declare it to you.* (John 16:13,14,15)

Holy Spirit glorifies Jesus.

Jesus described the operation of the Holy Trinity, the Godhead, the Sovereign one true God.

Being led by the Spirit of Christ, Paul wrote: *"For who knows a person's thoughts except the spirit of that person, which is in him? So also no one comprehends the thoughts of God except the Spirit of God."* (1 Corinthians 2:11)

Holy Spirit will supply you with all the "intel" you need to advance God's kingdom and to serve others for Him. He will reveal the Father's love and the depth of Jesus' salvation—to the uttermost. Now would be a great time to shout: "Thank You, God, for Your love, the gift of Your Son and the presence of Your Holy Spirit!"

"The friendship of the LORD is for those who fear him, and he makes known to them his covenant." (Psalm 25:14)

"There's a private place reserved for the lovers of God, where they sit near him and receive the revelation-secrets of his promises." (Psalm 25:14 TPT)

Read The Passion Translation's rendering of Psalm 25:14 one more time. *"There's a private place reserved for the lovers of God…"* Are you one of

How Do We Advance God's Kingdom through Blessing Declarations?

those *"lovers of God"*? It's within this *"reserved private place"* that God talks to me. We sit together and He shares with me revelation-secrets of His promises. You can enjoy His sweet fellowship as well.

Do you want Him in your life? Then, tell Him how much you desire His fellowship. Then, set aside time every day to meet with Him. Sit quietly; remove all distractions. Read His word; invite His Spirit to reveal "revelation-secrets of his promises" to you. Listen to Him.

Entrusting your life to God is the basis of "How Do We Advance God's Kingdom through Blessing Declarations." Trusting His love for you and for others is foundational.

Operating from the solid foundation of the **truth** of God, the Father; God, the Son; and God, the Holy Spirit, we advance God's kingdom with words of righteousness, peace, and joy in the Holy Spirit. We speak His Truth in love and expectation of the hope and life His word deposits into people and circumstances around them. We declare God's word of **truth** into their future because the LORD (Jehovah) is the Good Shepherd. He has already been in the future, prepared the way, and returns to guide and direct their paths into His provision every day. That's what a Good Shepherd does. He is the God Eternal, so He knows the future. No one else does. He informs us and others when He deems is "the right time."

David, the psalmist, spoke of Jehovah as his shepherd. Recall the name "Jehovah" describes and declares God as the "self-existent or eternal" one. He is God of the past, present, and future, eternally! *"Jesus Christ is the same yesterday and today and forever."* (Hebrews 13:8)

Every day as you read God's word, Holy Spirit will highlight a passage specifically for you.

Listen to Him. Write it down. Then, declare the living, active word of God over your life. He may show you a scripture of truth for your loved ones, a co-worker, or a neighbor. Write it down and date it. Release the word of truth over yourself or another person. Believe in the power of the living word of God to accomplish all that He purposed for it.

Your words, based on the living word of God, create life, a hope, and a future. As you speak and release the power of God's creative, life-filled word, you are laying down foundational stones along the path of a person's life. What path are you paving for others and yourself? God's word is a lamp unto your feet and a light unto your path. (Psalm 119:105)

Prepare the kingdom advancing path for yourself and others.

Lay foundational stones of God's truth as you speak blessing declarations. Release His light of truth upon their future steps. Remove stumbling stones of error and lies that hinder their journey and walk with God.

Tim Sheets' book reinforces this point.

He presents a scripture from Job 22:28 using the Amplified™ Bible:

"You shall also decide and decree a thing, and it shall be established for you; and the light [of God's favor] shall shine upon your ways (Job 22:28 AMP)."

> The word *thing* in the above verse is the Hebrew word *omer*, meaning "a word or promise" (Strong, H562). The heirs of God and the joint heirs of Christ have authority to decree words of Scripture, words of promise, words of prophecy (which are also words of God given through Holy Spirit enlightenment). Those words, in Jesus' name, will be established.
>
> *Established* is the Hebrew word *quwm*, meaning "to be made good, to perform, succeed, to raise up and come to be or to pass" (Strong, H6965). *Quwm* is used in the Hebrew language as a construction word. When you decree a word, you are constructing it into your life. You're building it to appear on your life's pathway. It becomes performed into your life's ways; it's why words are so important. When we decree a word of the Lord, when we speak a promise, when we speak a principle or a prophecy that is based upon God's Word, His favor anoints that word to come to pass in our lives.[1]

Let's carefully consider and construct our paths according to God's word of life and truth!

"Death and life are in the power of the tongue, and those who love it will eat its fruits." (Proverbs 18:21) May I ask you this—"what do you want to eat:" death or life?

---

1   Tim Sheets, *Prayers & Decrees that Activate Angel Armies*, p. 59

"The lips of the righteous feed many..." (Proverbs 10:21)

"The lips of the righteous know (speak) what is acceptable,..."
(Proverbs 10:32 AMP)

"The lips of the wise spread knowledge;..." (Proverbs 15:7)

"When wisdom speaks, revelation-knowledge is released..."
(Proverbs 15:7 TPT)

"Righteous lips are the delight of a king, and he loves him who speaks what is right." (Proverbs 16:13)

"Kings and leaders love to hear godly counsel, and they love those who tell them the truth." (Proverbs 16:13 TPT)

Whoa! Let's stop right here! You and I have a kingdom assignment to tell kings and leaders godly counsel based on God's truth. When you and I pronounce and declare truth, the hearts and affections of kings and leaders are directed toward us. There are examples throughout biblical history to reveal this fact. One of my favorite stories is found in the book of Daniel. Keep in mind that Daniel and three Hebrew friends were taken captive by the Babylonians when they were teenagers. They chose to keep themselves pure and devoted to Jehovah God, not accepting the pagan culture's foods and delicacies.

> *But Daniel resolved that he would not defile himself with the king's food, or with the wine that he drank. Therefore he asked the chief of the eunuchs to allow him not to defile himself. And God gave Daniel favor and compassion in the sight of the chief of the eunuchs.* (Daniel 1:8,9)

Notice: *"And God gave Daniel favor and compassion in the sight of the chief of the eunuchs."*

David declared this about God: *"For you bless the righteous, O LORD; you cover him with favor as with a shield."* (Psalm 5:12)

The psalmist wrote: *"He shall cover thee with his feathers, and under his wings shalt thou trust: his truth shall be thy shield and buckler."*
(Psalm 91:4 KJV)

Take note: We are given God's favor to accomplish His kingdom assignments. Let's advance within His favor and under His encompassing protection.

Let's continue with Daniel's story:

> *So he [chief of the eunuchs] listened to them in this matter, and tested them for ten days. At the end of ten days it was seen that they were better in appearance and fatter in flesh than all the youths who ate the king's food."* (Daniel 1:14,15, brackets added)

The number 10 is symbolic of testing and trial.[1]

Consider this initial commitment of Daniel and his three Hebrew friends to remain undefiled. This was their **first step of courage** into **making a difference** within the pagan culture. Each of us must take that first step of courage based upon our commitment to God.

Watch how God blessed these four courageous young men:

> *As for these four youths, God gave them learning and skill in all literature and wisdom, and Daniel had understanding in all visions and dreams. At the end of the time, when the king had commanded that they should be brought in, the chief of the eunuchs brought them in before Nebuchadnezzar. And in every matter of wisdom and understanding about which the king inquired of them, he found them ten times better than all the magicians and enchanters that were in all his kingdom. And Daniel was there until the first year of King Cyrus.* (Daniel 1:17,18,20,21)

Their courage was rewarded by God! He saw that they were faithful with a little, so He rewarded them with much. This sounds like a parable that Jesus presented:

> *He said therefore, "A nobleman went into a far country to receive for himself a kingdom and then return." Calling ten of his servants, he gave them ten minas, and said to them, 'Engage in business until I come.' When he returned, having received the kingdom, he ordered these servants to whom he had given the money to be called to him, that he might know what they had gained by doing business. The*

---

[1] Kevin J. Conner, p. 174

> *first came before him, saying, 'Lord, your mina has made ten minas more.' And he said to him, 'Well done, good servant! Because you have been faithful in a very little, you shall have authority over ten cities.' And the second came, saying, 'Lord, your mina has made five minas.' And he said to him, 'And you are to be over five cities.'"*
> (Luke 19:12,13,15-19)

Feel free to continue reading this parable that contains a sharp warning for all of us.

The third servant who was given one mina tucked it away in a handkerchief, that is, a "sweat cloth." If he had been working and using his one mina, he would have needed his "sweat cloth." But this third servant chose to be slack and careless with his master's assignment. Consequently, the master took away the one mina and gave it to his faithful servant who was to serve over ten cities! Sounds like the faithful servant was to have great authority within the master's kingdom! Commitment and faithfulness are rewarded.

Through a series of events, Daniel was elevated to a place of authority within that pagan society while maintaining his commitment to God. Even when the wickedness of people tried to sabotage his devotion to his God and his relationship with the king, **Daniel remained true to God**. He understood the "schemes of the devil" as the enemy used people against him. He did not allow his heart to become bitter against the king. Daniel discerned or recognized who and what was behind the evil edict.

Let's return to the book of Daniel to discover and hear the heart of the king towards Daniel.

> *It pleased Darius to set over the kingdom 120 satraps, to be throughout the whole kingdom; and over them three high officials, of whom Daniel was one, to whom these satraps should give account, <u>so that the king might suffer no loss</u>. [King Darius trusted Daniel.] Then this Daniel became distinguished above all the other high officials and satraps, <u>because an excellent spirit was in him</u>. And the king planned to set him over the whole kingdom. Then the high officials and the satraps sought to find a ground for complaint against Daniel with regard to the kingdom, but they could find no ground for complaint or any fault, because he was faithful, and no error or*

fault was found in him. (Daniel 6:1-4, underline and brackets added)

The other officials plotted a wicked scheme to trick King Darius and to bring an end to Daniel. They convinced King Darius to establish and sign a document stating that no one could make a petition or pray to any god except to the king. These evil officials knew the faithful habit of Daniel who prayed:

> *When Daniel knew that the document had been signed, he went to his house where he had windows in his upper chamber open toward Jerusalem. He got down on his knees three times a day and prayed and gave thanks before his God, as he had done previously.*
>
> (Daniel 6:10)

These high officials and princes delivered the news to the unsuspecting king. Notice King Darius' reaction:

"Then the king, when he heard these words, was much distressed and set his mind to deliver Daniel. And he labored till the sun went down to rescue him." (Daniel 6:14)

King Darius' hand was forced to execute the penalty for Daniel's opposition to his edict:

> *Then the king commanded, and Daniel was brought and cast into the den of lions. The king declared to Daniel, "May your God, whom you serve continually, deliver you!" "Then the king went to his palace and spent the night fasting; no diversions were brought to him, and sleep fled from him.* (Daniel 6:16,18)

Do you hear the heart of King Darius towards Daniel? Remember this:

"Kings and leaders love to hear godly counsel, and they love those who tell them the truth." (Proverbs 16:13 TPT)

Let's discover what the king did at sunrise:

> *Then, at break of day, the king arose and went in haste to the den of lions." "As he came near to the den where Daniel was, he cried out in a tone of anguish. The king declared to Daniel, "O Daniel, servant of the living God, has your God, whom you serve continually, been able to deliver you from the lions?* (Daniel 6:19,20)

How hard was the king's heart pounding? How fast were his feet running? How intently were his ears listening for the sound of Daniel's trustworthy voice?

> *Then Daniel said to the king, "O king, live forever! [Daniel spoke and released a Blessing Declaration!] My God sent his angel and shut the lions' mouths, [An angel was activated to save Daniel.] and they have not harmed me, because I was found blameless before him; and also before you, O king, I have done no harm." Then the king was exceedingly glad, and commanded that Daniel be taken up out of the den. So Daniel was taken up out of the den, and no kind of harm was found on him, because he had trusted in his God.* (Daniel 6:21-23, brackets and notes added)

Those high officials and princes "reaped what they sowed:"

> *"And the king commanded, and those men who had maliciously accused Daniel were brought and cast into the den of lions—they, their children, and their wives. And before they reached the bottom of the den, the lions overpowered them and broke all their bones in pieces."* (Daniel 6:24)

Listen to King Darius' heart and decree:

> *Then King Darius wrote to all the peoples, nations, and languages that dwell in all the earth: "Peace be multiplied to you."* [He blessed the people in his kingdom.] *I make a decree, that in all my royal dominion people are to tremble and fear before the God of Daniel, for he is the living God, enduring forever; his kingdom shall never be destroyed, and his dominion shall be to the end. He delivers and rescues; he works signs and wonders in heaven and on earth, he who has saved Daniel from the power of the lions."* [The living God of Daniel received praise and honor from a pagan king.]
> (Daniel 6:25-27, brackets and notes added)

"So this Daniel prospered during the reign of Darius and the reign of Cyrus the Persian." (Daniel 6:28)

Throughout his life Daniel continually **chose to remain faithful to God** and to **serve others** for Him. Daniel's godly counsel, his words of truth and honor paved the way for him to significantly influence the society in which he lived. Daniel served within the king's court for 66 years! **Daniel exalted the governance of God within a pagan society.**

You and I have spheres of influence into which we can speak and release God's wisdom, His unfathomable counsel. We can encourage others within their realms of employment, community, family, education and faith. We can assist them in advancing God's kingdom.

"The heart of the wise makes his speech judicious and adds persuasiveness to his lips." (Proverbs 16:23)

"Winsome words pour from a heart of wisdom, adding value to all you teach." (Proverbs 16:23 TPT)

Another young man was harshly and abruptly taken from his family and thrust into a pagan culture. Joseph was sold into slavery because of jealousy and resentment in the hearts of his brothers. "Sibling rivalry" ran rampant in mega doses! Joseph was required to make a choice, first in his heart, then through his actions and words. He could have become embittered because of the actions of others, yet he did not. Even when he was wrongfully accused of misconduct and thrown into prison, Joseph chose to remain faithful to God. Within the hard, cold walls of a prison cell, Joseph experienced God's faithfulness. God gave Joseph the gift of interpreting dreams. Within his years of confinement, Joseph recognized opportunities to engage this gift. Then, God opened another door of opportunity for Joseph to use this gift and to **speak words of wisdom** to Egypt's pharaoh. God used Joseph to execute His plan of salvation and advancement of His kingdom throughout many nations. His family, who would become a nation, was saved.

Joseph's siblings were unexpectedly reunited with him and confronted with their sin. Yet, Joseph's forgiveness towards them and his daily courage to remain faithful to God paved the way for God's kingdom to be advanced. Lives were saved, relationships restored.

Joseph's devotion to God literally saved nations from starving to death. God gave him favor with the pharaoh of Egypt. Joseph became the second in command of that nation. Joseph's **courage to speak paved the way** for his future and the future of millions.

How Do We Advance God's Kingdom through Blessing Declarations?

Joseph, Abraham's great-grandson, advanced God's revealed plan:

> *Now the LORD said to Abram, "Go from your country and your kindred and your father's house to the land that I will show you. And I will make of you a great nation, and I will bless you and make your name great, so that you will be a blessing. I will bless those who bless you, and him who dishonors you I will curse, and in you all the families of the earth shall be blessed."* (Genesis 12:1-3)

Notice the scope of God's plan: *"...and in you all the families of the earth shall be blessed."*

Yes, God planned to bless Abram and his wife, Sarai. Yet God's grand and sovereign purpose was for **generations of families** to live and thrive across the earth He had created. God's favor and protection covered and carried Abraham's great-grandson into a position in which he could thrive, not just survive. As Joseph presented his gift to Egypt's pharaoh, God's eternal purpose advanced.

"A man's gift makes room for him and brings him before the great."
(Proverbs 18:16)

"A man's gift [given in love or courtesy] makes room for him And brings him before great men." (Proverbs 18:16 AMP)

Joseph exercised his gift within the restrictive walls of the pharaoh's prison. And God caused the memory of his gift to be recalled for such a time when it was needed!

Do you recall this proverb? *"When wisdom speaks, revelation-knowledge is released..."* (Proverbs 15:7 TPT)

Read this proverb: *"The lips of the righteous feed many..."* (Proverbs 10:21)

Egypt's pharaoh recognized the wisdom provided by Joseph. He accepted Joseph's gift and elevated Joseph to enable him to use it. Joseph released God's wisdom across the earth.

You and I have the <u>gift of God's word</u>, and <u>His wisdom</u> found in the Scriptures. We can write, speak and release His word through Blessing Declarations. You and I can <u>ask God for the courage to speak!</u>

The Spoken Blessing II: Influencing Generations

Joseph advanced God's kingdom purposes. You and I can do likewise.

"Thy kingdom come. Thy will be done in (G1909) *earth, as it is in* (G1722) *heaven."* (Matthew 6:10 KJV, Strong's Concordance numbers added)

You may recognize this passage from the teachings of Jesus. He instructed His disciples to pray in this way. Many may know this passage as part of The Lord's Prayer included in the Gospel according to Matthew 6:9-13.

Within verse 10, I included two Strong's Concordance numbers. These references help reveal the mysteries of God's word. Holy Spirit prompted me to examine this passage. He showed me that the English word "in" was used twice; however, Jesus used different words. He spoke "**in** earth" using G1909 and "**in** heaven" using G1722.

Referencing Strong's Concordance, we discover this: G1909 [epi] expresses the idea of "superimposition (of time, place, order, etc.), as a relation of distribution…, that is, over, upon, etc.;…" (underline added)

G1722 [en] is "A primary preposition denoting (fixed) position (in place, time or state), and (by implication) instrumentality (medially or constructively), that (is, a relation of rest…" (underline added).

Using Strong's definitions we could add to our insight of Jesus' instruction to: Earnestly pray for the Father's royalty, rule and reign to appear, grow and be set; His purpose, decree and pleasure to come into being and be distributed across the earth as it is in a fixed position and in a relation of rest in heaven.

We must follow Holy Spirit's promptings as He leads us into deeper understanding and application of God's word. As we gain His "revelation-secrets," we employ them as we speak and release His word into people's lives and their situations.

Once I discovered the meanings of Jesus' original words, I began incorporating them into our prayers and Blessing Declarations. As my husband, Cal, and I pray, we call forth God's kingdom to be accomplished in the earth, superimposed across it. One day as we were praying, Holy Spirit gave me a visual representation of "superimposition."

Imagine that you are watching a weather channel. The meteorologist begins to explain the movement of a weather system across the map of the

United States of America. The computer program being used creates a visual representation of the mass of warm or cold air sweeping across the States. The individual states are visible as the system is superimposed over them. The computer program allows us to observe the progression of this air mass advancing across the face of our states. We can determine how and possibly when the weather system will affect our area. Its effect becomes personal.

The accompanying weather, whether it is rain, snow, hail, tornadoes, a hurricane, etc., is expected to be manifested across certain parts of the States. The meteorologist declares his or her forecast of what will occur in the upcoming days.

Read Matthew 6:10 in The Passion Translation: *"Manifest your kingdom realm, and cause your every purpose to be fulfilled on earth, just as it is fulfilled in heaven."*

Using the image of a weather system being superimposed across the face of the earth, declare that the kingdom of our God, which is righteousness, peace and joy in the Holy Spirit, will prevail. (Romans 14:17)

"Let faith forecast our future."[1]

Let the sound of VICTORY flow from the word of God out of our mouths, into others, across our land and within the atmosphere. We function within the kingdom of God from a place, posture and position of VICTORY. Angels are activated as "they hearken to and obey the Word of God that we declare."[2]

Our Blessing Declarations bring forth the life of God's word. Our Blessing Declarations release encouragement to others. Our Blessing Declarations advance God's kingdom authority across the earth and exalt His character before others.

> *But God, being rich in mercy, because of the great love with which he loved us, even when we were dead in our trespasses, made us alive together with Christ—by grace you have been saved—and raised us up with him and seated us with him **in** the heavenly places **in** Christ Jesus.* (Ephesians 2:4-6, emphasis added)

---

1 Pastor Steve Dow, All Nations Church, Tallahassee, FL
2 Tim Sheets, *Prayers & Decrees that Activate Angel Armies*, p. 57

The original Greek word used for our English word "in" was "en" (G1722). Recall that Jesus used this word to describe the Father's will being in a fixed position of rest in heaven. Using that explanation of "en," we recognize that God positions us in a place of rest in Christ Jesus, in a fixed and established position, and uses us as an instrument through which His word, truth and life flow to accomplish His kingdom and will in (distributed across) earth.

Read Ephesians 2, verses 5 and 6 from The Amplified™ Bible:

> *Even when we were [spiritually] dead and separated from Him because of our sins, He made us [spiritually] alive together with Christ (for by His grace--His undeserved favor and mercy--you have been saved from God's judgment). And He raised us up together with Him [when we believed], and seated us with Him in the heavenly places, [because we are] in Christ Jesus.* (Ephesians 2:5,6 AMP)

The *e-Sword X* app[1], offers this insight into Ephesians 2:1-10:

> Notice the past tense describing the finality of Christ's work. In the purpose of God we have been raised from the grave of sin and are seated with the risen Lord in the place of acceptance and victory. We were one with Christ when He lay in the grave and arose. **In God's thought** we **have already taken our seat with** the **glorified Christ upon the throne**; the pity is that we do not believe this or act as if we had done so. All this is the gift of God's unmerited love. By grace have we been brought into this position, and by grace are we maintained in it. We are of God's "making;" such is the Greek word for workmanship, Eph 2:10. **We have been created for good works**; they have been planned for us and we have only to walk in them. (emphasis added)

If you need to pause, do so. Read and re-read Ephesians 2:5-6. Take your time. Meditate on the goodness, grace and mercy of God. Tell Jesus how much you love and appreciate Him. Invite Holy Spirit to empower you to walk in God's good works.

"For we are his workmanship, created in Christ Jesus for good works, which God prepared beforehand, that we should walk in them." (Ephesians 2:10)

---

1 https://www.e-sword.net/

Would you like to read it from The Amplified™ Bible?

> *For we are His workmanship [His own master work, a work of art], created in Christ Jesus [reborn from above--spiritually transformed, renewed, ready to be used] for good works, which God prepared [for us] beforehand [taking paths which He set], so that we would walk in them [living the good life which He prearranged and made ready for us].* (Ephesians 2:10 AMP)

<u>We are God's "work of art."</u> We are joined together with His precious Son, Jesus. My heart is deeply touched with awe and reverence for God. Isn't yours? In God's eternity, we are. We have been born for such a time as this, planned in advance to accomplish the will and good pleasure of God. We are His delight. Doesn't knowing this encourage you?

Let's continue to consider how to walk in good works destined for us!

God's words of wisdom found in the book of Proverbs caution us:

"Keep your heart with all vigilance, for from it flow the springs of life." (Proverbs 4:23)

"So above all, guard the affections of your heart, for they affect all that you are. Pay attention to the welfare of your innermost being, for from there flows the wellspring of life." (Proverbs 4:23 TPT)

Jesus, the Eternal Word, affirmed this caution as He explained: *"...For out of the abundance of the heart the mouth speaks."* (Matthew 12:34)

The Passion Translation offers this: *"...For what has been stored up in your hearts will be heard in the overflow of your words!"* (Matthew 12:34 TPT)

Jesus continued: *"The good person out of his good treasure brings forth good, and the evil person out of his evil treasure brings forth evil."* (Matthew 12:35)

"When virtue is stored within, the hearts of good and upright people will produce good fruit. But when evil is hidden within, those who are evil will produce evil fruit." (Matthew 12:35 TPT)

Thus, we must <u>deposit God's word into our hearts</u> to have that <u>good treasure to share</u> with others. It is from that good treasure that Blessing Declarations flow.

We can add this to our understanding of "How Do We Advance God's Kingdom Through Blessing Declarations."

We must <u>make daily deposits of God's word into our hearts</u>. Another powerful point of Jesus' pattern for praying is: *"Give us this day our daily bread,"* (Matthew 6:11)

Jesus declared this about Himself: *"…"I am the bread of life; whoever comes to me shall not hunger, and whoever believes in me shall never thirst."* (John 6:35)

> *Jesus replied to them, "I am the Bread of Life. The one who comes to Me will never be hungry, and the one who believes in Me [as Savior] will never be thirsty [for that one will be sustained spiritually]."* (John 6:35 AMP)

Early on Sunday, December 22, 2024, I was spending time reading the Bible and listening to Abba Father's heart. Holy Spirit reminded me of the words of Christ: *"Give us this day our daily bread"* and *"I am the bread of life."* He also reminded me that healing is the children's bread. He continued to speak: "When you pray: 'give us this day our daily bread,' then pray 'give us our daily bread of healing.'" May I encourage you to immerse yourself in God's word every day. Allow Holy Spirit to lead your study and flow with Him. He will highlight passages and connect them in such a way that they become like the psalmist spoke:

"*NUN. Thy word is a lamp unto my feet, and a light unto my path.*"

Psalm 119:105 KJV

His revealing truth provides guidance and illumination for every step you take, even the steps you follow as you study and pray. Recall the instruction of Jesus:

"Therefore I tell you, whatever you ask in prayer, believe that you have received it, and it will be yours." (Mark 11:24)

Immanuel, God with us. Holy Trinity will freely share their time with you. What a gift!

Give others the gift of your time. As you receive the Bread of Life, share Him with others.

Freely we receive life and sustenance from reading and depositing God's word into our hearts; therefore, we can freely give to others.

(Matthew 10:8)

Please read that portion of verse 8 in The Message: *"You have been treated generously, so live generously."*

Let's recall one of the passages from the wise counsel of Proverbs 10:21— *"The lips of the righteous feed many…"* *"The lips of the righteous feed and guide many…"* (AMP).

Parents can speak Blessing Declarations over their children before the beginning of each school day. Our grandsons shared this about their parents speaking Blessing Declarations: "I feel safe, happy, and sure that nothing bad will happen." (Reed) "It makes me feel good about my day." (Charlie) "It makes me feel special." (Daniel Gleaton)

Our grandson, Andrew, commented about the Blessing scrolls: "I think it's cool that they teach about a certain theme…love, God's love for you."

Lovers of God, it is our privilege to feed many with the message of the Good News. One way the Bread of Life can be fruitful and multiplied within others is to speak and release Blessing Declarations over them.

Along your faith journey **in** Christ Jesus, you can begin with "five loaves and two fish." Present what you have to Abba Father and ask Him to bless it. He will cause the increase. Jesus, the Bread of Life, will perfectly meet each need. There will be twelve baskets leftover. (Matt 14:15-21) We should not despise the day of small beginnings. (Zechariah 4:10)

Join Jesus' heart of compassion as you walk **in** Him: *"So when Jesus landed he had a huge crowd waiting for him. Seeing so many people, his heart was deeply moved with compassion toward them, so he healed all the sick who were in the crowd."* (Matthew 14:14 TPT, underline added)

How many people do you see every day? How many people "crowd" your emails and text messages with needs? Consider the powerful message found in Proverbs 13:12 —*"Hope deferred makes the heart sick, but a desire fulfilled is a tree of life."* Your response to them could include a Blessing Declaration filled with hope, focusing on the Author and Finisher of our faith: Jesus.

Do you send Birthday cards to family and friends? Inscribe a Blessing Declaration within them. Use "Get Well" or "Sympathy" cards to share God's word of comfort and encouragement with others. May I offer examples?

Birthday Blessing Declaration:

As you celebrate your special day, may you give thanks to God for giving you life—I do!

> May you trust Him to cause you to excel and prosper in all that you do. May you recognize the hand of the Lord blessing you as you go out, and as you come in.
>
> May you give Him glory and honor in all your ways.
>
> In Jesus' Name. Amen.

Cal and I inscribe Blessing Declarations within our children's and grandchildren's Birthday cards. We first listen to Holy Spirit, hearing from Him the Father's heart for each person. Then, we declare His heart and vision for our loved one.

Charlie, our grandson, shared this: "I like it when every year for my birthday, I get to see which Blessing you put on each card and what it's about."

Daniel Gleaton, another grandson, commented: "…she doesn't copy and paste them from another card," indicating that each Birthday Blessing is unique.

Get Well Blessing Declaration:

> May God's presence cover you with His peace and comfort.
>
> May the stripes that Jesus bore on His back bring you full and complete healing.
>
> May Holy Spirit infuse your body with His restoration and wholeness.
>
> May you rest in His care, for He cares for you.
>
> In Jesus' Name. Amen.

Sympathy Blessing Declaration:

> May Holy Comforter envelope you with His presence.
>
> May He guide your thoughts and decisions as you face each day without your loved one.
>
> May His counsel be wise and precise, meeting every need.
>
> May you submit every care and concern to Him. He is more than able and always willing to be your Helper.
>
> In Jesus' Name. Amen.

Precious reader, these Blessing Declarations may have been written just for you! If one stirred your spirit, then grab it and receive it as yours. Join your faith in God with that declaration. You will receive a great benefit from it. Consider this: as you personally experience the richness and ministry of that Blessing Declaration, you will understand how others will feel when you write, speak and release God's word of truth to them. He deeply desires to minister to you and to others. Receive God's generous compassion, then give it to others in like manner.

Every Blessing Declaration focuses on God, including His word, His nature and His activity within people's lives. In writing, speaking and releasing Blessing Declarations, we direct others' attention to Him and encourage their trust in His goodness, mercy and grace. We can help others respond with faith that comes from God.

Peter proclaimed the power and life within God's word:

> *For you have been born again [that is, reborn from above--spiritually transformed, renewed, and set apart for His purpose] not of seed which is perishable but [from that which is] imperishable and immortal, that is, through the living and everlasting word of God.* (1 Peter 1:23 AMP)

Jesus spoke again about a mustard seed as He explained to His disciples the cause for their inability to cure the demonically controlled boy: *"He said to them:*

> *Because of your little faith. For truly, I say to you, if you have faith like a grain of mustard seed, you will say to this mountain, 'Move*

from here to there,' and it will move, and nothing will be impossible for you." (Matthew 17:20, underline added)

The KJV renders this wording: *"…because of your unbelief…"*

Ouch! Not many believers in Christ want to consider that they have unbelief. Take a moment to read Jesus' strong reprimand noted in an earlier verse: *"And Jesus answered, "O faithless and twisted generation, how long am I to be with you? How long am I to bear with you? Bring him here to me."* (Matthew 17:17)

Jesus pointed His words to those disciples who had been under His careful teaching, who had witnessed the power and love of God flowing through Him. These men had not placed total trust in His authority nor in the authority He had given to them. They were lacking spiritual understanding; thus, unable to execute His authority, His jurisdiction, over the evil, demonic forces. These disciples were <u>failing to advance</u> the kingdom of His Father.

This lack of faith and advancement of God's kingdom grieved Jesus. Mark, in his gospel writing, recorded a conversation between Jesus and the father of the demonically controlled son:

> *And it [demonic spirit] has often cast him into fire and into water, to destroy him. But **if you can** do anything, have compassion on us and help us. And Jesus said to him, "**If you can!** All things are possible for one who believes." Immediately the father of the child cried out and said, "I believe; **help my unbelief**"* (Mark 9:22-24, brackets and emphasis added)

Consider the father's request of Jesus: he asked for whatever power was needed, for compassion and sympathy, for relief and aid. Then, he asked Jesus to help him go beyond his unbelief. Do we need to ask Jesus to help us go beyond our unbelief? He is the Author and Finisher, the Completer and Perfecter of our most holy faith. <u>He inscribes faith</u> onto our hearts. Remember: faith is a gift from God. Every day Jesus is actively developing and maturing our faith in Him. <u>We must partner with Jesus to put His gift into action!</u>

Jesus honored the father's desperate cry for help. In like manner, Jesus will respond to our cries for help and our invitation for His working more faith in us. Jesus calls us to engage our faith within our daily lives. Every day <u>we make choices</u> that <u>propel us forward</u> within God's kingdom, **or** in <u>opposition to</u> His truth and righteousness. Let us choose wisely.

Joshua, Israel's leader, challenged the entire nation to make a personal decision and to follow it. This call was made as Joshua recognized that his life on earth was coming to an end. Listen to his challenge:

> *Now therefore fear the LORD and serve him in sincerity and in faithfulness. Put away the gods that your fathers served beyond the River and in Egypt, and serve the LORD. And if it is evil in your eyes to serve the LORD, choose this day whom you will serve, whether the gods your fathers served in the region beyond the River, or the gods of the Amorites in whose land you dwell. But as for me and my house, we will serve the LORD.* (Joshua 24:14,15)

Joshua provoked his fellow countrymen to action; to yield themselves to serve and join the LORD in His purpose and plans for their nation. Let's recall that the LORD's plan and purpose included blessing Abram in such a way that he and his family would bless others—*"and in you all the families of the earth shall be blessed."* (Genesis 12:3) God made a covenant, a "life agreement" with Abram whose name God changed to Abraham. Now, Abraham became the father of the nation of Israel for whom Joshua served as their leader. Generations of people have been included in God's covenant, His life agreement.

Joshua was a part of those generations. Decades earlier Joshua chose to follow God. He chose to "stay the course" wholeheartedly and to submit to God's leadership and chose to trust God's power to accomplish His will in and through his life. Joshua's faith needed growth and maturity.

How do we know that? Consider the words of the LORD as He **called** Joshua **to leadership**:

> *After the death of Moses the servant of the LORD, the LORD said to Joshua the son of Nun, Moses' assistant, "Moses my servant is dead. Now therefore **arise, go** over this Jordan, you and all this people, into the land that I am giving to them, to the people of Israel. Every place that the sole of your foot will tread upon I have given to you, just as I promised to Moses. From the wilderness and this Lebanon as far as*

> *the great river, the river Euphrates, all the land of the Hittites to the Great Sea toward the going down of the sun shall be your territory. No man shall be able to stand before you all the days of your life. Just as I was with Moses, so I will be with you. I will not leave you or forsake you.* ***Be strong and courageous****, for you shall cause this people to inherit the land that I swore to their fathers to give them.* ***Only be strong and very courageous****, being careful to do according to all the law that Moses my servant commanded you. Do not turn from it to the right hand or to the left, that you may have good success wherever you go. This Book of the Law shall not depart from your mouth, but you shall meditate on it day and night, so that you may be careful to do according to all that is written in it. For then you will make your way prosperous, and then you will have good success. Have I not commanded you?* ***Be strong and courageous. Do not be frightened****, and* ***do not be dismayed****, for the LORD your God is with you wherever you go."* (Joshua 1:1-9, emphasis added)

The LORD knew Joshua and the future challenges and opposition he would encounter, and the victories Joshua would achieve. The LORD spoke strength and courage into Joshua. The LORD **cast His vision before Joshua** for a future of strength and courage within his life. Joshua's faith, courage and trust in the LORD would grow and mature.

Jesus wants our faith to grow. For that to happen, we must **arise** and **go**. Who spoke this command to Joshua? The LORD, Jehovah, the eternal, self-existing God commanded His loyal co-worker, Joshua, to advance His plan and purpose across the land.

The command and directive of **arising** and **going** flows throughout God's word. He intends for His kingdom, His nature to be advanced. We read this same charge through the words of the prophet Isaiah:

> ***Arise****,* ***shine****, for your* ***light*** *has come, and the glory of the LORD has risen upon you. For behold, darkness shall cover the earth, and thick darkness the peoples; but the* ***LORD will arise upon you****, and his glory will be seen upon you. And* ***nations shall come to your light****, and* ***kings to the brightness of your rising****. Lift up your eyes all around, and see; they all gather together,* ***they come to you****; your sons shall come from afar, and your daughters shall be carried on the hip.* (Isaiah 60:1-4, emphasis added)

How Do We Advance God's Kingdom through Blessing Declarations?

Do you recall the declarations made by Jesus as He spoke to the multitudes around Him?

> *Seeing the crowds, he went up on the mountain, and when he sat down, his disciples came to him. And he opened his mouth and taught them, saying:* **You are the light of the world**. *A city set on a hill cannot be hidden. Nor do people light a lamp and put it under a basket, but on a stand, and it gives light to all in the house. In the same way,* **let your light shine before others**, *so that they may see your good works and* **give glory to your Father** *who is in heaven"* (Matthew 5:1-2, 14-16, emphasis added)

Let's return to the request of the father who needed help for his son. He asked Jesus for:

1. whatever power was needed to exercise dominion over the demonic spirit,
2. compassion and sympathy,
3. relief and aid,
4. relief from his faithlessness.

This father recognized the presence and power of the demonic spirit that worked against the life and future of his son, his successor, the **next generation** of his family line. Either he heard or witnessed the love, compassion, and authority of Jesus since he came in search of it. Bewildered when the disciples or students of Jesus were inept at doing the work of their Master Teacher, he pleaded with Jesus. Today, people are desperate for help.

Dear reader, you and I are disciples, students and followers of Jesus, our Master Teacher, our Redeemer, our Resurrected King, the One who has destroyed the works of the enemy.

Others will approach us with great needs and life-threatening situations. Will we or will we not assert dominion over the demonic realm and serve those in need with the love and compassion of our Master Teacher? I want to join the ranks of Joshua who declared: *"But as for me and my house, we will serve the LORD."* (Joshua 24:15)

How do we accomplish "serving the LORD?"

We must **trust Him**, then **arise** and **go**. We must take the first step towards sowing. Write, speak and release the measure of God's word that you know. Give it to others. Sow it into the soil of others' lives. James, the half-brother of Jesus, challenged us in our daily walk:

"But be doers of the word, and not hearers only, deceiving yourselves."
(James 1:22)

Now read it in The Passion Translation: *"Don't just listen to the Word of Truth and not respond to it, for that is the essence of self-deception. So always let his Word become like poetry written and fulfilled by your life!"*
(James 1:22 TPT)

How do we make room for God's word of truth to become poetry inscribed on the tablets of our hearts, then fulfilled in and through our lives? How can we truly engage His life-depositing word into the lives of others and in the earth?

Consider this:

1. **Seek God in the early morning.** Enjoy His fellowship as you read His word of truth.
2. **As you read, listen for and be attentive to Holy Spirit's promptings and questions.**
3. **He will guide your reading.** He will highlight a word or passage and invite you to investigate its meaning or connection to another scripture. As you dig deeper, you will discover great treasure and insightful application of God's word for your life.
4. **As you fellowship with Him, the Spirit will deposit that treasure of understanding into your heart.** From that reservoir of truth, that fountain of life, you draw as you serve others. You speak and release Blessing Declarations which become a "cup of cool water" to refresh their soul. Recall the power and impact of our words:

"The mouth of the righteous is a fountain of life,…" (Proverbs 10:11)

"On the lips of him who has understanding, wisdom is found,…"
(Proverbs 10:13)

"The mouth of the righteous brings forth wisdom,…" (Proverbs 10:31)

May I share a very personal, right-this-moment, experience? As I wanted to provide a scripture to support the idea of offering a "cup of cool water," Holy Spirit reminded me of the scriptures I referenced earlier. As I reviewed those, He encouraged me to read the entire chapter of Proverbs 10. As I followed His guidance, I discovered more treasures to share with you! Thus, you just read verses 11, 13 and 31.

This is just one example of the operation and activity of God's Spirit within our lives.

"You make known to me the path of life; in your presence there is fullness of joy; at your right hand are pleasures forevermore." (Psalm 16:11)

5. **Acknowledge the truth of Proverbs 18:21 and apply it to your life.** Make intentional choices of words as you send emails, texts, greeting cards, posts on social media. Ask Holy Spirit to place a guard on your heart, not allowing offenses to remain that would taint your thoughts and words. As you speak with others, invite Holy Spirit, the Spirit of Christ, to minister to them through you.

   Please read The Passion Translation's version of Proverbs 18:21: *"Your words are so powerful that they will kill or give life, and the talkative person will reap the consequences."*

6. **Acknowledge and activate your delegated authority to advance God's kingdom in earth as it is in heaven.** Live inside the position purchased for you by the shed blood of Jesus Christ, His victory over the enemy of our souls, and His resurrection from the dead to new life. Jesus Christ is seated at the right hand of the Father in heaven. He is our pleasure forevermore as Psalm 16:11 identifies.

   Paul helps us understand how and where we live: *"If the Spirit of him who raised Jesus from the dead dwells in you, he who raised Christ Jesus from the dead will also give life to your mortal bodies through his Spirit who dwells in you."* (Romans 8:11)

   The Bible study app *e-Sword X*, provides this note on Romans 8:10-17:

   But there is another most blessed function of the divine Spirit, Rom 8:14. He is willing to lead us, to prompt our actions, to inspire our purposes, and to mold our characters. The more we yield to Him, the deeper becomes our awareness of that filial relationship with God which breathes in the cry, *Abba, Father*. But note the wonderful climax, Rom 8:17. If we yield to the Holy Spirit, He will conduct us into the divine treasure-house and bid us avail ourselves of the infinite resources which are there stored for our use, not in the *next* life, but in *this*.

Let's reread the passage written by the apostle Paul, through the inspiration of Holy Spirit:

Even when we were dead in our trespasses, made us alive together with Christ—by grace you have been saved—and raised us up with him and seated us with him in the heavenly places in Christ Jesus. (Ephesians 2:5-6)

It is within that position purchased for us that we are seated in Christ Jesus, who is seated at the right hand of Abba Father. It is within that position that we gain access to the infinite resources for our present life! The benefits and joy of our restored relationship to Abba Father through His Son, Jesus, are without measure.

Our Abba takes great delight in pouring forth His blessings and allowing us to share them with others. <u>One way</u> we can share His gifts is by speaking and releasing Blessing Declarations! It is <u>one instrument</u> to utilize as we serve others for God.

On September 17, 2024, our son-in-law, Kyle, was given a dream by God. This dream served as a confirmation of something he would be invited to participate in later that day. Many times, dreams that are given by God prepare us for something ahead. This is Kyle's dream with his interpretation and application:

> **Dream:** I was working on a project for my father in the dream. I was wearing a hat, my carpenter tool belt and was working on what seemed to be the exact project I am currently working to complete. I was walking around the worksite and noticed that instead of sliding my pencil into my hat right in front of my ear, I did so with one of your blessings (scroll) and the dream ended shortly after.

Interpretation: (at least for me, possibly others): I have been working for the Father for a while now, and He has remained quiet in most of my labor, but has been blessing me to continue working and has been faithful to provide in ways through my Handyman business, but has been teaching me to hear blessing, and realize what He desires to give others. While also circumcising my ear to hear what He is saying without mixture. That not only have I been His project, but that He has been preparing me for all the things I had lost sight of, or have gotten too busy to remember He has had them in His heart for me.

Location of the Blessing: in front of my ear where my pencil would normally sit. In carpentry, the pencil and tape measure are of vital importance in the work that needs to be accomplished. So, while the blessing represents blessing, it also represents the very thing that helps "mark" places, people and time with God's covering and provision. It also represents a place where God reinforces His covenant that He has cut with us. A pencil often makes a mark where material will be cut. (Kyle A. Del Vecchio)

7. **Let's spend a few moments with Kyle's interpretation of his dream.** He mentioned working for the Father. *"For we are God's fellow workers. You are God's field, God's building."* (1 Corinthians 3:9) The Amplified™ Bible offers this insight: *"For we are fellow workmen (joint promoters, laborers together) with and for God; you are God's garden and vineyard and field under cultivation, [you are] God's building. [Isa. 61:3]"*

The Bible study app *e-Sword X* suggests this idea:

> Let us think of ourselves only as God's instruments, and in a humble way as God's fellow-workers. It is a most helpful thought. Constantly when engaged in tilling the soil as evangelists or in building character as preachers and teachers, let us count on success, because of the all-power of our great Partner. He must give the policy and direction; it is our part to conform wholly to His will and guidance.[1]

---

1 *e-Sword X*, note on 1 Corinthians 3:1-9

The commentator for *e-Sword X* encourages us to operate from a submitted posture before God and in total reliance upon Him, our Partner. *The Amplified™ Bible* stresses our partnership with God which was Adam's purpose in the Garden of Eden. Adam was created in God's image and would represent Him and promote His kingdom as he went forth. I believe that you and I can function within a balance of these perspectives. Daily, we request, invite and then follow God's leadership and guidance provided through the presence of His Holy Spirit.

Reading Isaiah 61, we recognize that our Messiah, Jesus Christ, is described. Following the flow of Isaiah's prophecy, multiple contrasts of "before" and "after" the preaching of the good news are presented. The desolate and forlorn has been exchanged for restoration and refreshment. Jesus presented the same shift from darkness to light within the kingdom of God. We have experienced such liberation with our new birth in Him. We can spread His light to others. We can alleviate burdens (heaviness) with our encouraging words of Blessing Declarations.

As Jesus was sent by the Father, you and I are sent by Jesus to bind up and heal the broken-hearted, to proclaim and declare freedom from oppressive mindsets and to set free those bound by maledictions and word curses. As we speak and release Blessing Declarations, we can replace the ashes of sorrow for beautifully adorned garlands of God's truth. The time of God's favor and blessings is now.

As you and I read God's word, Holy Spirit will cause a passage to become "alive," "highlighted," or "quickened" within our hearts and minds. This happens frequently for me. In Chapter 5 we reviewed the explanation of the Rhema word. When Holy Spirit prompts us with a passage, receive it and write it. That scripture has a purpose that God wants to fulfill. Ask Him for His purpose. He may instruct us to pray it first, then, create it into a Blessing Declaration for someone. The recipient may be US!

Read again Kyle's statement:

"That not only have I been His project, but that He has been preparing me for all the things I had lost sight of, or have gotten too busy to remember He has had them in His heart for me."

I am reminded of Paul's reassurance of God's steadfastness to His beloved as he wrote to the believers in Philippi and in Thessalonica:

> *I pray with great faith for you, because I'm fully convinced that the One who began this glorious work in you will faithfully continue the process of maturing you and will put his finishing touches to it until the unveiling of our Lord Jesus Christ!*
> (Philippians 1:6 TPT)

> *Faithful and absolutely trustworthy is He who is calling you [to Himself for your salvation], and He will do it [He will fulfill His call by making you holy, guarding you, watching over you, and protecting you as His own].* (1 Thessalonians 5:24 AMP)

Not only is God continually working on our behalf, but He will also help us remember previous conversations and guidance He has offered. You and I may choose to do "life" our own way, but out of deep love and compassion for us, God will redirect our steps to more closely follow His. He truly wants what is best for us.

8. **The location of "the Blessing" was significant to Kyle as he noted.** An explanation of "the Blessing" might be needed. Several decades ago, Holy Spirit gifted me with the idea of writing Blessings on a scroll. He called it a "witty invention." He also gifted me with faithful friends, Laura Mann and Dena Woodburn, who undergirded me with their love, ideas and writings. Kyle has experienced the timeliness of these Blessing scrolls. One of his favorites included Jeremiah 29:11 which he needed at that very moment. Read his Blessing:

> *May you know that the thoughts God has for you are continual, considering your past, present and future. May you feel reassured to know His plans for you are for peace and not calamity, to give you a hope and a future. You are loved.* (Jeremiah 29:11)

Review with me Kyle's thoughts on the location of the Blessing: "it [the Blessing scroll] also represents the very thing that helps "mark" places, people and time with God's covering and provision." When Kyle was given the Blessing scroll bearing Jeremiah 29:11, he received it for himself and believed it. He didn't toss it aside. He needed and wanted the power and promise of that scripture to become a reality in his young life. He believed God, even if his faith was the size of a mustard seed. Kyle trusted God to honor His word. God's covering and provision are inscribed within every Blessing. The Blessing Declarations cause God to be remembered.

Please make note of the psalmist's making mention, marking the trustworthiness of the LORD. Psalm 20:7 KJV describes David's confidence: *"Some trust in chariots, and some in horses: but we will remember [H2142] the name of the LORD our God.* (brackets added) Remember [H2142] means to "recount, mark, put in remembrance of, record, recount,"

David brings to his and others' remembrance the "name [H8034] of the LORD;" His position, honor, authority and character.[1]

Over the years of writing, distributing, speaking and releasing Blessing Declarations, I have witnessed how God always meets the need. He is faithful and true to His Name.

9. **To engage Blessing Declarations within the lives of others, we join Jesus' heart of compassion.** This word "compassion" is used twelve times in the New Testament; all are found within the writings of Matthew, Mark and Luke. Five of those usages are found in the Gospel according to Matthew. Who was Matthew? He was the wayward Jew who accepted a tax-collector's job within the Roman government. He became despised by his fellow Jews. They viewed him as a contemptible traitor.

Who was Matthew? He was a recipient of the compassion of Jesus who called him by name to follow Him. As Matthew had freely received forgiveness and compassion, he made careful note of that same compassion extended by Jesus to others. He quickly recognized it because he had experienced it.

> *Then Jesus called his disciples to him and said, "I have compassion on the crowd because they have been with me now three days and have nothing to eat. And I am unwilling to send them away hungry, lest they faint on the way.* (Matthew 15:32, underline added)

---

1 Strong's Concordance, H2142: remember and H8034: name

We discover Jesus' compassion meeting a different need: *"<u>Moved with compassion</u>, Jesus touched their eyes; and immediately they <u>regained their sight</u> and followed Him [as His disciples]."* (Matthew 20:34 AMP, underline added)

Mark shared another outpouring of the compassion of Jesus. *"When he went ashore he saw a great crowd, and he <u>had compassion</u> on them, because they were like <u>sheep without a shepherd</u>. And he began <u>to teach them</u> many things."* (Mark 6:34, underline added)

These three passages reveal the actions of Jesus Christ that flowed from His heart of compassion: feeding the natural hunger of people, healing the blind, and shepherding those in need of care, provision, protection and guidance for their "todays" and their "tomorrows."

10. **As we speak and release Blessing Declarations over others, we place before them God's word as a guiding light.** *"NUN. Thy word is a lamp unto my feet, and a light unto my path."* (Psalm 119:105) *"Truth's shining light guides me in my choices and decisions; the revelation of your word makes my pathway clear."* (Psalm 119:105 TPT)

Zachary, our grandson, confirmed this about the Blessing scrolls: "I like reading them…because it reminds me of the Bible. It's a certain verse. It helps me with my decisions."

As we speak and release Blessing Declarations, we teach others about the kingdom of God. Consider the example and directive set before us by Jesus: *"And he called the twelve together and gave them power and authority over all demons and to cure diseases, and he sent them out to proclaim the kingdom of God and to heal."* (Luke 9:1,2,)

Using Strong's Concordance to gain insight into Luke's description, we understand that Jesus committed, bestowed, granted to His twelve disciples the force, ability, strength and delegated influence, jurisdiction, competency over every demonic being and to relieve and heal infirmities and sicknesses. Additionally, Jesus sent them forth to preach, publish, herald the royalty, rule and reign of the Supreme Deity and to cure and make whole.

11. **"For it is Christ's love that fuels our passion and motivates us, because we are absolutely convinced that he has given his life for all of us. This means all died with him,"** (2 Corinthians 5:14 TPT)

What "fuels our passion and motivates us?" Christ's love emboldens us because we are "absolutely convinced that he has given his life for all of us."

How do we advance God's kingdom through speaking Blessing Declarations? We remain solid in our faith in His love, His completed work on Calvary and His resurrected life. We remain *"absolutely convinced…that those who live should no longer live self-absorbed lives but lives that are poured out for him—the one who died for us and now lives again."* (2 Corinthians 5:14,15 TPT)

How do we "no longer live self-absorbed lives?" Hear the answer found within the truth of God's word—2 Corinthians 5:17 in The Passion Translation:

"Now, if anyone is enfolded into Christ, he has become an entirely new creation. All that is related to the old order has vanished. Behold, everything is fresh and new." Our old selves have "vanished," washed away by the all-powerful, ever-merciful, completely forgiving Blood of our Lord and Savior Jesus Christ. The old is gone, the new life reigns within us. Those "self-absorbed lives" no longer have us bound. We are set free! We are set free to tell others about the All-Sufficient Grace of God.

You may ask: "How is that possible?" Read Paul's declaration: *"And God has made all things new, and reconciled us to himself, and given us the ministry of reconciling others to God."* (2 Corinthians 5:18 TPT)

Our ability to speak to others is made possible because God has made us new. He has reconciled us to Himself and He has given, committed, ordained us with "the ministry of reconciling others" to Himself. Our DNA has been regenerated.

Let's continue to read Paul's power-packed message about this ministry: *"that is, in Christ God was reconciling the world to himself, not counting their trespasses against them, and entrusting to us the message of reconciliation."* (2 Corinthians 5:19)

Read The Passion Translation's wording for the ending phrase: *"... and he has entrusted to us the ministry of opening the door of reconciliation to God."* As we speak and release Blessing Declarations, we are "opening the door of reconciliation to God."

Beloved of God, may I share with you that over the years of releasing Blessing Declarations, countless people have commented that the message of God's word arrived just at the right time, not a minute too soon, nor too late. Our compassionate God is a right now, right on time God. His timeliness creates something beautiful.

He never fails. His love endures forever. His purpose for us is eternal. He who calls and ordains us is Faithful.

Hold onto the word of encouragement and purpose for your life:

> *We are ambassadors of the Anointed One who carry the message of Christ to the world, as though God were tenderly pleading with them directly through our lips. So we tenderly plead with you on Christ's behalf, "Turn back to God and be reconciled to him."* (2 Corinthians 5:20 TPT)

12. **When we and others turn back to God and receive reconciliation, what should our response be?** Listen to King David's charge to the covenant people of God: *"And David said to all the congregation, 'Now bless the LORD your God.' And all the congregation blessed the LORD God of their fathers, and bowed down their heads, and worshipped the LORD, and the king."* (1 Chronicles 29:20 KJV)

As believers in the Lord Jesus Christ, we are the new covenant people of God. During His final Passover Meal with His disciples prior to His sacrificial death on the Cross, Jesus spoke: *"for this is my blood of the covenant, which is poured out for many for the forgiveness of sins."* (Matthew 26:28) The Passion Translation offers this: *"For this is the blood that seals the new covenant. It will be poured out for many for the complete forgiveness of sins."* (Matthew 26:28 TPT)

In Paul's first letter to the believers living in Corinth, he wrote: *"In the same way also he took the cup, after supper, saying, "This cup is the new covenant in my blood. Do this, as often as you drink it, in remembrance of me."* (1 Corinthians 11:25)

Consider King David's charge to the congregation or assembly of God's covenant people: he called them to "bless the LORD your God." The word bless is barak which means to kneel, by implication to bless God as an act of adoration.[1]

The people of God bowed down their bodies in reverence to their Eternal, Self-existent, Supreme Magistrate. In their worship, the people of God's covenant, prostrated themselves on the ground with a heart of submission to their Sovereign God. Their physical bodies served as a sign of their inward commitment to honor and obey Him, to love Him and Him only.

You and I are given a choice. As Joshua charged the assembly *"… choose you this day whom you will serve,"* we make our choice to worship King Jesus, to lay down our lives to follow Him in service to the Father and to others for the advancement of God's kingdom "here in earth, as it is in heaven." We have a choice to remember Jesus' sacrifice for us and others, then, to share His life's message.

What is your choice? How will you express your worship to God? Read the complete prayer given by Jesus to His disciples when they asked how they should pray:

"And it came to pass, that, as he was praying in a certain place, when he ceased, one of his disciples said unto him, Lord, teach us to pray, as John also taught his disciples." (Luke 11:1 KJV)

> *And he said unto them, When ye pray, say, Our Father which art in heaven, Hallowed be thy name. Thy kingdom come. Thy will be done, as in heaven, so in earth. Give us day by day our daily bread. And forgive us our sins; for we also forgive every one that is indebted to us. And lead us not into temptation; but deliver us from evil. For thine is the kingdom and the power and the glory, forever. Amen.* (Luke 11:2-4 KJV, some manuscripts add the last line)

Jesus honored the holiness of His Father, so should we. We recognize the Father's place and position of authority and dominion in heaven. He rules and reigns from the highest heaven. His kingdom, His will

---

[1]   *e-Sword X* and Strong's Concordance

is being accomplished <u>in</u> earth as He rules and reigns <u>in</u> heaven. We can proclaim that authority and dominion: "You, Father, reign over the heavens and the earth. You are high and lifted up! You are Great and greatly to be praised. Majesty! Kingdom authority is Yours and only Yours. There is none like You! You are all we want and need! You love us with an everlasting love. Your mercies are new and fresh and abundant every day! Great is Your faithfulness! We love You, Abba!"

How do we pray and worship? We honor Who our heavenly Father is. He is the Great I AM. We magnify His greatness, His lovingkindness, His faithfulness to <u>all generations</u>. We ascribe to Him all praise that is due His Holy Name. We forget none of His benefits. We acknowledge His provisions for our lives. We cast all our cares upon our Abba, for He cares for us. We thank Jesus for His sacrifice for us, His taking of our sins upon His sinless body, His going to Hell for three days instead of us. We ask Holy Spirit to help us forgive others as Jesus Christ has forgiven us. We thank Holy Trinity for being active and very present in our lives.

We humble ourselves before our Father, trusting Him to deliver us from evil.

Would you return with me to the story of Daniel and his three young companions? Shortly after Daniel, Hananiah, Mishael, and Azariah had been given great favor by God, King Nebuchadnezzar had a disturbing dream. When the king's magicians, enchanters, sorcerers and Chaldeans could not tell him the dream with its interpretation, King Nebuchadnezzar issued a <u>death warrant for all the wise men</u> of Babylon to be destroyed. This edict included Daniel and his friends.

Daniel <u>chose to take another step of courage</u> and requested the king to allow him a designated time in which he might show the interpretation to the king. Daniel's request was granted. He informed his friends of the urgent need to:

> *Seek mercy from the God of heaven concerning the mystery, so that Daniel and his companions might not be destroyed with the rest of the wise men of Babylon. Then the mystery was revealed to Daniel in a vision of the night. Then Daniel blessed the God of heaven.* (Daniel 2:18,19)

Read how **Daniel blessed God**:

> *Blessed be the name of God forever and ever, to whom belong wisdom and might. He changes times and seasons; he removes kings and sets up kings; he gives wisdom to the wise and knowledge to those who have understanding; he reveals deep and hidden things; he knows what is in the darkness, and the light dwells with him. To you, O God of my fathers, I give thanks and praise, for you have given me wisdom and might, and have now made known to me what we asked of you, for you have made known to us the king's matter.* (Daniel 2:20-23)

After Daniel blessed and exalted God, he spoke with Arioch, the king's captain, who was to execute the king's deadly edict. Then, Daniel was taken to the king. Listen to the king's question and Daniel's response. It serves as a powerful example for us and how we should conduct our lives.

> *The king declared to Daniel, whose name was Belteshazzar, "Are you able to make known to me the dream that I have seen and its interpretation?" Daniel answered the king and said, "No wise men, enchanters, magicians, or astrologers can show to the king the mystery that the king has asked, <u>but there is a God in heaven who reveals mysteries</u>, and he has made known to King Nebuchadnezzar what will be in the latter days. Your dream and the visions of your head as you lay in bed are these: To you, O king, as you lay in bed came thoughts of what would be after this, and he who reveals mysteries made known to you what is to be. But as for me, this mystery has been revealed to me, not because of any wisdom that I have more than all the living, but in order that the interpretation may be made known to the king, and that you may know the thoughts of your mind."* (Daniel 2:26-30, underline added)

How do we conduct our lives? We seek God, the all-wise God. We declare to Him that He is all we want and need. We assure God that we love Him with all our hearts, souls and minds and our neighbors as ourselves. Amen and amen.

Would you like to write a prayer as you worship Him?

Oh, Lord, how majestic is Your name in all the earth. You are high and lifted up in the heavens!

_____

Beloved reader, during times of worship the Lord has revealed answers I have been seeking. How do I respond? I am drawn into a deeper love and reverence of Abba Father, His loving nature and His faithful character.

There is truly none like Him.

Holy Spirit reminded me of a deeply worship-filled song written by Lenny LeBlanc: "There is None Like You." I encourage you to locate that song and worship God.

"How do we advance God's Kingdom through Blessing Declarations?"

- We entrust our lives to God, trusting His love for us and for others.
- We commit our hearts to loving Him and living in fellowship with Him.
- We consecrate our future, hopes and dreams as we seek first His Kingdom and His righteousness, trusting Him to provide all our needs according to His riches in glory in Christ Jesus.
- We make daily deposits of God's word into our hearts from which we draw His good treasure.
- We continually submit to the sanctifying work of Holy Spirit.
- We ask Him to work in us courage and confidence to carry out the Father's assignments.
- We activate the ministry of reconciliation that Father God has given and assigned to us.
- We ask God for the nations, so that they might be saved and encouraged in their faith.
- We communicate the love of Christ and His salvation as we write, speak and release life-depositing, heart-reviving Blessing Declarations.

How Do We Advance God's Kingdom through Blessing Declarations?

My Blessing Declaration for you:

May you know the breadth and length and height and depth of God's love for you.

May you enjoy His presence every day, knowing that "in His presence is fullness of joy, at His right hand are pleasures forevermore."

May you be assured that by the richness of God's mercy and grace, we have been made alive in Christ.

May you be confident that the Father has raised us up with Him and has seated us with Him "in the heavenly places in Christ Jesus."

May you arise and go proclaiming, declaring the love and truth of our Lord Jesus Christ.

May others hear the word of salvation released through you.

May they believe on the Lord Jesus Christ!

In Jesus' Name. Amen.

Advancing God's Kingdom within Your Life:

1. What area of your life needs releasing to God's care?

_____

_____

_____

2. What steps are you taking to improve your fellowship with God?

_____

_____

_____

3. How are you seeking God's kingdom first in relationship to your hopes and dreams?

___

4. What part of God's word have you recently deposited within your heart?

___

5. What area of your life needs the sanctifying work of Holy Spirit?

___

6. Within your sphere of influence, how will you activate the ministry of reconciliation?

___

7. Identify which nations for whom you are asking God to use you.

___

8. What is a step of courage you will take in writing and releasing Blessing Declarations?

___

Chapter 7

Engaging Blessing Declarations by the Next Generations

For the Pure and Shining One. A song of poetic praise, by King David. I waited and waited and waited some more, patiently, knowing God would come through for me. Then, at last, he bent down and listened to my cry. He stooped down to lift me out of danger from the desolate pit I was in, out of the muddy mess I had fallen into. Now he's lifted me up into a firm, secure place and steadied me while I walk along his ascending path. (Psalm 40:1,2 TPT)

Beloved of God, years ago Cal and I were sinking in the "desolate pit" of speaking self-defeating words that flowed from hearts of frustration, criticism and condemnation. At that point in time, our three young children did not hear words of kindness nor attitudes based on patience. Anthony, Peyton and Elizabeth heard words that did not honor them. Our Abba Father did not hear words that pleased Him. Cal and I focused on the challenges of raising our children instead of the blessings that they were to us. We failed to trust God.

Feeling trapped in a downward spiral, we cried out to God. Our loving Father sent His co-laborer, Dr. Bill Ligon, and His Son's crimson cord to save us. In Chapter 5, I mentioned that a guest speaker, Dr. Ligon, extended his message of truth and hope that pulled us out and up into God's marvelous freedom and victory. Cal and I grabbed hold of the biblically based principle of speaking blessings and depositing them into our children. This shepherding pastor offered us the rod and staff of God's word and encouraged us to engage this principle daily.

Dr. Ligon challenged us to repent of harboring anger, resentment, unbelief and fear within our hearts. He invited Cal and me to allow God's Holy Spirit to "*Create in me a clean heart, O God; and renew a right spirit within me.*" (Psalm 51:10 KJV)[1]

Cal and I needed to admit our sin of not trusting God with our children and their future. "*The sacrifices of God are a broken spirit; a broken and contrite heart, O God, you will not despise.*" (Psalm 51:17) Our hearts were broken. God knew what He wanted to accomplish within us, not only for our benefit, but for the benefit and future of our precious children, the next generation.

Please read that verse from The Amplified™ Bible: *My [only] sacrifice [acceptable] to God is a broken spirit; A broken and contrite heart [broken with sorrow for sin, thoroughly penitent], such, O God, You will not despise.*" (Psalm 51:17 AMP) We were humbled and remain so.

Do you recall the cry of the father whose son was being controlled by a demonic spirit? Read the passage again:

> *And it [demonic spirit] has often cast him into fire and into water, to destroy him. But if you can do anything, have compassion on us and help us. And Jesus said to him, "If you can'! All things are possible for one who believes." Immediately the father of the child cried out and said, "I believe; help my unbelief!"* (Mark 9:22-24, brackets added)

Please take a moment and read this passage from The Amplified™ Bible:

> "*The demon has often thrown him both into fire and into water, intending to kill him. But if You can do anything, take pity on us and help us!" Jesus said to him, "[You say to Me,] 'If You can?' All things are possible for the one who believes and trusts [in Me]!" Immediately the father of the boy cried out [with a desperate, piercing cry],*

---

1   See www.reasonsforhopeJesus.com to read "Got Questions?" article on "How Are the Shepherd's Rod and Staff Different?"

saying, "I do believe; help [me overcome] my unbelief."
(Mark 9:22-24 AMP)

This short passage is packed with a powerful message! Parents, grandparents, aunts, uncles, guardians, teachers, pastors, marriage and family therapists, daycare workers, principals, police officers, take note and learn from Jesus. Yes, demonic spirits can overpower people—people who are our next generation. These can be within the lineage of our families, or they can be within the next generation of our Christian faith. We are called to be "fruitful and to multiply." We are called to help others reach their God-given destinies.

Matthew, an eyewitness of this event, was inspired by Holy Spirit to describe it in this manner:

And Jesus rebuked the demon, and it came out of him, and the boy was healed instantly. Then the disciples came to Jesus privately and said, "Why could we not cast it out?" He said to them, "Because of your little faith. For truly, I say to you, if you have faith like a grain of mustard seed, you will say to this mountain, 'Move from here to there,' and it will move, and nothing will be impossible for you."
(Matthew 17:18-20)

Recall the words of Jesus: "*The thief comes only to steal and kill and destroy. I came that they may have life and have it abundantly.*" (John 10:10)

Jesus was referring to the enemy of our soul and our future: Satan, the devil. He schemes to steal, kill and destroy people and their kingdom purposes and destinies.

Did you notice the father's desperate cry for help? He was not only distraught over the condition of his son, but he also anguished over his lack of faith. Both father and son needed help. This describes the condition and circumstances of our family when God sent His best help through Dr. Bill Ligon, who obediently followed Holy Spirit's leading. On that Sunday night, Dr. Ligon shared the message found within God's word of speaking and releasing His truth, goodness, and authority over and into people.

On that night, Dr. Ligon's divine appointment was a set of desperate parents! At the right time, Cal and I heard the heart and compassion of Jesus through His obedient shepherd, Dr. Bill Ligon. I am confident that the father in Mark 9:22-24 took the instruction and admonishment of Jesus and grew in his faith. Jesus saw fertile soil into which He sowed faith, truth, love and authority to cast out the father of lies, Satan. Cal and I grabbed Dr. Ligon's message and put it into action. As our hearts changed, so did the words and confessions of our mouths. Jesus explained: *"…For out of the abundance of the heart the mouth speaks."* (Matthew 12:34)

Jesus did not stop with that revealing statement. He placed before us the consequences of speaking good versus evil—that is, words of faith based on His goodness or hurtful words that demean and condemn His creation. *"I tell you, on the day of judgment people will give account for every careless word they speak, for by your words you will be justified, and by your words you will be condemned."* (Matthew 12:36,37)

Knowing that there are serious consequences for faithless, destructive words should cause every reader to "stop in your tracks" and do a "heart and mouth check." It did for Cal and me. Hearing Jesus' words of warning created a much-needed fear and reverence for the principles of God's kingdom. Reverence for God's holiness and righteousness has been sorely missing in our society. God is holy, and He calls us to be as well.

In the apostle Peter's first letter, he presented this admonition: *"But as he which hath called you is holy, so be ye holy in all manner of conversation; since it is written, 'You shall be holy, for I am holy.'"* (1 Peter 1:15,16 KJV)

Peter pressed his point with the reason we should choose to conduct our lives in holiness. You, I and others have been redeemed not by our works, *"But with the precious blood of Christ, as of a lamb without blemish and without spot:"* (1 Peter 1:19 KJV)

Cal and I began making choices in our hearts and mouths to honor Jesus' sacrifice for us, our children and for others. Peter explained the choice each of us can make:

> *Since by your obedience to the truth you have purified yourselves for a sincere love of the believers, [see that you] love one another from the heart [always unselfishly seeking the best for one another], for you have been born again [that is, reborn from above--spiritually trans-*

> *formed, renewed, and set apart for His purpose] not of seed which is perishable but [from that which is] imperishable and immortal, that is, through the living and everlasting word of God.*
> (1 Peter 1:22,23 AMP)

Transformation occurred within our family. God's designed destinies for our children would not be destroyed or perverted by the enemy. We prayed and declared: "Thy kingdom come, Thy will be done, here in earth, within our children, as it is in heaven."

We wanted our family to feel safe and secure within the walls of our home. We wanted the rooms of our house to be filled with laughter, joy and delight. Our children needed that.

> *"By wisdom a house is built, and by understanding it is established; by knowledge the rooms are filled with all precious and pleasant riches."*
> (Proverbs 24:3,4)

> *Wise people are builders—they build families, businesses, communities. And through intelligence and insight their enterprises are established and endure. Because of their skilled leadership the hearts of people are filled with the treasures of wisdom and the pleasures of spiritual wealth.* (Proverbs 24:3,4 TPT)

As a mother, my part in ensuring their security was vital. Listen to the wise counsel found in Proverbs 14:1 KJV: *"Every wise woman buildeth her house: but the foolish plucketh it down with her hands."* Please read it in The Passion Translation: *"Every wise woman encourages and builds up her family, but a foolish woman over time will tear it down by her own actions."*

I had to recognize and acknowledge the power and effect of my words. I had the power to edify, encourage and build up our children. I had already witnessed the destructive consequences of my hurtful words that originated from a heart filled with unforgiveness, anger and resentment. My heart was broken by sin and filled with sadness. I needed the Healer's touch. Do you recall Isaiah's description of the coming Messiah:

> *The Spirit of the Lord GOD is upon me, because the LORD has anointed me to bring good news to the poor; <u>he has sent me to bind up the brokenhearted</u>, to proclaim liberty to the captives, and the opening of the prison to those who are bound;* (Isaiah 61:1, underline added)

I needed the joy of the LORD to fill my heart. I had to spend more time in His word; more time in His presence:

You make known to me the path of life; in your presence there is fullness of joy; at your right hand are pleasures forevermore. (Psalm 16:11)

I had to become a woman in and of God's word. I needed to treasure it in my heart. "…*Your word is a lamp to my feet and a light to my path.*" (Psalm 119:105)

"*By your words I can see where I'm going; they throw a beam of light on my dark path.*" (Psalm 119:105 The Message)

"*For you bring me a continual revelation of resurrection life, the path to the bliss that brings me face-to-face with you.*" (Psalm 16:11 TPT)

The path of resurrection life was set before me in God's word. Joy came in the morning.

"*A joyful heart is good medicine, but a crushed spirit dries up the bones.*" (Proverbs 17:22)

"*A joyful, cheerful heart brings healing to both body and soul. But the one whose heart is crushed struggles with sickness and depression.*" (Proverbs 17:22 TPT)

Jesus paid for and paved the path of resurrection life for you, me and others. Join me along that path. Diligently seek God in His word, in prayer and in conversation with Him.

"*I love those who love me, and those who seek me diligently find me.*" (Proverbs 8:17)

"*I will show my love to those who passionately love me. For they will search and search continually until they find me.*" (Proverbs 8:17 TPT)

I love them that love me; and those that seek me early [H7836] shall find me. (Proverbs 8:17 KJV, brackets added)

I found it interesting to note the King James Version included the Hebrew word **sh'char** [shaw-khar'] which is defined: "A primitive root; properly to dawn, that is, (figuratively) be (up) early at any task (with the implication of earnestness); by extension to search for (with painstaking): - [do something] betimes, enquire early, rise (seek) betimes, seek (diligently) early, in the morning)."[1]

The Psalm writer, David, began seeking God in the early morning hours:

"*O LORD, in the morning you hear my voice; in the morning I prepare a sacrifice for you and watch.*" (Psalm 5:3)

Consider the Hebrew word for **watch**: "ts™ph™h (tsaw-faw') A primitive root; properly to lean forward, that is, to peer into the distance; by implication to observe, await: - behold, espy, look up (well), wait for, (keep the) watch (-man)." (Strong's Concordance, H6822: watch)

In the morning, O LORD, You will hear my voice; In the morning I will prepare [a prayer and a sacrifice] for You and watch and wait [for You to speak to my heart]. (Psalm 5:3 AMP)

Arise early, while the house is still quiet, seek God and keep seeking Him. Keep watch for Him to be active in and through your life, every day! You will experience and receive treasures of His lovingkindness, His goodness, mercy and grace.

> *Unending wealth and glory come to those who discover where I dwell. The riches of righteousness and a long, satisfying life will be given to them.*
>
> *What I impart has greater worth than gold and treasure, and the increase I bring benefits more than a windfall of income.*
>
> *I lead you into the ways of righteousness to discover the paths of true justice.*
>
> *Those who love me gain great wealth and a glorious inheritance, and I will fill their lives with treasures.* (Proverbs 8:18-21 TPT)

Cal and I have gained great wealth in and through our relationship—yes, our friendship—with God, the Father, God, the Son, and God, the Holy Spirit. God has filled our lives with an overflowing treasure of His goodness. We consider our children, their spouses and our grandchildren to be a large portion of God's goodness, grace and mercy towards us.

Our families are Jesus' inheritance.

---

[1] Strong's Concordance, H7836: early

Please read Hebrews 12:2 from The Amplified™ Bible:

> *[Looking away from all that will distract us and] focusing our eyes on Jesus, who is the Author and Perfecter of faith [the first incentive for our belief and the One who brings our faith to maturity], who for the joy [of accomplishing the goal] set before Him endured the cross, disregarding the shame, and sat down at the right hand of the throne of God [revealing His deity, His authority, and the completion of His work].*

May you and I focus our eyes on Jesus, allowing Him to inscribe upon our hearts His love for us and others. May our hearts be focused on the joy of knowing and sharing Him. May you read our family's stories and hear the lovingkindness, grace and goodness of God through their words and testimonies. May He touch your heart.

I invited Cal and our adult children to describe and discuss their recollections of our family's interactions with each other. Their birth order is Anthony, Peyton, Elizabeth, Victoria and David. Please note that Victoria lives in Heaven. There will be references that mention the older three, as there is a space between Victoria's passing and the birth of David. There are 18 years between the birth of Anthony and David.

Cal described our family:

> We were a happy-looking family on the outside, but on the inside we (I) knew there were things that had to change inwardly. We would differ on views as to how to discipline, and it felt that the kids were always finding ways to push my buttons. Adding to that, a teacher labeled one of our sons 'attention deficit.' In reality, he was just a kid.

Peyton shared his earliest memories:

> I remember that we yelled a lot…it was stressful for you…running a business, raising three kids…I had a fiery temper…we weren't as cautious about our word choices…I remember that we began to change…we had blessings every morning. I was frustrated with life in general…there was consistency in discipline… you guys had rules…loving family, had our challenges, …but overall, there was consistency and discipline…we were a good family…with challenges.

Anthony recalls Peyton's teachers being challenged by Peyton's unique personality. He added this insight: "…having kids now, I believe that some of the 'problems' we went through were part of just having kids, kids exploring boundaries, busy parents, financial/job stresses that impact family, unique child personalities—as there were specific challenges with Peyton."

Additionally, Anthony remembered our long parental conversations with Peyton. At some point, Anthony noticed that our talking changed to blessing Peyton, "a mindset that we shifted to."

Anthony recalled a specific event held at our church that occurred at the end of his 5th grade. At that time, Kathy Palmer served as the Children's Church Pastor for Christian Heritage Church in Tallahassee, FL. Kathy, her husband Steve, and other volunteers designed a powerful and impactful Blessing Service for the graduating 5th graders and their families. In preparation for this service, Kathy and Steve met with the 5th graders' parents. Cal and I were among those parents. They assisted us in writing Blessings we would speak over our graduate. We were also encouraged to help siblings write a Blessing to speak over the graduate during the upcoming service.

Please hear Peyton's heart as he relates his memory of that service:

> I remember writing Blessings for Anthony's graduation…we then spoke them (the Blessings) during the service we had at Christian Heritage and (we) put hands on Anthony…I remember that it was very emotional…I'm an emotional guy and I remember crying.…
>
> (I remember) getting choked up for Anthony's for sure…burying the hatchet of old stuff…moving forward…letting 'bygones be bygones,' forgiveness…ultimate way that you do that is blessing someone. You can't have hostility in your heart if you're able to sincerely bless someone. You have to go through some sort of forgiveness if somebody has wronged you if you want to bless them.…
>
> Because I took the time to write…(a Blessing), I was able to go through a period of forgiveness to help be able to write it. So

when I blessed (Anthony) that was the emotional release. While I was blessing…I was also forgiving…without telling (Anthony) I forgave (him).

Side note: we participated in similar Blessing Services to honor Peyton, Elizabeth and David during their 5th grade graduations.

Peyton stressed an important aspect of creating, writing and releasing a Blessing Declaration: "You can't have hostility in your heart if you're able to sincerely bless someone. You have to go through some sort of forgiveness if somebody has wronged you if you want to bless them….."

Offenses we harbor must be surrendered to the Lord. Preparation precedes the "pen." All of us need those "come to Jesus" times, allowing Him to remove the ash heap of offenses and to replace them with the beauty of His grace and mercy. As you cast aside grievances and pain, He enters to refresh and renew you. Then, you are ready to pick up that pen and write! Listen closely to the beauty of His presence filling your heart. <u>He composes the Blessing Declaration <u>for</u> you because He has a message for the recipient. He is speaking through you to touch that person's heart. <u>Your</u> reconciliation becomes a path for <u>theirs</u>.

Pause for a moment to consider this "path of reconciliation." Do you recall that we have been given the ministry (path) of reconciliation? Read our assignment, one more time:

> *All this is from God, who through Christ reconciled us to himself and gave us the ministry of reconciliation; that is, in Christ God was reconciling the world to himself, not counting their trespasses against them, and entrusting to us the message of reconciliation.*
>
> (2 Corinthians 5:18,19)

The King James Version describes our purpose in this way: "*…and hath committed unto us the word of reconciliation* (G2643)." Therefore, we are to speak and communicate God's reconciliation back to Him through Christ's sacrifice. Consider Strong's definition for reconciliation: (G2643) "katallagē from G2644; exchange (figuratively adjustment), that is, restoration to (the divine) favor: - atonement, reconciliation(-ing)."

Our words of Blessing Declarations have the power to direct others back to God through Christ Jesus. We show Jesus to others through our words and declarations. As we advance God's kingdom purpose within others, they can do the same. The recipients of your Blessing Declarations can participate and become fruitful within God's kingdom.

Please consider the "good fruit" that was produced within Peyton's young life. His recollections continued:

> I remember being more conscious of my word choices growing up with friends, trying to be as positive as I could. In my high school junior year, we had a 'meet around the pole' kind of thing and it evolved into every morning meeting on the Band Field, and we started praying with some of the FCA [Fellowship of Christian Athletes] members. In the beginning it was just a few of us and that was really scary. What was really cool is that we kept it going and more and more people came. ….maybe we had 60-80 kids and it started with me, Tom Coogle, Adam Coogle and a couple of other people, maybe 4 or 5 of us and it spread from there. It was a really cool thing because it brought our school together…. there was a moment of silence then some of us would pray. A lot of my prayerfulness then was blessing our school, blessing the kids. The words I used to pray every morning were to watch out for us and protect us, keep us safe, let us be good friends and good people, let us watch out for one another, and be conscious of others' feelings and be gracious to one another. It translated over to how I prayed was like how you guys blessed us. It seemed natural to pray that way, too, especially when praying for other people, not selfishly praying. That year was more like not speaking ill of one another and then, that we set an example for other people in the school by these certain characteristics that we portray are Christ-like. I would speak them out loud as I would pray.

Beloved of God, as I heard Peyton's memories, I was humbled. I was reminded of the influence parents exercise within their child's life. We deposit within them seeds which bear fruit. Our words, our attitudes, our actions produce fruit; they bear consequences, good or bad.

Do you recognize a need for change in your life, within your family's life? Honestly, it's time.

Cal recalls our path of reconciliation, our allowing a change to occur within our hearts and mouths.

> After hearing Bill Ligon present the biblical concept on blessing versus cursing our kids, as well as each other, things began to change. It is hard to change from an attitude you experienced as a kid, to now being careful as to what you say to your wife and children. It is always a work in progress through prayer and patience. Blessings worked and probably saved our family unit.

Does your family need saving? Do they need to hear words of reconciliation, the words of Christ?

Cal described it in this way: "It was a change in lifestyle. Ann would correct me as I spoke over the kids. It was hard as you find yourself in an angry incident. I began to be more careful as to what came out of my mouth."

As a parent, I purposefully looked for something positive to say to our children. I had focused on their rough places instead of seeing the diamonds below the surface. It is truly a mindset adjustment that follows a heart change.

Dr. Bill Ligon delivered the way and word of reconciliation to Cal and me. We were <u>his next generation</u> of faith, hope and love. Our children became the subsequent generation. The principle of speaking and releasing Blessing Declarations is a powerful way of following God in His original directive: "be fruitful and multiply."

Cal and I followed God as He led us into green pastures, along quiet waters that restored our souls. He continues to be our Good Shepherd. In following Him, I applied for and was offered the position and privilege of serving the children of Christian Heritage Church as their pastor. Cal served as my right-hand man in much the same way as Steve served Kathy. They paved the way and provided a wonderful example for us.

During this time of service, I asked the Lord for a creative way to incorporate the Advent Wreath within our Christmas Celebration. I was familiar with this special wreath as my childhood church included it during the Advent season. This is when the Lord gifted me with His "witty invention" of writing Blessings on scrolls. With Holy Spirit's leading,

Engaging Blessing Declarations by the Next Generations

I wrote the first set of Blessings based on the word of God. These small scrolls were attached to our Blessing Wreath. During the Advent Season, our Children's Church service incorporated teachings to prepare our hearts in celebration of Christ's coming. Children were invited to select a Blessing scroll from the wreath. Cal and I would speak their Blessing over them. We sowed seeds of God's word into their lives.

It was powerful. Children's hearts were touched. So were ours.

Beloved of God, I simply asked God for help. I wanted to offer the children something special, something meaningful and impactful for their lives. Matthew recorded Jesus' teaching on the consequence of asking:

> *Ask, and it will be given to you; seek, and you will find; knock, and it will be opened to you." "For everyone who asks receives, and the one who seeks finds, and to the one who knocks it will be opened.* (Matthew 7:7,8)

"If you then, evil (sinful by nature) as you are, know how to give good and advantageous gifts to your children, how much more will your Father who is in heaven [perfect as He is] give what is good and advantageous to those who keep on asking Him." (Matthew 7:11 AMP)

In this teaching, Jesus presented the dynamics of God's kingdom that was heard by God's people in the days of Jeremiah:

> *"Call to me and I will answer you, and will tell you great and hidden things that you have not known."* (Jeremiah 33:3)

Prior to this message, Jeremiah had delivered God's word of hope and restoration:

> *And they shall be my people, and I will be their God. I will give them one heart and one way, that they may fear me forever, for their own good and <u>the good of their children after them</u>. I will make with them an everlasting covenant, that I will not turn away from doing good to them. And I will put the fear of me in their hearts, that they may not turn from me. <u>I will rejoice in doing them good</u>, and I will plant them in this land in faithfulness, with all my heart and all my soul.* (Jeremiah 32:38-41, underline added)

Do you hear the heart of God in Jeremiah's message? God's everlasting covenant comes through Jesus. Did you notice that God is deeply desirous of doing good for the children as well? Blessing us and our children, <u>the next generation</u>, with His goodness causes Him to be full of cheer and joy! Doing good for us delights God!

Sharing the heart of God with our children through Blessing Declarations allowed His character of doing good to be cultivated within them.

Reflecting on his position as a Physician Assistant in a local hospital's Emergency Department, Peyton shared this:

> I encourage people that I work with. We have downtime where we talk about personal things. I try to be a positive person and be kind to them. I generally care about the people I work with. I enjoy getting to know them and impart wisdom where I can. When I speak to someone, I speak positivity, life and wealth, prosperity and good judgment and favor, giving them confidence, guidance and direction. I think it's well received. If you speak plainly and you're positive in your words and in your counsel, that goes a long way in a workplace setting.
>
> That's how I see Blessing Declarations with an Emergency Department in those conversations that happen all the time with people. It's more indirect, but it seems to work. I've had these interactions where people have come to me, sat down and asked how I would deal with something on a personal level. People are receptive as I give them guidance from a biblical perspective because that's how I was raised.

Did you hear Peyton's words? "I give them guidance from a biblical perspective because that's how I was raised." Seeds of truth, words from God's heart, were sown into Peyton's life. Good fruit developed; now others enjoy that good and wholesome spiritual food. Those around Peyton are experiencing what David wrote in his psalm:

"O taste and see that the LORD is good: blessed is the man that trusteth in him." (Psalm 34:8 KJV)

Peyton added that he purposefully orders pizza for the ER on a weekly basis:

I want them to know they are valued and that I'm thankful for them. I care about them and I appreciate them. Food comes from a generous heart that has purpose to make them feel valued. I bless them (with free pizza) because I am blessed and move that blessing forward, then that helps other people do something as well.

The apostle Paul revealed the dynamics of God's kingdom as he wrote to the Galatians:

"*Do not be deceived: God is not mocked, for whatever one sows, that will he also reap.*" (Galatians 6:7)

"*Make no mistake about it, God will never be mocked! For what you plant will always be the very thing you harvest.*" (Galatians 6:7 TPT)

Follower of God, you and I have the privilege and purpose of sowing God's word of hope, truth and life into others. We are His ambassadors, reconciling the world back to Him through His Son, Jesus Christ. The path and process of reconciliation may look and sound different through the lives of His saints, yet God's purpose is being fulfilled.

Within a former work environment, Anthony encountered opportunities to shield associates from critical attitudes and condemning judgments that arose. As a young boy, he learned to recognize demeaning, destructive "word curses" and how to counter them. He is now equipped to combat any maledictions with positive, expectant attitudes and words. He looks for the strengths within others and anticipates seeing good being developed within his associates. There are times when others recognize Anthony's efforts on their behalf, yet many times they are unaware of his intervention. However, God sees it all.

David's workplace is at home. His job involves monitoring medical tests and assessments of patients' hearts. Recently David shared:

With my new promotion, I am discovering that a lot of patients have chronic illnesses and may only have a few more years to live, being on the older side. Sometimes I will speak a quick prayer or Blessing over the patients, in hope that they will get better, because it is very easy to say that 'you are going to die in a few years.' The main point is that a diagnosis is not your destiny.

Do the words we speak and release affect others when they can't hear and receive our Blessing Declarations? That answer is discovered along a dusty road of Capernaum.

> *When he had entered Capernaum, a centurion came forward to him, appealing to him, "Lord, my servant is lying paralyzed at home, suffering terribly." And he said to him, "I will come and heal him." But the centurion replied, "Lord, I am not worthy to have you come under my roof, <u>but only say the word</u>, and my servant will be healed. For I too am a man under authority, with soldiers under me. <u>And I say</u> to one, 'Go,' and he goes, and to another, 'Come,' and he comes, and to my servant, 'Do this,' and he does it.'" When Jesus heard this, he marveled and said to those who followed him, "Truly, I tell you, with no one in Israel have <u>I found such faith</u>." And to the centurion Jesus said, "Go; <u>let it be done for you as you have believed</u>." And the <u>servant was healed</u> at that very moment.* (Matthew 8:5-10,13, underline added)

Distance in our natural realm is overshadowed by the authority of Jesus and His word of life, healing and restoration. The centurion recognized Jesus' authority. That the centurion sought Jesus' help indicated that he had already heard about Jesus and possibly had witnessed Jesus' compassion and power since He lived in Capernaum. (Matthew 4:13)

Before I apply this kingdom principle to our family's lives, may I share with you the *FireBible's*™ note on Matthew 8:10—"The centurion's faith was more impressive than anything that Jesus had seen among the Jews because it combined a loving concern for another person with complete trust in Christ's authority and power." (p. 1533)

Cal, Peyton, Anthony and David combine a loving concern for others and trust in Christ's authority and power. Some of their words of life and truth are spoken directly to people, while other prayers and declarations are made and released into the spiritual realm.

I strongly encourage faith-filled believers to speak and release Blessing Declarations into people and situations regardless of their awareness. During Elizabeth's teenage years, much tension developed between us. I had my ways of managing our household which did not accommodate much flexibility. Did you think: drill sergeant?

Yes, we butted heads a lot! Our heads smacked together so frequently that Elizabeth's heart began to harden towards me. She would not allow me to touch nor hug her. Admittedly, I still had things to learn about parenting, "managing our household" and covering her with God's grace.

Cal and I chose to speak and release Blessing Declarations over Elizabeth during our morning prayer times. Her bedroom was on the opposite side from ours, yet we were confident in the power of God's word to deposit His seeds of life and truth. As Peyton indicated, one's heart must forgive in preparation for blessing someone. Cal and I needed to forgive her defiance. May I stress this: Jesus instructed us to forgive as we also sought His forgiveness for our attitudes. As He provided a powerful prayer for His disciples to incorporate within their daily lives, Jesus added:

"*For if you forgive others their trespasses, your heavenly Father will also forgive you, but if you do not forgive others their trespasses, neither will your Father forgive your trespasses.*" (Matthew 6:14,15)

> *For if you forgive others their trespasses [their reckless and willful sins], your heavenly Father will also forgive you. But if you do not forgive others [nurturing your hurt and anger with the result that it interferes with your relationship with God], then your Father will not forgive your trespasses.* (Matthew 6:14,15 AMP)

The *FireBible*™ provides this note on "If you forgive":

> The Greek term aphiemi, which means 'forgive'…, is found in various forms in the NT (over 140 times). It sometimes means 'to let go,' 'to leave behind,' 'to dismiss,' and even 'to cancel a debt.' It is used for the forgiveness of sins by God (implying also the canceling of guilt). We are to forgive others in the same way God forgives us.[1]

Additional insight is provided on "If you do not forgive": "Jesus teaches that there should be no compromise in our readiness or willingness to forgive the offenses of others. Holding on to unforgiveness is a sin because of the bitterness and destruction it can bring in one's own spirit and because it fails to reflect God's character in our lives. If we refuse to forgive others, Christ will not forgive us—nor will he answer

---

[1] *FireBible*™, p. 1527, note on Matthew 6:14

our prayers—because we choose to hold on to sin. This is an important principle because God uses it as a measure for forgiving us (18:35; Mark 11:26; Luke 11:4)."[1]

Jesus stressed the weightiness of forgiveness as He related a parable concerning the unforgiving servant:

"So also my heavenly Father will do to every one of you, if you do not forgive your brother from your heart." (Matthew 18:35)

I recommend reading Matthew's entire narrative found in Matthew 18:21-35. It's eye-opening and heart penetrating. Referencing the *FireBible's*™ notes, the sin of unforgiveness paves a path full of rocky bitterness, destructive stumbling blocks and disfigurement of one's countenance. That is, when unforgiveness rules our lives, we no longer carry God's image within us. When people are around us, they don't hear nor see Jesus through us. We fail to accomplish God's original plan: to be fruitful and multiply His image across the earth.

Beloved of God, unforgiveness is reinforced through repetitive thinking and saying: "I'm right, they're wrong." Unforgiveness is based in pridefulness. The word of God says:

"Pride goes before destruction, and a haughty spirit before a fall."
(Proverbs 16:18)

"Your boast becomes a prophecy of a future failure. The higher you lift up yourself in pride, the harder you'll fall in disgrace." (Proverbs 16:18 TPT)

During a conversation with the LORD, the prophet Habakkuk was told:

"Behold, his soul is puffed up; it is not upright within him, but the righteous shall live by his faith." (Habakkuk 2:4)

"Behold, his soul which is lifted up is not upright in him: but the just shall live by his faith." (Habakkuk 2:4 KJV)

You and I live in a time and culture that cultivates haughtiness and arrogance. We are called to separate ourselves from this culture of offense. Forgiveness is based upon our view or perception of the greatness or smallness of God. So may I ask you: "How big is our God in your eyes?"

---

1   *FireBible,*™ p. 1527, note on Matthew 6:15

The psalmist shared his view of God:

> *For the LORD is a great God, and a great King above all gods. In one hand he holds the mysteries of the earth and in the other he holds the highest mountain peaks. The sea is his, for he made it, and his hands formed the dry land. Oh come, let us worship and bow down; let us kneel before the LORD, our Maker!* (Psalm 95:3-6)

Are you harboring unforgiveness towards someone in your immediate family? Have you allowed resentment to reign within your heart? Has a root of bitterness become a large, looming tree over your life? Jesus hung on a cross hewn from a tree. That tree held <u>our Maker</u>, <u>our Redeemer</u>, the One who forgives us and all those who have caused us pain. Our God is big enough and loving enough to forgive ALL who call upon His Name for salvation. We all need saving from our sin.

Would you like to pause for a moment and jot down those in your life who need your forgiveness? As Peyton mentioned: forgiveness must precede speaking and releasing Blessing Declarations. We must forgive as Christ has forgiven us.

Do you recall the verse in Philippians that I spoke over Elizabeth as I drove her to middle school?

"May you, Elizabeth, be confident of this very thing: that He who has begun a good work in you will perfect and complete it until the day of Jesus Christ. In Jesus' Name. Amen." (Philippians 1:6 KJV)

As you read The Passion Translation's wording of that verse, notice in Whom Paul placed his confidence:

> *I pray with great faith for you, because I'm fully convinced that the One who began this glorious work in you will faithfully continue the process of maturing you and will put his finishing touches to it until the unveiling of our Lord Jesus Christ!* (Philippians 1:6 TPT)

Paul's faith was in "the One who began this glorious work." In Paul's eyes, heart and confession of faith, God was and is a big, big God. You and I can trust God to accomplish His marvelous work and plan within our lives and within the lives of others! Yes, He will faithfully continue the process of maturing us. His love for us is exponentially big.

Being "confident of" and trusting in God has been a "good work" that Elizabeth has experienced and recognized within her life. She shared: "Sometimes when I am frustrated or feel stuck in a situation, I am reminded to watch my words and speak life and not death. To not dwell on what I see with my physical eyes but remember how God sees that person or situation. It (is) challenging for sure and it takes trust, but God can deal with things a lot quicker if we trust him to handle things His way and not push our way."

Elizabeth continued to reflect:

> After Kyle and I got engaged, I asked my mom if she could have blessings at each table for our guests to enjoy. Our flower choice was the lily, so from our wedding, the blessing set 'Lily of the Valley' was created. At our service we chose the song, 'Light of your Face' to be (sung) as we had our family members pray/bless our union. This song quotes Numbers 6:24-25 (the Aaronic Blessing/Priestly Blessing) which was a perfect fit.

May I pull back the curtain on this memorable wedding to share what one of our wedding guests heard from the Lord? Frank Voran watched our family members surround Kyle and Elizabeth as we spoke and released Blessing Declarations over them. Our words were not audible to our guests. They could only hear the song. Yet, during this Blessing time, Frank heard the Lord say:

> My heaven is echoing, resounding with agreement with the blessings that are being spoken. Resources of every kind are dispatched and are now in place for Elizabeth and Kyle and all whom their lives will touch. The reciprocal blessing will resound from earth to heaven and back.[1]

"Resounding" means "shouting, triumph; joyful noise; acclamation of joy or a battle-cry; alarm; loud noise."[2]

"Reciprocal" means "(of an agreement or obligation) bearing on or binding each of two parties equally."[3]

---

1 May 12, 2012—Frank Voran
2 https://www.oxfordlearnersdictionaries.com/us/definition/english/resounding
3 ibid

The Lord heard every word spoken over that young couple. He rejoiced and shouted with excitement that He was being trusted and magnified within the lives of Kyle and Elizabeth. He will accomplish His mighty plans, purposes and delights within and through their lives. He is faithful to fulfill the word of life released and received that day. (Deut. 30:9; Isaiah 55:11)

Angels were dispatched with "resources of every kind" and were set "in place for Elizabeth and Kyle and all whom their lives will touch." God's blessings flow into and through them.

During Kyle and Elizabeth's reception, our guests inquired about the family time on the platform, wanting to know what was being said. Every time we were asked, a door of opportunity opened for us to share the power of speaking and releasing God's word. Several guests commented that they planned to duplicate that special and powerful time. Seeds of engaging God's word within the lives and futures of young people were sown. God will bring the harvest. Apply the meaning of reciprocal to our lives—as we believe in and declare His word, He fulfills it.

Part of our Blessing Declarations over Kyle and Elizabeth was for their house to be filled with precious and pleasant riches, which includes many children. Over the years, Isaac, Noah, Joseph, Daniel and Victoria have been born. Partnering with God, Kyle and Elizabeth are training up their children in the way they should go so that when they are old, they will not depart from it. (Proverbs 22:6) These five children receive great benefit from their training: *"All your children shall be taught by the LORD, and great shall be the peace of your children."* (Isaiah 54:13)

Elizabeth's reflections continued:

> My children love having the blessings around this house. I make sure to have them available for them to read themselves or even at times, they pick them up and bring them to Kyle and me. They loved to give them as gifts to their teachers each year at school, and sometimes we were able to share with teachers from previous years who loved them as well. Kyle and I continue to pray and bless our children daily. Each day is different, but they know without a doubt that they are loved and covered spiritually.

Kyle and Elizabeth's "tent pegs" have been expanded into training and teaching the children of their church family. She explained:

> Kyle and I are the Children's Directors at our church, and we have been able to supply the Blessing Gifts to our families in different events throughout the year (such as) Mother's Day, Father's Day and Christmas. The kids love to 'shop' for their parents and in return, these families are exposed to the Blessings each day.

As we have witnessed generations advancing through the years and decades, may I add another dimension to the generations of speaking and releasing Blessing Declarations? Do you recall Steve and Kathy Palmer, the couple I mentioned earlier in this chapter? Kathy was serving as Children's Church Pastor when we joined the body of believers at Christian Heritage Church in 1987. Under the Palmers' discipling, Anthony, Peyton and many other children were nurtured in their personal faith and relationship with the Lord. In 1991, Kathy, Steve and other volunteers hosted a Blessing Service for Anthony and other graduating 5th graders. That was the Blessing Service which Peyton described.

Fast forward to today. Steve and Kathy Palmer and several of the faithful Children's Church volunteers attend LifePoint Church along with Kyle and Elizabeth. These champions of speaking Blessing Declarations into and over people are enjoying the fruit of their sowing eternal seeds of God's truth and labors of love. They are witnessing the multiple generations who have been nurtured by God's word being released and deposited into their lives. This is God's reward to these devoted workers: seeing a bountiful harvest come forth!

"…to sow seeds of righteousness will bring a true and lasting reward."
(Proverbs 11:18 TPT)

"And the fruit of righteousness is sown in peace of them that make peace." (James 3:18 KJV)

"And the seed whose fruit is righteousness (spiritual maturity) is sown in peace by those who make peace [by actively encouraging goodwill between individuals]." (James 3:18 AMP)

"And the effect of righteousness will be peace, and the result of righteousness, quietness and trust forever." (Isaiah 32:17)

Elizabeth's reflections of her five children echo Isaiah's message: "Each day is different, but they know without a doubt that they are loved and covered spiritually." Isaac, their eldest son, described his parents' blessings as causing him to "feel protected." Noah, their second son, explained feeling "safe" because of the blessings spoken by Kyle and Elizabeth.

Kyle and Elizabeth's children trust in their parents' love for them as well as God's love.

"One generation shall commend your works to another, and shall declare your mighty acts." (Psalm 145:4)

"<u>Generation after generation</u> will declare more of your greatness and declare more of your glory." (Psalm 145:4 TPT, underline added)

Let's reflect upon our lives for a moment. Are we helping others know our Father God?

Jesus did. Throughout His earthly life, Jesus spoke of His Father. As the time of Jesus' humanity on earth was ending, He spoke directly to Thomas:

> *I am the way, and the truth, and the life. No one comes to the Father except through me. If you had known me, you would have known my Father also. From now on you do know him and have seen him.* (John 14:6-7)

Do you recall Philip's response? Listen to this disciple: *"Lord, show us the Father, and it is enough for us."* (John 14:8)

Can you relate to Jesus' amazement as He had been nurturing and teaching these disciples for over three years? Hear Jesus' astonished words:

> *Have I been with you so long, and you still do not know me, Philip? Whoever has seen me has seen the Father. How can you say, 'Show us the Father'? Do you not believe that I am in the Father and the Father is in me? The words that I say to you I do not speak on my own authority, but the Father who dwells in me does his works. Believe me that I am in the Father and the Father is in me, or else believe on account of the works themselves. Truly, truly, I say to you, whoever believes in me will also do the works that I do; and greater works*

than these will he do, because I am going to the Father. Whatever you ask in my name, this I will do, that the Father may be glorified in the Son. If you ask me anything in my name, I will do it.

(John 14:9-14)

"Greater works than these" are prepared beforehand for those of us who believe in Him. Let's recall the metaphor that Jesus engaged as He taught the crowd who surrounded Him.

You are the light of the world. A city set on a hill cannot be hidden. Nor do people light a lamp and put it under a basket, but on a stand, and it gives light to all in the house. In the same way, <u>let your light shine before others</u>, so that they may see your good works and give glory to your Father who is in heaven. (Matthew 5:14-16, underline added)

Listen, again, to Isaiah's words about the light:

Arise, shine, for your light has come, and the glory of the LORD has risen upon you. For behold, darkness shall cover the earth, and thick darkness the peoples; but the LORD will arise upon you, and his glory will be seen upon you. And nations shall come to your light, and kings to the brightness of your rising. (Isaiah 60:1-3)

I recognize that Isaiah was speaking about Israel and her future, yet Jesus used the metaphor to speak forth purpose and future for those listening to Him. Jesus taught the multitudes about His Father's kingdom being experienced on earth and how they could be instrumental in bringing that into fruition. Jesus' desire was for these people to know His Father as He did and does. He calls us to show others the Father as well.

Let's jump from the hillside filled with crowds of people to a band room filled with young teenagers. Cassidy, Anthony's wife, followed the call of God on her life when she accepted the position as Trinity Catholic High School's Band Director, in Ocala, Florida, in 2005. When Cassidy began serving in this position, she strategically placed the Blessing scrolls on her desk. Out of curiosity, her students asked about the small scrolls. Cassidy encouraged them to take one and read it. The Blessings were later incorporated into her year-ending banquet.

Please read her email dated May 4, 2015.

"Hi Ann! I place one of your blessings each year on the Senior Band Award plaques, and we speak it over them at the banquet."

Let me pause for a moment to emphasize something: the Blessing is engraved on each Senior band member's plaque. God's word used in creating the Blessing is inscribed permanently on their commemorative plaque and the Blessing is spoken over these students in the presence and hearing of their parents and other band members. This is powerful.

Let's continue with Cassidy's email:

> They (the Blessings) are all taken from the Hope and a Future or You Are Loved set, but sometimes I pull a sentence from one and a sentence from another to fit the particular class. The printer always puts the copyright symbol at the end of the blessing. Will you approve this one?

Let's pause again to consider: Cassidy (1) engaged the principle of speaking and releasing Blessings (based on God's word) into her students' lives and (2) personalized the Blessing to "fit the particular class."

Returning to Cassidy's email:

> Blessing: May you love the Lord your God with all your heart, with all your soul, and with all your strength. May you excel in all that you do that others might notice and glorify God. May you be confident that nothing, absolutely nothing, can separate you from God's love. Remember this: you are loved.© Genesis 39:1-6; Philippians 2:14-15; Romans 8:39   May 4, 2015

> Funny story—my percussion class has chosen to read the same blessing every day since January. They have developed some fun quirks with this one. They read one that ends with the ending above—'May you be confident that nothing' (the class says out loud 'Absolutely nothing') 'can separate you from God's love. Remember this:' (class says: 'You are loved.') It's fun. How they have made it their own, but important that these words have been spoken over them every day, pushing their way into their hearts. One of the boys is an atheist, so that is even more pow-

erful. Please continue to pray for all these students. They need to experience God's love just like public school kids do, and I believe they have unknowingly chosen this particular blessing for a reason. Thanks, Cassidy.

Quite honestly, I am awed by God. Aren't you? <u>Generation to generation</u>, God's word is being deposited into young lives. We may not know until we move into our eternal destinies all the lives we have touched. Yet, we embrace great hope and expectation as we share the love of Christ and the heart of His Father! Our pastor, Steve Dow, recently declared: "We are purveyors of hope." You and I spread the Gospel of Hope found in Jesus Christ.

Another noteworthy aspect of Cassidy's percussion class was their desire to speak and release a certain blessing of God's love and faithfulness <u>over themselves</u>. The biblical passage they referenced is found in Romans 8. Please read this powerful declaration:

> *Who shall separate us from the love of Christ? Shall tribulation, or distress, or persecution, or famine, or nakedness, or danger, or sword? No, in all these things we are more than conquerors through him who loved us. For I am sure that neither death nor life, nor angels nor rulers, nor things present nor things to come, nor powers, nor height nor depth, nor anything else in all creation, will be able to separate us from the love of God in Christ Jesus our Lord.*
> (Romans 8:35, 37-39)

The Passion Translation provides this edifying wording:

> *So now I live with the confidence that there is nothing in the universe with the power to separate us from God's love. I'm convinced that his love will triumph over death, life's troubles, fallen angels, or dark rulers in the heavens. There is nothing in our present or future circumstances that can weaken his love. There is no power above us or beneath us—no power that could ever be found in the universe that can distance us from God's passionate love, which is lavished upon us through our Lord Jesus, the Anointed One!* (Romans 8:38,39 TPT)

Do you recall your teenage years—the struggles and challenges of just being a teenager? Consider the power and importance of clothing young people with this garment of truth. Every day these students declared God's truth over themselves. They heard their words based on God's word. Let's recall another passage in Paul's letter to the Roman believers: *"So faith comes from hearing, and hearing through the word of Christ."* (Romans 10:17)

Every day these students were building and strengthening their faith in the word of Christ. <u>When</u> will they draw upon that word which richly dwells within them—<u>when</u> the trials of life and the challenges of adulthood come, <u>when</u> they are persecuted for their faith in God.

Their words of faith have paved the way for them to declare: "May you be confident that nothing" (the class says out loud "Absolutely nothing") "can separate you from God's love. Remember this:" (class says: "You are loved.").

That's how they extend their Shield of Faith that quenches the fiery darts of the enemy. That defeated foe is a liar, and these students know the truth that sets them free from torment and deception. They are <u>more than conquerors</u> in Christ Jesus.

Let's return to Peyton's recollections of engaging Blessing Declarations in his life.

> I remember in college and in PA School, I would pray a lot to have focus, that God would give me 'Holy Spirit highlights' like you used to pray for me. I really feel that that worked. When I would pray over myself, I was trying to impart Blessings upon myself. That sounds really selfish, but if you don't have anybody else to pray over you all the time like I grew up with, but you inherently still want those Blessings, you are going to, in your prayerfulness,…to claim those Blessings for your life. I am going to pray over my life, that I'm going to have it. I feel like it helped me.

As a child of God, Peyton believed in and embraced God's word of life and truth for his life. Peyton strengthened himself in the Lord as David did:

> *And David was greatly distressed, for the people spoke of stoning him, because all the people were bitter in soul, each for his sons and*

> *daughters. But David <u>strengthened</u> himself in the LORD his God.* (1 Samuel 30:6, underline added)

> *And David was greatly distressed; for the people spake of stoning him, because the soul of all the people was grieved, every man for his sons and for his daughters: but David <u>encouraged</u> himself in the LORD his God.* (1 Samuel 30:6 KJV, underline added)

Just as David encouraged himself in the LORD, Peyton did likewise. We should do the same. We declare God's powerful and effective word over ourselves. The Appendix includes the document: "Declare Who You Are In Christ Jesus." It states, "Our declarations and prayers can change the atmosphere around us!" This list provides a treasure trove of biblical passages to speak and release over oneself! Engage these biblical truths and embrace them for yourself and others!

> *"Dedicate your children to God and point them in the way that they should go, and the values they've learned from you will be with them for life."* (Proverbs 22:6 TPT)

"Dedicate your children to God and point them in the way that they should go" carries a compelling principle for us. While the 16-year span between Peyton and David included different family dynamics, their application of speaking blessings and positive affirmations remained constant. Drawing again from Peyton's recollections:

> I encourage people that I work with. I try to be a positive person and be kind to them. When I speak to someone, I speak positivity, life and wealth, prosperity and good judgment and favor….giving them confidence…guidance and direction. In that counsel I see that being imparted in people, in a passive way in conversation. I think it's well received. If you speak plainly and you're positive in your words and in your counsel…I think that goes a long way in a workplace setting.

Referencing David and Carolina's thoughts, please read a similar application: "We have noticed that only Christians want to read the Blessing scrolls, unfortunately. However, almost all people respond positively to the idea of the declarations. We have been able to engage many people in conversation about why how you speak to yourself and others matters deeply. We hope it plants a seed in those around us to reach out with questions in the future."

Planting seeds of hope, truth and compassion remain foundational in our children's lives.

"The values they've learned from you will be with them for life."
(Proverbs 22:6 TPT)

From generation to generation, God's word stands steadfast, mighty and true. Build your family and others upon the sure and secure foundation of God's sovereign word, for it is settled in the heavens. Declare His sovereignty over yourself and others.

View Him for Who He is: Lord of all.

Throughout our children's lives, they have recognized the importance of viewing and affirming that truth: *God is Lord of all.*

When your world is turned upside down, *He is Lord of all.* Even when a loved one is killed, when a baby dies, God is sovereign, and He is still good. Do we understand the pain, grief and suffering? No, but Jesus does. What shall we do when the pain is more than we can bear? Fall on Him. Cry out to Him. He hears us.

Following the heartache of losing Victoria in 1989, God promised me another child. Holy Spirit gave me the gift of faith. He showed me the future, and He called me to follow Him into it. He gave me this gift to combat the opposing forces that would lie against God's promise being accomplished. Cal and I began speaking life and fruitfulness over my womb. We engaged and declared the words of Christ over my body and our future. As we walked through the months and years of waiting, Cal and I helped each other look beyond the present circumstances. A three-strand cord is not easily broken. (Ecclesiastes 4:12)

We held onto our confidence in Holy Spirit's intercession that joins Jesus' intercession before the Throne of God. Our prayers and declarations added the third strand. God fulfilled His promise on March 30, 1998: David Weber Gleaton was born.

Other couples have deeply desired to have children. Their efforts have ended in heartaches and disappointments. These friends have asked us to pray and to speak Blessing Declarations over them. Several have read *The Spoken Blessing: A Spiritual Posture* in which they learned how to use life-depositing scriptures to speak Blessing Declarations over themselves. As the years have progressed, we have heard from these couples who have been given God's precious gifts of children. "*Behold, children are a heritage from the LORD, the fruit of the womb a reward.*" (Psalm 127:3)

Brett and Deb Cooper learned how to speak God's word over their union and Deb's body. They released Blessing Declarations daily, weekly, faithfully entrusting the future of their family to God. Recently, I had the pleasure of reconnecting with Brett and Deb as they introduced me to their two children, Isaac and Bella! To God be the glory! Amen.

Many friends have received the power of God's word through Blessing Declarations. These friends have chosen to share them with customers, within Christian conferences, during birthday parties, wedding and baby showers, Bible study groups, at home over a meal. As God's words of life and truth are released and activated over an individual, He moves to fulfill His plan and purpose within them. "*Thy kingdom come. Thy will be done, in earth as it is in heaven.*" (Matthew 6:10 KJV)

Let's recall a portion of Kyle's dream and application as he compared a carpenter's pencil to a blessing scroll: "So, while the blessing represents blessing, it also represents the very thing that helps 'mark' places, people and time with God's covering and provision."

How will you respond to God's word inscribed within this book? Will you take and run with the principle, focus and vision of speaking and releasing Blessing Declarations?

Consider this counsel: "*The wise of heart will receive commandments, but a babbling fool will come to ruin.*" (Proverbs 10:8)

Please read it from The Amplified™ Bible: "*The wise in heart [are willing to learn so they] will accept and obey commands (instruction), But the babbling fool [who is arrogant and thinks himself wise] will come to ruin.*" (Proverbs 10:8 AMP)

The writer of these words of wisdom continued: "*Whoever heeds instruction (H4148) is on the path to life, but he who rejects reproof leads others astray.*" (Proverbs 10:17, Strong's number added)

Heeding God's instruction causes us to advance along the path of life! Did you notice the second part of this wise counsel: if we reject *instruction*, warning, restraint, correction, rebuke and chastisement, we will lead a life full of error and deception. The fallacies within our lives adversely affect others.[1]

You and I have a choice to make. Read Proverbs 10:31: *"The mouth of the righteous brings forth (H5107) wisdom…"* (Strong's number added)

With our mouths we sow either seeds of good, beneficial truth for living life or seeds of despair, destruction and condemnation which propagate death. The Hebrew word that is translated as "brings forth" is "nûb: A primitive root; to germinate, that is, (figuratively) to (causatively make) flourish; also (of words), to utter: - bring forth (fruit), make cheerful, increase."[2]

Others need to hear words of life and truth, filled with the grace and mercy of God.

A prayer that Cal and I often pray is:

> Holy Spirit, we ask for <u>Your divine appointments</u> and opportunities today. Order our steps throughout our day, for we know that the steps of a righteous man (and woman) are ordered by You. We ask that You help us <u>recognize these appointments</u> and follow Your leading in how to respond. We want to continually advance the kingdom of God: Thy kingdom come. Thy will be done, in earth as it is in heaven. Help us be fruitful and multiply God's kingdom today within the lives and hearts of people. Holy Spirit, bring to our remembrance the word of truth that richly dwells within us. Help us speak and release Blessing Declarations. In Jesus' Name. Amen.

Walking in partnership with God, we choose to follow His prompting and leading.

Let's follow Jesus and the crowd accompanying Him as they walk through Jericho. Jesus has a divine appointment with a man we met earlier in the Introduction.

---

1   Strong's Concordance, H4148: instruction
2   Strong's Concordance, H5107: brings forth

> *And behold, there was a man named Zacchaeus. He was a chief tax collector and was rich. And he was seeking to see who Jesus was, but on account of the crowd he could not, because he was small in stature. So he ran on ahead and climbed up into a sycamore tree to see him, for he was about to pass that way.* (Luke 19:2-4)

"When Jesus got to that place, he looked up into the tree and said, 'Zacchaeus, hurry on down, for <u>I am appointed</u> to stay at your house today!'" (Luke 19:5 TPT, underline added)

Will you join me at the house of Zacchaeus? Let's keep in mind that this man was despised and ostracized due to his greedy business dealings for the Romans. This occupation provided Zacchaeus with great wealth, yet he was an impoverished soul. His spiritual coffers were empty, and he knew it. He wanted what Jesus offered. Listen to the transformation that occurred within his heart:

> Zacchaeus <u>joyously welcomed</u> Jesus and was amazed over his gracious visit to his home. Zacchaeus stood in front of the Lord and said, "Half of all that I own I will give to the poor. And Lord, if I have cheated anyone, I promise to pay back four times as much as I stole." (Luke 19:8 TPT, underline added)

Zacchaeus' actions reflected his true repentance and his heart's new focus and purpose. From that point, he planned to follow Christ, recognizing Him as Lord, having supreme authority over his life. Zacchaeus changed his allegiance and service from the Roman government and the love of money to the governance of God's kingdom. He stepped out of darkness into the marvelous light and under the leadership of his Savior, Jesus.

To confirm Zacchaeus' salvation, listen to the words of Jesus:

"*And Jesus said to him, 'Today salvation has come to this house, since he also is a son of Abraham.'*" (Luke 19:9)

"*Jesus said to him, 'Today salvation has come to this household, because he, too, is a [spiritual] son of Abraham.'*" (Luke 19:9 AMP)

Remain with me in Zacchaeus' house for another moment. Consider the depth of wisdom we can receive from this life-altering encounter with Jesus: (1) to obtain a better view or perspective of Him, we must not allow others and their opinions to hinder our pursuit; (2) we must climb higher and discover ways to overcome our personal barriers as we seek to know Him better; (3) we must surrender our expectations of "life" and "our future" to Jesus and His kingdom authority; (4) we must not be one who prejudges others and Jesus' love for them.

What are your "takeaways" from Zacchaeus' conversion, his stepping into the light of God's kingdom, casting aside his old mindsets and "mode of operation?"

Following the life-altering visit to Zacchaeus' heart and home, Jesus deposited an important message and kingdom principle within the lives of His followers. He presented a timely parable using minas as a commodity to confront His disciples' expectation that He was their political Savior delivering them from the bondage of Roman control.

"As they heard these things, he proceeded to tell a parable, because he was near to Jerusalem, and <u>because they supposed</u> that the kingdom of God was to appear immediately." (Luke 19:11, underline added)

"So he told them this story <u>to change their perspective</u>: 'Once there was a wealthy prince who left his province to travel to a distant land, where he would be crowned king and then return." (Luke 19:12 TPT, underline added)

"And he called his ten servants, and delivered them ten pounds, and said unto them, '<u>Occupy</u> till I come." (Luke 19:13 KJV, underline added)

"Calling ten of his servants, he gave them ten minas, and said to them, '<u>Engage in business</u> until I come." (Luke 19:13, underline added)

"Before he departed he summoned his ten servants together and said, 'I am entrusting each of you with fifty thousand dollars <u>to trade with</u> while I am away. <u>Invest it</u> and <u>put the money to work</u> until I return." (Luke 19:13 TPT, underline added)

As we pause for a moment, let's consider what the "mina" is within our lives? What is it that our Wealthy Prince, King Jesus, distributes to each of us, His servants, <u>equally</u>?

"And he said to them, '<u>Go</u> into all the world and <u>proclaim the gospel</u> to the whole creation." (Mark 16:15, underline added)

> Then he opened their minds to understand the Scriptures, and said to them, "Thus it is written, that the Christ should suffer and on the third day rise from the dead, and that <u>repentance for the forgiveness of sins</u> should be proclaimed in his name to all nations, beginning from Jerusalem." (Luke 24:45-47, underline added)

"Now you must go into all the nations and <u>preach repentance</u> and <u>forgiveness of sins</u> so that they will turn to me. Start right here in Jerusalem."
(Luke 24:47 TPT, underline added)

"And Jesus came and spake unto them, saying, All power is given unto me in heaven and in earth." Matthew 28:18 KJV

> Go therefore and <u>make disciples</u> of all nations, <u>baptizing</u> them in the name of the Father and of the Son and of the Holy Spirit, <u>teaching</u> them to observe all that I have commanded you. And behold, I am with you always, to the end of the age. (Matthew 28:19-20, underline added)

You and I may recognize these last verses of the Gospel according to Matthew as "The Great Commission." A Google search from Oxford Languages produced this definition of the noun <u>commission</u>: *"an instruction, command, or duty given to a person or group of people."*

As Jesus' disciples, it is our duty to follow His command and instruction to take His mina, the Gospel, to every nation. Jesus gives <u>equally</u> to each of us His mina that we are to *<u>put to work</u>* to advance the kingdom of God.

We are to conduct the business of His Father as He did.

It was the Father's will for Jesus to pour out His precious blood to pay for, to reconcile the debt that His brethren owed for their sin. Would you walk with me in following Jesus and the eleven disciples as they walk towards the Mount of Olives at the conclusion of their meal?

> And they went to a place called Gethsemane. And he said to his disciples, 'Sit here while I pray.' And he took with him Peter and James and John, and began to be greatly distressed and troubled. And he said to them, 'My soul is very sorrowful, even to death. Remain here and watch.' And going a little farther, he fell on the ground and prayed that, if it were possible, the hour might pass from him. And

> he said, 'Abba, Father, all things are possible for you. Remove this cup from me. Yet not what I will, but what you will. (Mark 14:32-36)

Anguishing in prayer under the ancient olive trees, Jesus submitted Himself to the Father's will as He had taught and instructed His disciples:

"After this manner therefore pray ye: Our Father which art in heaven, Hallowed be thy name. Thy kingdom come. Thy will be done in earth, as it is in heaven." (Matthew 6:9-10 KJV)

Jesus' entire life on earth was devoted to accomplishing His Father's will, advancing His kingdom in earth. Do you recall the significance of His using "in" as He spoke? Strong's Concordance provides:

"G1909 [epi] expresses the idea of: *"superimposition* (of time, place, order, etc.), as a relation of distribution …, that is, over, upon, etc.;…" (emphasis added).

You and I are commanded and instructed to <u>distribute</u> His Good News and to advance the kingdom of God across the nations. Let's return to the parable in Luke 19:15:

> *When he returned, having received the kingdom, he ordered these servants to whom <u>he had given</u> the money to be called to him, that he might know what they <u>had gained by doing business</u>. The first came before him, saying, "Lord, <u>your</u> mina has made ten minas more."* (Luke 19:15,16, underline added)

> *The first one came forward and said, "Master, I took <u>what you gave me</u> and <u>invested it</u>, and it multiplied ten times." "Splendid! You have done well, my excellent servant. Because you have shown that <u>you can be trusted</u> in this small matter, I now <u>grant you authority to rule</u> over ten fortress cities."* (Luke 19:16,17 TPT, underline added)

The servant was awarded <u>delegated influence</u> over a larger area!

Do you and I desire to hear our Savior, King Jesus' words of affirmation and receive His greater assignments? Then, we must be "about our Father's business" in sharing the Gospel of His Son and in gaining ground for His kingdom. Every believer and follower of Jesus has been given His Gospel, the Good News of His saving grace which provides eternal life.

The Spoken Blessing II: Influencing Generations

Every disciple of Jesus is called to promote and strengthen the influence of God's kingdom. What are we doing with our *mina*?

Writing, texting, speaking Blessing Declarations based on His Good News is one way to superimposition His kingdom within the lives of others. Will you join our family and friends in releasing Blessing Declarations? Thy kingdom come. Thy will be done in earth as it is in heaven.

> *May the Father grant you to be strengthened with power through His Spirit in your inner being. May Christ dwell in your hearts through faith. May you be rooted and grounded in love and be strengthened to comprehend what is the breadth and length and height and depth, and to know the love of Christ that surpasses knowledge. May you be filled with all the fullness of God.* (Ephesians 3:16-19)

In an interview with Steve Shultz on Elijah Streams, Johnny Enlow commented that we must "learn to advance God's kingdom in the face of challenges." (August 5, 2024)

As believers in Christ Jesus, let us be intentional in helping others face challenges and embrace a new mentality based on foundational truths from the word of God. These truths become foundational strengths within their hearts, within their thinking and within their verbal confessions concerning their future and the future of others.

Jesus set before us the example of transformation and renewal.

In earlier chapters, we have read Isaiah's prophecy regarding the Messiah's transformative work: ashes to beauty, mourning to gladness, despondency to praise <u>so that</u> these people may be called and recognized as strong towers (oaks) of His righteousness. As Messiah transforms lives, bringing God's kingdom to earth, the Father is glorified.

Let's take note of how the "transformed ones" will be used:

"They shall build up the ancient ruins; they shall raise up the former devastations; they shall repair the ruined cities, the devastations of many generations." (Isaiah 61:4)

Transformation of <u>generations</u> will occur. According to the tender mercies of God we are transformed. Read Titus 3:5: *"He saved us, not because of works done by us in righteousness, but according to his own mercy, by the washing of regeneration and renewal of the Holy Spirit…"*

Those who have had their minds renewed and their lives transformed assist others. You and I are those who have received *"the washing of regeneration and renewal of the Holy Spirit."* (Titus 3:5)

As we have freely received, let us freely give to others that the Lord God will be glorified.

Let us advance God's kingdom with His word of truth, pushing back the darkness with the light and life of the Gospel of Jesus Christ. We speak and release His life-depositing word.

> *Do not be conformed to this world, but be transformed by the renewal (G342) of your mind, that by testing you may discern what is the will of God, what is good and acceptable and perfect.*
> (Romans 12:2, Strong's number added)[1]

The renewal of our minds is accomplished by the power and presence of Holy Spirit. Ask Him to fill, and refill you. Invite Him to empower you to go forth in the power of God. May the Lord God receive all honor and glory! Amen.

Please hear and receive this Blessing Declaration from the set: "To God be the Glory:"

> *May your faith in Jesus Christ compel you to reach forward to achieve a more intimate relationship with Him. May your outstretched hands meet His as your heart ignites with passion for His Gospel. May your faith-filled prayers be like arrows that reach beyond your natural scope entering the supernatural realm of God's provision and promises. May God be glorified throughout your walk of faith.*
> (Matthew 8:10; 9:29; 15:28 Hebrews 11:1,6,32-34)

---

[1] Strong's Concordance, G342: renovation; renewing

Looking to the Author and Finisher of Our Faith:

We look away from the natural realm and we fasten our gaze onto Jesus who birthed faith within us and who leads us forward into faith's perfection. His example is this: Because <u>his heart was focused</u> on the <u>joy of knowing that you would be his</u>, he endured the agony of the cross and conquered its humiliation, and now sits exalted at the right hand of the throne of God! (Hebrews 12:2 TPT, underline added)

1. What must happen within your life for you to "fasten" your "gaze onto Jesus?"

   _____

   _____

   _____

2. What steps will you take to allow Jesus to become the Author and Finisher of your faith?

   _____

   _____

   _____

3. How will you follow Jesus' example of focusing on the joy of sharing Him with others?

   _____

   _____

   _____

4. What will you do to create one-on-one time for you and Holy Spirit?

   _____

   _____

   _____

5. Whose birthdays, anniversaries, and weddings occur within the next few months? Will you write and release Blessing Declarations over their lives? What are your plans?

_____

_____

_____

6. How has Jesus transformed your life?

_____

_____

_____

7. Would you like to thank Him for His love and sacrifice for you?

_____

_____

_____

Chapter 8

Creating Blessing Declarations

Let us encompass others with the atmosphere of the eternal, ever-alive word of God. Let us engage generations in the promises and empowerment of God's word. Let us enlarge God's sovereignty within the minds and hearts of people.

Consider upcoming special days and occasions that will occur this year. Every year family, friends and business associates celebrate birthdays and anniversaries. Select a greeting card or create your own, then ask Holy Spirit to share His heart for them. Ask Him for His message, His word of encouragement, His living and abiding word for them. He will bring to your remembrance the words of Christ (John 14:26). Follow His leading through the Scriptures. Make notes. Your "walk with Holy Spirit" will enlarge your love for Him and for the recipient of your Blessing Declaration. Remember, you are a co-partner with God.

As Jesus explained to His disciples the work of Holy Spirit, He reassured them:

> *I still have many things to say to you, but you cannot bear them now. When the Spirit of truth comes, he will guide you into all the truth, for he will not speak on his own authority, but whatever he hears he will speak, and he will declare to you the things that are to come. He will glorify me, for he will take what is mine and declare it to you.*

All that the Father has is mine; therefore I said that he will take what is mine and declare it to you. (John 16:12-15)

This passage of John 16:12-15 clearly identifies that Jesus had more to tell His beloved followers. Holy Spirit will serve as the agent of the Holy Trinity to share, tell, declare and reveal future knowledge and information. We are to trust and rely on the operation and activity of Holy Spirit.

Please read John 16:15 in The Passion Translation:

"Everything that belongs to the Father belongs to me— that's why I say that the **Divine Encourager** *will receive what is mine and reveal it to you."* (emphasis added)

Trust the *Divine Encourager* to share the heart of the Father so that **you** can "do greater works than these" (John 14:12) to <u>encourage</u> others and <u>glorify</u> the Father.

You may ask, "How do I glorify the Father by writing, speaking and releasing Blessing Declarations based on God's word?" Listen to Jesus' explanation:

"If you abide in me, and my words abide in you, ask whatever you wish, and it will be done for you." "<u>*By this my Father is glorified,*</u> *that you bear much fruit and so prove to be my disciples."* (John 15:7-8, underline added)

Ask Him to reveal the Father's heart for others. As you share His heart with others, you bear much fruit and prove to be Jesus' disciple. Thus, you <u>glorify</u> the Father.

> *But if you* <u>*live in life-union with me*</u> *and if my words live powerfully within you— then you can ask whatever you desire and it will be done."* "*When your lives bear abundant fruit, you demonstrate that you are* <u>*my mature disciples who glorify my Father*</u>*!*
> (John 15:7-8 TPT, underline added)

Jesus was quite plain: <u>we live in life-union with Him</u> through Holy Spirit's presence living within us. Living in life-union with Holy Spirit allows the joy of Jesus to be in us and for His joy to be made full (John 15:11). <u>Living in life-union with Holy Spirit</u> empowers and directs our Blessing Declarations to be aligned with the mind and heart of Christ, which is the heart of the Father.

Writing, speaking and releasing Blessing Declarations becomes a true joy. As you have freely received, be a conduit of His joy and freely give. Allow His joy to overflow onto and into others. Celebrate their special days.

Jesus does.

As Jesus shared His joy, He also showed His compassion for the hurting. Whatever the need was, Jesus recognized it and offered His words of comfort and actions of compassion.

In Chapter 6, we saw the heart and hands of Jesus reaching people (Matthew 14:14; 15:32; Mark 6:34). Within your realm of relationships, you may know someone who has recently lost a loved one to illness or tragedy. Another friend or business associate may have gone through a divorce. A neighbor may have been "let go" or given "early retirement" due to a company's "downsizing." A parent may be struggling with a wayward child.

As you hear about the needs of a friend, relative, neighbor or business associate, begin to pray for those in need of support. Ask Holy Comforter to come alongside and assist you in creating Blessing Declarations to cover them with encouragement and consolation.

Recall that Jesus referred to Holy Spirit as the Comforter.

> *And I will pray the Father, and he shall give you another Comforter, that he may abide with you for ever… But the Comforter, which is the Holy Ghost, whom the Father will send in my name, he shall teach you all things, and bring all things to your remembrance, whatsoever I have said unto you.* (John 14:16,26 KJV)

Use your Bible's concordance to locate scriptures related to the need. If your Bible does not include a concordance, obtain a copy of *The New Strong's Exhaustive Concordance of the Bible*. Another option is to purchase a Bible that includes a concordance. One of the Bibles I use is the *FireBible*™, *English Standard Version*™. It includes a concordance.

The *FireBible*™ provides several scriptures under the word: comfort. Consider this entry for 2 Corinthians 1:3-4:

> *Blessed be the God and Father of our Lord Jesus Christ, the Father of mercies and God of all comfort, (4) who comforts us in all our*

affliction, so that we may be able to <u>comfort</u> those who are in any affliction, with the <u>comfort</u> with which we ourselves are <u>comforted</u> by God." (emphasis added)

This passage provides a powerful beginning to a Blessing Declaration! Consider this:

> May the God and Father of our Lord Jesus Christ comfort you.
>
> May the Father of mercies comfort and console your heart.
>
> May His tenderness touch your emotions and calm your thoughts.

To add to the depth of my understanding of verses 3 and 4, I looked up the Greek meanings for <u>comfort</u> and <u>affliction</u>. As you follow this method, take note that there will be occasions when the same English word is used for different Greek words. This is not meant to confuse you. It can serve to add insight into the original intent of the message.

Examples of Blessings:

Bridal Shower:

Create and distribute Blessing Declarations to be spoken over the Bride-to-Be. The focus of the Bridal Shower will shift as God's blessings and favor are released over the couple. The following are several Blessing Declarations from the set: "Come Away My Beloved."©

> *May your love grow more perfect and complete as you live together with Christ.*
>
> *May Christ always be the third partner in your marriage, as a three-strand cord is not easily broken.*
>
> *May He do exceedingly abundantly more than you ask or think.* ©
>
> 1 John 4:17; Ecclesiastes 4:12; Ephesians 3:20
>
> *May you cheerfully help each other, for two are better than one because they have a good return for their labor.*
>
> *For if you fall, the other will lift you up. In your work, prayer or play, two cannot be overpowered,*
>
> *united by the Holy Spirit.* ©
>
> Ecclesiastes 4:9,10,12
>
> *May you be harmonious, sympathetic, brotherly, kind-hearted, and humble in spirit; not returning evil for evil,*
>
> *or insult for insult, but giving a blessing instead;*
>
> *for you were called for the very purpose that you might inherit a blessing.* ©
>
> 1 Peter 3:8,9

Rehearsal Dinner:

A Blessing for (Groom's name) and (Bride's name)

May you, (groom) recognize (bride) as a fellow heir of the grace of life—founded and grounded in Lord Jesus, that your prayers may not be hindered. May you pray for (bride).

May the Lord hear and respond to your prayers. (Groom), may you dwell with (bride) offering her understanding, giving honor to her as your wife.

May you regard (bride) as fine, delicate, expensive china, handling her with great care and tenderness.

May you, (groom) and (bride), be imitators of God, as beloved children, and walk in love, just as Christ also loved you, and gave Himself up for you.

May you walk in the light of the Lord, allowing His goodness, righteousness and truth to be formed within you.

May you walk in the wisdom of the Lord, making the most of your time, understanding what the will of the Lord is.

May you clothe yourselves with humility toward one another, for God is opposed to the proud but gives grace to the humble.

May you be subject to one another in the fear and reverence of Christ.

(Bride), may you gracefully accept the covering of (groom) and his leadership within your marriage.

(Groom), may you love (bride), your wife, just as Christ also loved the church and gave Himself up for her.

(Groom), may you love (bride), nourishing her with the water of God's Word.

May you cherish her as a priceless gift from God.

(Groom) and (bride), may you walk in a manner worthy of the calling with which you have been called,

*with all humility and gentleness, with patience, showing forbearance to one another in love,
being diligent to preserve the unity of the Spirit in the bond of peace. In Jesus' Name. Amen.* ©

1 Peter 3:7; 5:5; Ephesians 4:1-3; 5:1-2,8-9,15-17,21,23,25,28-29

Baby Shower:

To the fun and joy of a Baby Shower, add the power of speaking Blessing Declarations. Select scriptures and create Blessing Declarations that are meaningful to the Mother-to-Be. Invite her guests to speak and engage God's word into the lives of the entire family. The following Blessing Declarations are from "Reflections of His Love,"© Blessing set.

*Precious mother, may God complete and perfect the good work He has begun in you;
for it is God who is at work in you, both to will and to work His good pleasure.
May you be known as a daughter of God.* ©

Philippians 1:6; 2:13

*Sweet mother, may all that you do be done in love. May you become an ambassador for Christ,
sharing His gospel with others who are lost.* ©

1 Corinthians 16:14; 2 Corinthians 5:20

*Blessed baby, may you dwell in the shelter of the Most High and abide in the shadow of the Almighty.
May you say to the Lord, "You are my refuge and my fortress, my God, in whom I trust."* ©

Psalm 91:1,2

Baby Dedication:

Child's Name

Date

(Child's name), may you always remember that you are God's workmanship, created in Christ Jesus to do good works.

May God show you the path for your life as He has prepared for you and ordained every day for good works which will honor and glorify Him.

May you draw close to Him, your Creator, that your joy is deepened.

May you take great pleasure in knowing Jesus and simply being with Him. He loves your company.

May God cause you to prosper and excel in whatever you do.

May you always remember that the Lord, your God, is the One who gives you power to make wealth so that He may confirm His everlasting covenant with you.

May you give God the glory for your success.

May He be honored by your tithes, gifts and offerings.

May you walk in the blessings of the Lord all the days of your life, as He opens the windows of heaven and pours out His abundant love until it overflows.

In Jesus' Name. Amen. ©

Ephesians 2:10; Psalm 16:11; 139:16; Genesis 39:2-5; Malachi 3:8,10; Deuteronomy 8:18

Examples of Blessings

Graduation:

As family and friends gather in celebration of a graduation, personalize Blessing Declarations for the graduate. As you create their Blessing Declarations, insert his or her name. The following examples are from "A Hope and A Future"© Blessing set.

May God instruct you and teach you in the way which you should go.

May God counsel you with His eye upon you.

May you be glad as you trust in the Lord.

May His lovingkindness surround you.

May His favor be about you like a shield.©

Psalm 32:8,10; Proverbs 30:5

May your confidence and faith in Lord Jesus help you to do great things for His kingdom.

May your faith grow into a mighty tree which offers refuge, nourishment and shelter for the needy and afflicted.

May you discover that as you walk with God you will find that all things are possible. ©

John 14:12; Matthew 17:20,21; Mark 10:27

May your faith in God surpass the mind of man as did Abraham's as he believed
what God declared to him concerning a son.

May your message to others be the demonstration of the Spirit and His power working within and through you.

May your faith in Lord Jesus be reckoned to you as righteousness.©

Corinthians 2:4-5; Genesis 15:1-6; Romans 4:6-8

Thanksgiving Meals:

Consider creating Blessing Declarations that celebrate God, His goodness and provision. At each place setting, provide the guests with a Blessing Declaration they can speak and release over each other. Please read the Blessing Declarations from the set: "His Harvest."©

May you sing praise to the Lord and give thanks to His Holy Name.
May His favor abide with you for a lifetime.
May a shout of joy in the morning replace your weeping at night.
May you call to the Lord for his grace and help.
May He exchange your mourning into victorious dancing.
May He discard your sackcloth and clothe you in gladness.
May you give thanks to the Lord, your God, forever. ©
Psalm 30:4,5,8,10-12

May the hand of the Lord be with you and the power of His might prepare the way for you.
May His presence draw multitudes to believe in Him.
May you go and make disciples of all nations, baptizing them in the name of the Father
and the Son and the Holy Spirit.
May you teach them all that Jesus commanded. ©
Acts 11:21; Matthew 28:19-20

May God give you wisdom and knowledge as you go out and minister to His people.
May you be blessed with every spiritual blessing in heavenly places in Christ
that you would be holy and blameless, serving as a beacon, a light set on a hill which cannot be hidden.
May Christ's love abiding within you shine forth, drawing men to Him.

Examples of Blessings

May your harvest of souls be fruitful and multiplied. ©
2 Chronicles 1:10; Ephesians 1:3; Matthew 5:14-16; John 4:35-39

[Use your concordance to locate scriptures related to thank, thanks, thanksgiving, provide, provided, heart, harvest. Ask Holy Spirit to help you create Blessing Declarations to share.]

Charlie, our grandson, shared his favorite thing about the Blessing scrolls: "…when we pass them out to each family member we get to read them every year, to see which one everybody gets, to see what it's about…it's on love and different things."

Christmas and Hanukkah Celebrations:

A dear friend, a Messianic Jew, asked me to create a Blessing set based on Jesus being the Light. Within Michelle Freilich's faith in Jesus as Yeshua, she continues to celebrate Hanukkah with a deeper understanding and love for the Lord who saves.

I searched scriptures related to His announcement: *"I am the light of the world."* (John 8:12) Holy Spirit helped me create this set.

The following Blessing Declarations are from "The Glow of His Light."©

May you recognize God as the Creator of all light, both natural and supernatural.

May you look to Him as your source for light, in your daily tasks, in your spiritual matters.

May God impart His truth within your heart, giving you understanding and insight.

May His wisdom be resident within you.

May the decisions and choices you make reflect His light that dwells in the depths of your being. ©

Genesis 1:3; Proverbs 14:33

May the Lord give you a balanced understanding of His compassion.

May you be concerned for the rights of the poor and encourage the wealthy with wisdom.

May the Lord give light to your eyes so that you may see His vision, His kingdom purposes for you and for others.

May you continue in an attitude of humility before God and men, trusting in God's justice and provision.

May your confidence in God be established, giving you a strong sense of security. ©

Proverbs 29:7,13,18,23,25,26

May you weep no longer over the empty tomb, over disappointments in your life.

May you turn and see your hope, your risen Savior.

May you recognize His face as the light of a new day shines brilliantly upon Him.

May He call your name. May you fall before Him, worshipping and adoring Him.

May you arise and boldly tell others about His resurrection and everlasting life. ©

John 20:11-18

Our grandson, Reed, values the messages on the Blessing scrolls. He commented: "I like them because they're a lot about Jesus, God, (and) good things They've done."

Examples of Blessings

Birthdays:

Ask, listen, write, then send a Blessing Declaration from the heart of the Father. Please read examples taken from the Blessing set: "You Are Loved."©

May you understand and know the Lord as the One who takes great delight

in exercising His lovingkindness, justice and righteousness on earth.

May you be fruitful and steadfast in your love for the Lord as He will abundantly shower you with blessings.

You are loved. ©

Jeremiah 9:24; Proverbs 28:20,25

May God lead you in His triumph in Christ.

May He manifest through you the sweet aroma of the knowledge of Him in every place.

May you be a fragrance of Christ to God among those who are being saved and among those who are perishing.

May you be kind to one another, tender-hearted, forgiving each other, just as God in Christ also has forgiven you.

You are loved. ©

2 Corinthians 2:14-15; Ephesians 4:32

Anniversaries:

Celebrate the couple's love, commitment and sacrifice for each other. Release God's word of light unto their path as they walk united in Christ Jesus. The following are Blessing Declarations from: "The Secrets of the Heart."©

May your beloved helpmate, your spouse, be your best friend.

May you trust the other to meet your deepest needs.

May you feel secure enough in their love that you can share your intimate secrets;

your hurts, your hopes, the longings of your heart.

May you be one who encourages the other to reach for the vision God has placed within them.

May you walk arm-in-arm, supporting each other through the trials and testings of life. ©

Song of Solomon 1:15,16; 2:4,16; 4:10; Philippians 3:14

May you do nothing from selfishness or empty conceit,

but with humility of mind may you regard others as more important than yourself.

May you not simply look out for your own personal interests, but also for the interests of others.

May you do all things without grumbling or disputing.

May all that you do be done in love. ©

Philippians 2:3-4, 14; 1 Corinthians 16:14

Pastor Appreciation Month:

Ask Heavenly Father to share His love and heart for your pastor. Give honor where honor is due. Write and release the Father's love for His under-shepherd.

Please read these examples from the Blessing set: "A True and Faithful Witness."©

May you continue to serve as God's true and faithful witness as you proclaim the essence of eternal life:

loving the Lord your God with all your heart and with all your soul and with all your strength and with all your mind.

May you love your neighbor as yourself.

May the witness of God's own Son be lifted up before all men. ©

Luke 10:24; John 12:32

Examples of Blessings

As you serve God as His true and faithful witness, may others recognize that you have been with Jesus.

May your life resemble His.

May your union with Him be evident in your heart's motives, your actions and your speech.

May you be a mirror image of the Father's True and Faithful witness, His Son—Jesus. ©

Acts 4:13; Revelation 19:11

Promotions:

Celebrate with loved ones and friends their accomplishments and advancements. Honor and bless them with the guiding light of God's word. The following Blessing Declarations are included in: "Walking in the Covenant."©

May your heavenly Father be glorified by men when they see your good works as your light shines before them.

May you shine forth as the sun, in your Father's kingdom, as you wear Jesus' robes of righteousness.

May you be a peacemaker as others recognize the nature and character of Jesus within you. ©

Matthew 5:16; 13:43; 5:9

May you press on toward the goal for the prize of the upward call of God in Christ Jesus.

May you run in such a way that you may win.

May you press on to maturity, so as to realize the full assurance of hope, being imitators of those who through faith and patience inherit the promises. ©

Philippians 3:14; 1 Corinthians 9:24; Hebrews 6:1,11,12

Healing and Restoration Needs:

Invite Holy Spirit, the Spirit of Christ, to share Jesus' heart with those in need. Read how Jesus showed His compassion towards two blind men:

> *And behold, there were two blind men sitting by the roadside, and when they heard that Jesus was passing by, they cried out, "Lord, have mercy on us, Son of David!" The crowd rebuked them, telling them to be silent, but they cried out all the more, "Lord, have mercy on us, Son of David!" And stopping, Jesus called them and said, "What do you want me to do for you?" They said to him, "Lord, let our eyes be opened." And Jesus in pity touched their eyes, and immediately they recovered their sight and followed him.* (Matthew 20:30-34)

Consider the admonition of Peter, a disciple of Jesus, one who had been with Him, watching His Savior cover others with tender mercies and restoration:

"Finally, be ye all of one mind, having compassion one of another, love as brethren, be pitiful, be courteous:" (1 Peter 3:8 KJV)

"Finally, all of you be like-minded [united in spirit], sympathetic, brotherly, kindhearted [courteous and compassionate toward each other as members of one household], and humble in spirit;" (1 Peter 3:8 AMP)

The word used for compassion has its roots in a word meaning: <u>to experience pain jointly or of the same kind; to suffer with</u>. (Strong's Concordance) Jesus came alongside, stopped to listen, and extended His heart towards those in need. Shall we not do the same?

Read examples of Blessing Declarations from the set: "A Place of Refuge."©

> *May you place your hope in God as He is your rock and your salvation, your stronghold.*
>
> *May you not be shaken.*
>
> *May you trust in Him at all times, pouring out your heart before Him.*©
>
> Psalm 62:5,6,8

Examples of Blessings

May you draw near to God and He will draw near to you.

May your friendship and intimacy with the Lord be so precious that you are the 'apple of His eye.'

May you be so close and personal to Him that you breathe in as He exhales.

May your life be strengthened and renewed by His breath.©

James 4:8; Deuteronomy 32:10

Precious believer in the Lord Jesus Christ, you have His Holy Spirit indwelling you. Continue to rely on Holy Spirit's wisdom, counsel and instruction. Ask Him to remind you of the words of Christ. Seek the Father every day and rest on Him. He cares for you. Cultivate a deeper attitude of gratitude for Jesus, your Redeemer, your Savior. He gave His everything **for** you, and **to** you. *He laid down His life for you.* Thank Him every day.

Share your heart with Him:

_____

_____

_____

_____

Please read Paul's exhortation for his son in the faith, Timothy:

"Keep and follow the pattern of sound teaching (doctrine) which you have heard from me, in the faith and love which are in Christ Jesus."

(2 Timothy 1:13 AMP)

We can speak God's words of life and power into people's lives through releasing Blessing Declarations. His words are eternal and do not diminish in their power and authority to bring life, hope and salvation.

May you walk, talk, listen and respond to what the Spirit of Christ is saying. May His joy be made full and complete in you! In Jesus' Name. Amen.

Appendix

Declare Who You Are In Jesus Christ

Our declarations and prayers can change the atmosphere around us!

- **I am a child of God.** John 1:12; Romans 8:16-17
- **I am redeemed from the hand of the enemy.** Psalm 106:10
- **I am forgiven.** Psalm 130:4; Acts 10:43; Ephesians 1:7
- **I am saved by grace through faith.** Ephesians 2:5,8
- **I am justified.** Matthew 12:37; Romans 5:1; Galatians 2:16
- **I am sanctified.** 1 Thessalonians 5:23; Hebrews 10:10
- **I am a new creature in Christ Jesus.** Romans 6:4; 2 Corinthians 5:17
- **I am a partaker of God's divine nature.** Ephesians 4:24; 2 Peter 1:4
- **I am redeemed from the curse of the law.** Galatians 3:13
- **I am delivered from the power of darkness.** Psalm 18:17
- **I am living and led by the Holy Spirit.** John 14:26; Romans 8:13,14; Galatians 5:16
- **I am kept in safety.** Psalm 4:8; 16:9; Psalm 91
- **I have the divine favor of God.** Psalm 90:17; Psalm 147:11; Proverbs 3:3,4
- **I am getting all my needs met in Jesus.** Psalm 23:1; Philippians 4:19
- **I am casting all my cares on Jesus.** Psalm 55:22; 1 Peter 5:7

- **I am strong in the Lord and in the power of His might.**
  Romans 4:20,21; Ephesians 6:10
- **I am doing all things through Him who strengthens me.**
  2 Corinthians 12:9; Philippians 4:13
- **I am an heir of God and a joint heir with Jesus Christ.**
  Romans 4:7; 8:17; Titus 3:7
- **I am the light of the world.** Matthew 5:14-16; Philippians 2:15
- **I am observing and doing the Lord's commandments.**
  Deuteronomy 10:12,13; John 14:21; 15:10
- **I am blessed coming in and blessed going out.** Deuteronomy 28:1-6; Psalm 121:8
- **I am an heir of eternal life.** Titus 3:7
- **I am blessed in Christ with all spiritual blessings.** Ephesians 1:3
- **I am healed by the stripes of Jesus.** Isaiah 53:5; 1 Peter 2:24
- **I am exercising my authority over the enemy.** Matthew 10:1; Mark 6:7; Luke 9:1, 10:19
- **I am more than a conqueror.** Romans 8:31, 37
- **I am establishing God's word here in earth.** Isaiah 55:11; 2 Timothy 4:2
- **I am casting down vain imaginations.** 2 Corinthians 10:5
- **I am being transformed by the renewing of my mind.**
  Romans 12:2; Titus 3:5; Ephesians 4:23
- **I am a co-laborer with God.** Mark 16:20; 1 Corinthians 3:9; 2 Corinthians 6:1

Author's Notes

Days, weeks, and months comprise the twenty years since the writing of my first book. That time has transpired *within* and *through* the Grace-filled, Mercy-releasing hands of God.

I have exponentially grown in my love for Abba, Father, Jesus, the Living, Redeeming Word, and Holy Spirit, the Spirit of Christ, my Counselor, Teacher and Friend.

Our God is a Faithful God. He has woven pastors, teachers, guest speakers, books, live-streaming sessions, songs, missionaries, family and friends to instruct, correct and love me. Our God is an awesome God. He has woven my life and our family's lives together with yours. For this, I am grateful. God is worthy of all praise.

As I mentioned in the Preface of this book, we invite you to share with us your thoughts and personal application of our message. Please use: *www.spokenblessing.com*.

We value your time and efforts to respond. We honor your journey in discovering a deeper love for our holy God. He loves you and desires to walk *with* you every day. May you continue to enjoy and abide in the benefits of His Salvation.

Abiding in His love,

Calvin Clifton and Ann Dews Gleaton
Anthony, Cassidy, Andrew, Zachary and Daniel Gleaton
Peyton, Amy, Charlie, Reed, Ruby and Rhett Gleaton
Kyle, Elizabeth, Isaac, Noah, Joseph, Daniel, Victoria Del Vecchio
David and Carolina Gleaton

About the Author:

Ann Dews Gleaton and family were introduced to the principle and the practice of speaking Blessings in 1991. Their family needed a major attitude adjustment! Learning to speak Blessings met this urgent need. Ann and her husband, Cal, followed the example of Jesus in declaring Blessings over their children. The attitude of their hearts and the atmosphere of their home changed.

Ann's passion is to teach men, women and children how to make The Spoken Blessing an integral part of their lives. She has multiplied this understanding and practice within numerous lives. Ann has taught within various settings: college courses, women's conferences, and Bible studies for men and women. She and Cal minister to others the life-changing words of Christ as they follow His example of speaking and releasing Blessings.

Ann and Cal currently live in Cairo, Georgia. Their four children, now married, deposit God's word into their children's lives. The principle and practice of speaking Blessings is propelled into the next generation, for the glory of God.

To order Ann's first book: *The Spoken Blessing—A Spiritual Posture* and to learn more about available Blessing sets, please visit: *www.spokenblessing.com*

The Gleaton Family

Cal and Ann Gleaton

Kyle and Elizabeth Del Vecchio
Joseph, Isaac, Victoria, Noah and Daniel (Left to Right)

Peyton and Amy Gleaton
Charlie, Rhett, Ruby and Reed
(Left to Right)

Anthony and Cassidy Gleaton
Andrew, Daniel and Zachary
(Left to Right)

David and Carolina Gleaton

References

Conner, Kevin. *Interpreting the Symbols and Types, Completed Revised and Expanded.* Portland: BT Publishing, 1980.

Gleaton, Ann D. *The Seed of God's Word.* 1999.

Gleaton, Ann D. *Intimacy with Jesus.* 1999.

Gleaton, Ann D. *You Are Loved.* 2004.

Gleaton, Ann D. *Come Away My Beloved.* 1999.

Gleaton, Ann D. *Reflections of His Love.* 1999.

Gleaton, Ann D. *A Hope and A Future.* 1999.

Gleaton, Ann D. *His Harvest.* 1999.

Gleaton, Ann D. *The Glow of His Light.* 2004.

Gleaton, Ann D. *The Secrets of the Heart.* 2004

Gleaton, Ann D. *A True and Faithful Witness.* 2012.

Gleaton, Ann D. *Walking in the Covenant.* 1999.

Gleaton, Ann D. *A Place of Refuge.* 1999.

Gleaton, Ann Dews. *The Spoken Blessing—A Spiritual Posture.* True Potential, Inc., 2025.

Hayford, J., Chappell, P., Ulmer K., Hayden, R., Huntzinger, J. and Matsdorf, G. (eds.) (2002).

New Spirit-Filled Life™ Bible: New King James Version. Nashville: Thomas Nelson Publishers.

Keener, Craig. *The IVP Bible Background Commentary New Testament.* Downers Grove: InterVarsity Press, 1993.

Keller, Tim. *Discovering the Gospel in Job, youtube.com.*

LeBlanc, Lenny. *There is None Like You.* Mobile: Integrity's Hosanna! Music, 1991.

Lockyer, Herbert. *All the Divine Names and Titles in the Bible.*
  Grand Rapids: Zondervan Publishing House, 1975.

Lockyer, Herbert. *All the Men of the Bible.*
  Grand Rapids: Zondervan Publishing House, 1958.

Meyers, Rick. *e-Sword X the Sword of the LORD with an electronic edge,* (9.5 version), 2025.

Peterson, Eugene. *THE MESSAGE: The Bible in Contemporary Language.*
  Colorado Springs: NavPress Publishing Group, 2002.

Ribble, John. *The Hymnbook.*
  Philadelphia: Presbyterian Church in the United States, MCMLV.

Simmons, Brian. *The Passion Translation*™
  BroadStreet Publishing™ Group, 2020.

Sheets, Tim. *Prayers & Decrees that Activate Angel Armies.*
  Shippensburg: Destiny Image Publishers, Inc., 2022

Stamps, D. and Adams, J. (Eds.) (2011). FireBible™*: English Standard Version*™,
  Hendrickson Publishers Marketing, LLC.

Strong, James. *The New Strong's Exhaustive Concordance of the Bible.*
  Nashville: Thomas Nelson Publishers, 1990.

The Lockman Foundation. *E-Sword X New American Bible Study Set, NASB, 2020 Text and NASB, 1995.*

The Lockman Foundation. *E-Sword X Amplified Bible Study Set, 2015 and AMPC, 1987.*

The Lockman Foundation. *The Amplified Bible, Expanded Edition,*
  Grand Rapids: Zondervan Publishing House, 1987 and 2015.

Wikipedia, reference for *Rhema and Logos,* noted on pp. 77-78.

Google: Oxford Languages: *DNA.*

www.reasonsforhopeJesus.com Got Questions? *"How are the Shepherd's Rod and Staff Different?"* Noted on page 146.

References

(www.heavolutionintl.org) "Decree" explained. Noted on page 14.

www.nature.com. DNA explained. Noted on page 13.

www.thescottspot.wordpress.com. Altrogge, Mark. *I Stand In Awe Of You.* 1987.

"The Boys in the Boat" (film), Amazon.com.

www.ingramcontent.com/pod-product-compliance
Lightning Source LLC
Chambersburg PA
CBHW070639160426
43194CB00009B/1504